Swearing in English

Swearing in English uses the spoken section of the British National Corpus to establish how swearing is used, and to explore the associations between bad language and gender, social class and age. The book goes on to consider why bad language is a major locus of variation in English and investigates the historical origins of modern attitudes to bad language. The effects that centuries of censorious attitudes to swearing have had on bad language are examined, as are the social processes that have brought about the associations between swearing and a number of sociolinguistic variables.

Drawing on a variety of methodologies, including historical research and corpus linguistics, and a range of data such as corpora, dramatic texts, early modern newsbooks and television programmes, Tony McEnery takes a sociohistorical approach to discourses about bad language in English. Moral panic theory and Bourdieu's theory of distinction are also utilised to show how attitudes to bad language have been established over time by groups seeking to use an absence of swearing in their speech as a token of moral, economic and political power. This book provides an explanation, not simply a description, of how modern attitudes to bad language have come about.

Tony McEnery is Professor of English Language and Linguistics at Lancaster University, UK, and has published widely in the area of corpus linguistics.

Routledge advances in corpus linguistics
Edited by Tony McEnery
Lancaster University, UK

and

Michael Hoey
Liverpool University, UK

Corpus-based linguistics is a dynamic area of linguistic research. The series aims to reflect the diversity of approaches to the subject, and thus to provide a forum for debate and detailed discussion of the various ways of building, exploiting and theorising about the use of corpora in language studies.

Swearing in English

Bad language, purity and power from 1586
to the present

Tony McEnery

Routledge
Taylor & Francis Group

LONDON AND NEW YORK

First published 2006
by Routledge
2 Park Square, Milton Park, Abingdon, Oxon, OX14 4RN

Simultaneously published in the USA and Canada
by Routledge
270 Madison Ave, New York NY 10016

Routledge is an imprint of the Taylor & Francis Group

Transferred to Digital Printing 2009

© 2006 Tony McEnery

Typeset in Garamond by Wearset Ltd, Boldon, Tyne and Wear

British Library Cataloguing in Publication Data
A catalogue record for this book is available from the British Library

Library of Congress Cataloging in Publication Data
A catalog record for this book has been requested

ISBN10: 0–415–25837–5 (hbk)
ISBN10: 0–415–54404–1 (pbk)

ISBN13: 978–0–415–25837–1 (hbk)
ISBN13: 978–0–415–54404–7 (pbk)

Publisher's Note
The publisher has gone to great lengths to ensure the quality of this reprint
but points out that some imperfections in the original may be apparent.

This book is dedicated to those who struggle to have their views heard

Contents

Figures

Tables

Acknowledgements

I cannot think of anything that I have ever written which owes so much to the comment and insight of others. I have spent the past eight years, on and off, talking about the ideas in this book to a range of researchers. Because of the nature of this book, the researchers I have spoken to have spanned a range of disciplines. I have also had many audiences, some shocked, some reflective, listen to and comment on the ideas presented here. While the list of people I would like to thank is enormous, I will limit myself here to people who have either suffered my musings on this topic at length, or whose contribution to this work, whether they know it or not, has been significant. From Linguistics at Lancaster I would like to thank Paul Baker, Norman Fairclough, Costas Gabrielatos, Andrew Hardie, Willem Hollman, John Heywood, Geoff Leech, Mark Sebba, Jane Sunderland, Andrew Wilson, Ruth Wodak and Richard Xiao in particular. Four other Lancastrians who deserve a mention are a historian, Michael Seymour, two of my colleagues from Religious Studies, Ian Reader and Linda Woodhead, and Paul Rayson from Computing. All four read parts of this book and gave me very useful comments from the perspective of their own disciplines. Beyond Lancaster, I would like to thank the following academics: Mike Barlow, Lou Burnard, Ron Carter, Angela Hahn, Mike Hoey, John Kirk, Merja Kyto, John Lavagnino, Barbara Lewandowska, Willard McCarty, Ruslan Mitkov, Geoffrey Sampson, Mike Scott, Harold Short, Joan Swann and Irma Taavitsainen. I also need to thank Matthew Davies who assisted me with library research for this book and Dan MacIntyre who helped to construct the corpora used in Chapter 7.

On an institutional level, I would like to thank the Faculty of Social Sciences at Lancaster who provided me with two small grants to construct some of the corpora used in this book and a third grant to conduct work at the British Library. I must also thank the British Academy which has funded my work on seventeenth-century newsbooks as used in part in Chapter 3.

The Libraries of Cambridge and Oxford Universities, as well as the British Library, were of enormous assistance in the writing of this book, particularly Chapters 3 and 4. I am indebted to them for their willingness to help. Additionally, Lancaster University Library, by giving me access to both its rare books archive and Early English Books Online, made my work much, much easier.

1 Bad language, bad manners

Bad language

Consider the word *shit*. Simply being asked to do this may have shocked you. Even if it did not, most speakers of British English would agree that this is a word to be used with caution. Because of prevailing attitudes amongst speakers of the English language, using the word may lead any hearer to make a number of inferences about you. They may infer something about your emotional state, your social class or your religious beliefs, for example. They may even infer something about your educational achievements. All of these inferences flow from a fairly innocuous four-letter word.

Shit, and all other words that we may label as bad 'language', are innocuous in the sense that nothing particularly distinguishes them as words. They are not peculiarly lengthy. They are not peculiarly short. The phonology of the words is unremarkable. While it might be tempting to assume that swear words are linked to 'guttural' or some other set of sounds we may in some way impressionistically label as 'unpleasant', the fact of the matter is that the sounds in a word such as *shit* seem no more unusual, and combine together in ways no more interesting, than those in *shot, ship* or *sit*.[1] A study of bad language would be relatively straightforward if this were not the case.

So how is it that such an innocuous word is generally anything but innocuous when used in everyday conversation? How is it that such words have powerful effects on hearers and readers such as those you may have experienced when you read the word *shit* in the first sentence of this book? The use of bad language is a complex social phenomenon. As such, any investigation of it must draw on a very wide range of evidence in order to begin to explain both the source of the undoubted power of bad language and the processes whereby inferences are drawn about speakers using it. The potent effects of words such as *shit* can only be explained by an exploration of the forces brought to bear on bad language in English through the ages. It is in the process of the development of these attitudes that we see taboo language begin to gain its power through a process of stigmatisation. This process leads a society to a point where inferences about the users of bad language are commonplace. The following chapters will aim to add weight to this observation. For the moment, the reader must take this hypothesis on trust, as before we can begin the process of outlining evidence to support this hypothesis, a refinement of the goals of this book, and some basic matters relating to the sources of evidence I will use, need to be dealt with.

The focus of this book is bad language in English, with a specific emphasis on the study of swearing. Bad language, for the purposes of this book, means any word or phrase which, when used in what one might call polite conversation, is likely to cause offence. Swearing is one example of bad language, yet blasphemous, homophobic, racist and sexist language may also cause offence in modern England. However, this book will not study changes in what has constituted bad language over the centuries. Books such as Montagu's (1973) *Anatomy of Swearing* and Hughes' (1998) *Swearing* have explored these changes already. Nor will this book work through a history of the changing pattern of usage of swear words as Hughes and Montagu have. Rather, this book has three distinct goals. First, it will study the effect of centuries of censorious attitudes to bad language. Following from this, this book will explore how bad language came to be viewed as being associated with a range of factors such as age, education, sex and social class. The passing parade of words that constitute bad language seems to have had little or no effect on what is associated with the users of bad language over the past three centuries or so. This book aims to look beyond the words that have caused offence to look for the social processes that have brought about the associations between bad language and a number of sociolinguistic variables. Finally, this book will seek to demonstrate that the roots of modern English attitudes towards bad language lie in the late seventeenth and early eighteenth centuries. It is in this period that we can find a social and moral revolution occurring which defined attitudes to bad language for centuries to come and established a discourse of purity as a discourse of power.

In pursuit of the later two goals, this book explores the ways in which the public perception of bad language over the past 400 years has changed. The review is not comprehensive in the sense that I do not slavishly work through each decade and century. Rather I seek, by a study of three periods (1586–1690, 1690–1745 and 1960–1980), to outline the role that bad language has played in public life and public discourse in England. In doing so, I will investigate how the state has used bad language as an excuse for censorship (1586–1690), how bad language became associated with a number of sociolinguistic variables such as age, sex and social class (1690–1745), and how a discourse of power based on the absence of bad language was reinforced and defended in the debate over bad language in the media (1960–1980). In looking at these three periods, I will also argue that the studies presented are cumulative – in the later period the discourse of purity that was being defended was that established in the period 1690–1745, and in turn that linguistic purity was used as a tool of censorship in a way just as effective as any act of state censorship in the period 1586–1690.

The goals link to the organisation of this book. The book is split into three major parts. In the first part, I pursue the first goal of the book by looking at the way in which modern English reflects historical processes which have formed attitudes to bad language. In the second part of the book, I will explore in detail what these historical processes were and how those processes have linked bad language to the demographic variables studied in Part 1. In exploring these historical processes I will look at both the establishment of these attitudes (1690–1745) and a recent example of the maintenance of these attitudes (1960–1980). In the final part of the book, I will look at the discourses which were used to establish and to maintain these attitudes.

These three sections support a number of claims about bad language in modern British English. I summarise these claims here, though for the moment I will not seek to justify them – that is the work of the rest of this book. My claims are:

1   modern attitudes to bad language were established by the moral reform movements of the late seventeenth and early eighteenth centuries;
2   these attitudes were established to form a discourse of power for the growing middle classes in Britain;
3   the moral and political framework supported by a discourse of power can be threatened by the subversion of that discourse.

In pursuit of my goals, I will need to use a wide range of sources of data if any explanation of modern attitudes to bad language is to be attempted. The sources used in this book are social and political history, sociological theory and corpus linguistics.

Social and political history

The British people and its government through the ages have forged the attitude to bad language current in British society today. Such a statement is clearly uncontroversial. Yet accepting this statement entails a serious examination of bad language in the context of British social and political history. This in turn leads to significant problems. Discerning the processes behind political actions and social attitudes in the twenty-first century is difficult enough. Considering such factors from the sixteenth century onwards ushers in many practical difficulties. A whole range of methodologies which may be used in the present day are clearly inapplicable when considering the sixteenth century. Focus groups, questionnaires and the full panoply of techniques in modern social science are of no use at all to the researcher in such an investigation. The limited range of data available is accessible only via the tools of the historian's trade – dealing with old texts, government documents and whatever information other sources of documentary evidence may yield.

Sociological theory

It should be clear by now that my approach to bad language views it as being as much a social/historical phenomenon as a linguistic one. In trying to account for how a society develops attitudes and beliefs which problematises language, I will draw on modern sociological theory which seeks to provide an explanatory framework for such events, most notably Bourdieu's theory of distinction and moral panic theory. Bourdieu's theory of distinction, as will be shown shortly, is useful in explaining any differences in language use by different social classes. Moral panic theory is the basis of the approach taken in this book to discourses about bad language.

Corpus linguistics

Corpora are used in two distinct ways in this book. In the third part of the book, corpora are mainly used as sources of evidence to explore the development of attitudes to bad language and discourses surrounding bad language use. This contrasts somewhat with the first part of the book where corpora are used as sources of evidence related to swearing in British English. So, in the third part of this book, corpora are not being used in ways which many readers will typically be familiar with. The way corpora are used in Part 3 differs from the way in which they are used in areas more familiar with corpus use, e.g. language pedagogy, lexicography or theory-neutral linguistic description. This difference arises because my aim here is to show that corpus linguistics as a methodology allows one to couple corpus data with theories and supporting data from beyond linguistics. Yet in coupling corpus data with sociological theory and historical data, I believe that we gain a deeper insight into a question which should be of interest to linguists – the source and origin of the attitudes to bad language prevalent in modern British English.

The first, and to some extent the second, part of the book covers a more familiar, descriptive, use of corpus data. However, it is in the contrast of the different parts of the book that I hope that the need for a deeper, historical and sociological exploration of bad language becomes apparent. While corpus data allows us to describe swearing in English, for example, it does not begin to provide an explanation for anything that we see within the corpus. Description in tandem with explanation is a powerful combination in linguistics. The separation of one from the other is damaging. An explanation of something which is not described in some credible fashion may be no explanation at all. Description without explanation is at best a first step on the road to a full investigation of some linguistic feature. In this book, corpora have a role to play in both explanation and description. The explanations for the attitudes to bad language which corpora help to flesh out in the third part of this book flow directly from the corpus-based description of bad language in the first part of the book. The explanation helps one to understand the description. The description becomes the key to lending cre-dence to the abstract explanation.

So, in this book, corpora are being used as a medium for an exploration of hypotheses arising from social and political history as well as sociological theory. Having mentioned sociological theory, it seems appropriate to return to the theories drawn on in this book: moral panic theory and Bour-dieu's theory of distinction.

Moral panics

The sociologist Stanley Cohen developed moral panic theory in the late 1960s to account for episodes where the media and society at large fasten on a particular problem and generate an alarmist debate that, in turn, leads to action against the perceived problem. The response to the problem is typ-ically disproportionate to the threat posed. Cohen (2002: 1) introduces the idea of a moral panic by saying that:

> Societies appear to be prone, every now and then, to periods of moral panic. A condition, episode, person or group of persons emerges to become defined as a threat to societal values and interests; its nature is presented in a stylised and stereotypical fashion by the mass media; the moral barricades are manned by editors, bishops, politicians and other right-thinking people; socially accredited experts pronounce their diag-noses and solutions.

Though moral panics are far from new, moral panic theory is. In spite of the relative recency of moral panic theory, it is somewhat fractured. Goode and Ben-Yahuda (1994) outline three forms of moral panic as part of an attempt to provide a grand unified theory of the topic. The problem with their approach is that it may be that in trying to produce an over-arching theory, they are forcing a separation between what may be intertwined processes, or are forcing fundamentally different processes to sit unhappily together under the umbrella term 'moral panic theory'. Nonetheless, as the different vari-eties of moral panic are of minimal relevance to the main goals and claims of this book, I will exemplify moral panic theory here solely with reference to the so-called interest group moral panic theory, both because it was the first model developed and because it links most clearly to the events discussed in Parts 2 and 3 of this book.[2]

Cohen (1972) put forward an early version of moral panic theory focused on a media scare related to the activities of two rival groups, 'Mods' and 'Rockers', who clashed occasionally in England, most famously in British south-coast seaside towns in 1964.[3] The model put forward by Cohen is essentially a cultural account of moral panics. It has four basic elements. First, the moral panic must have an object, i.e. what is the moral panic about? Second, a moral panic needs a scapegoat, also termed a 'folk devil' –

> The power of television first impressed me when I lived near a school. Every morning as a stream of children passed by I was treated to advertising jingles, catch-phrases, unarmed combat play-acting or 'bang, bang, you're dead' dialogue with bad language from the previous night's tv programmes. I began to take a closer look at what I was watching. Did the playground echo an escalation of violence, sex and language? It led me to National VALA with its world wide findings, the concerns of others like myself and the fight to maintain common sense standards of good behaviour, decency and moral values in public communications.
>
> Ten years on the pattern has become clear. 'Adult' television material with its rise in violence, increasing sexual explicitness and filthy expression has abandoned responsibility for viewers of every age. Too extreme a view? Films like Natural Born Killers, Reservoir Dogs, Pulp Fiction and Trainspotting (and hundreds of similar examples shown since 1988) all on television must give any responsible citizen cause for worry.
>
> If on screen assaults, beatings, killings, shootings, woundings and brutal behaviour accompanied by revolting language and profanity and often linked with explicit sexual detail, female degradation and drugs are not considered to have a debasing influence on viewers then monitoring is pointless. But I do not think so. Knowledge has fuelled my indignation with the irresponsible response from broadcasting channels, weak regulation laid down by Government and excuses from public bodies who should know better.
>
> Good positive thinking will ensure that decency, morality and good standards return to the screen when you, the viewer, insist. After all, it is the nation and our children at risk.

Figure 1.1 A letter appearing in the autumn 1999 issue of the *National Viewer and Listener*.

should be regulating output, as well as the Government which should be imposing stronger regulatory guidelines. These are also scapegoats. Yet encoded in the attack on the secondary scapegoats is the *corrective action* that the writer is seeking – the imposition of regulatory frameworks both voluntary (from broadcasting channels and public bodies) and statutory (from the Government) which would eliminate the objects of offence. This action will only occur if further corrective measures are taken, in the form of 'viewers' agitating for this change through letter writing. The claim of the letter is that, in the absence of such corrective action, there are clear *consequences* – the children of Britain, in particular, and the nation in general, will be harmed.

Should the corrective action be taken, however, the consequences will be avoided and the desired outcome will be achieved, a Britain in which 'decency, morality and good standards' return to the television screen. The viewer is appealing also to an abstract *moral entrepreneur* – the National Viewers' and Listeners' Association – which is the main driver behind this particular moral panic. As a result of analysing texts such as this, I decided to introduce an additional category – moral panic rhetoric – to my analysis of the lexis of moral panics. While moral panic rhetoric is clearly different from the other categories, in that it does not identify a discourse role, it does capture an essential feature of a moral panic, as I argue that the moral panic is a distinct register marked by a strong reliance on evaluative lexis that is polar and extreme in nature. The existence of such a register is hinted at by Cohen (2002: 19–20) when he notes, when reviewing press coverage of the 'Mods and Rockers' panic, that:

> The major type of distortion ... lay in exaggerating grossly the seriousness of the events, in terms of criteria such as the number taking part, the number involved in violence and the amount and effects of any damage or violence. Such distortion took place primarily in terms of the mode and style ... of most crime reporting: the sensational headlines, the melodramatic vocabulary and the deliberate heightening of those elements of the story considered as news. The regular use of phrases such as 'riot', 'orgy of destruction', 'battle', 'attack', 'siege', 'beat up the town' and 'screaming mob' left an image of a besieged town.

While Cohen's observations are not those of a linguist, he is clearly aware that the intentional manipulation of language to evoke specific hearer/reader responses is an intrinsic part of a moral panic, i.e. that there is a moral panic rhetoric. Indeed, in the example given in Figure 1.1, I would argue that the writer adopts *moral panic rhetoric* – for example, negatively loaded modifiers such as *filthy, revolting, brutal, irresponsible, weak* and *degradation* are used to amplify the objects of offence and the sins of the scapegoat. Positively-loaded words are used to describe the desired outcome that the writer and the National Viewers' and Listeners' Association are seeking, with talk of *decency, morality, good standards, common sense* and *moral values* establishing the moral supremacy of the writer and the National Viewers' and Listeners' Association and, by implication, suggesting that those who disagree with the writer are at least tacitly supporting indecency, immorality, bad standards, foolishness and the abandonment of moral values. All of these claims are based on the flimsiest of evidence – the musings of a person hearing a passing group of schoolchildren and wondering whether their behaviour might have been influenced by the previous night's television. Rather than wondering whether the television was now more accurately portraying everyday language use, the writer chose to believe that television was setting new standards *for* everyday language use. Whichever of these two arguments is true, the fact that the writer does not admit the possibility that views other than their own may have validity reveals another feature of this moral panic in particular, and one that is arguably a feature of many, if not all, moral panics – the reliance on moral absolutist beliefs. As will be shown later, particularly in Chapters 5 and 7 of this book, terms such as *decency* and *morality* do not need to be defined for this writer, as they assume the meanings of these words based on a pre-existing moral framework, in the case of the National Viewers' and Listeners' Association, conservative Christianity. Yet the power of certainty that this gives the moral entrepreneurs and associated activists also pervades their writings – the need to explore opposing views, the need to work within a framework of moral relativism, is absent. The answers provided within a framework of moral absolutism are, by their very nature, absolute. It is that which, in part, gives strength to the rhetoric of a moral panic of this sort. Consequently in Chapters 6 and 7 I will also explore the rhetoric and discourse roles of moral panics.[8]

Bourdieu's theory of distinction

Another important explanatory framework adopted in this book is the theory of social distinction drawn from the work of the French sociologist, Pierre Bourdieu. Bourdieu's work, while admittedly drawn from his research on French society and relating largely to features of culture such as art, food and manners, nonetheless is relevant to language, as Bourdieu himself acknowledges. Bourdieu's claim is a relatively simple one: features of culture are used to discriminate between groups in society, establishing a social hierarchy based on a series of social shibboleths. The consequences of the establishment of such a hierarchy are both to allow members of groups to be readily identified and to impose the hierarchy itself. For example, if a taste for fine wine is supposed to be a token of high social status, then on seeing somebody pouring a drink from such a bottle of wine, other factors aside, one might assume they were of a certain social class. Similarly, if one sees somebody drinking a pint of beer, and this is a marker of low social class, other factors aside, one may also infer their social class. However, if fine wine is priced so as to exclude the lower orders from purchasing it, the social hierarchy has nothing to do with taste as such. Rather, those tokens of taste are controlled in such a way as to impose the social structure that they are a token of. Transporting this argument to language is somewhat straightforward. If there are forms of language which are identified with a refined form of speech, then those aware of the perception of this form of language, who are able to invest either the time or the money in order to acquire that 'refined' form of language, will be able to identify themselves with a particular group in society. Yet more perniciously, if that type of speech is already associated with a particular social class, then there is a zero cost for that social class in using that form of speech, while the speech associated with lower classes is devalued and the onus is placed on them to adapt the way that they speak. In making that adaptation they are tacitly acknowledging the supposedly superior form of speech that they are shifting to when that shift takes place. To Bourdieu, in language this process leads to:

> opposition between popular outspokenness and the highly censored language of the bourgeois, between the expressionist pursuit of the picturesque or the rhetorical effect and the choice of restraint.[9]

In seeking shibboleths of taste, groups distinguish themselves from one another in society in order to set boundaries which identify difference. For Bourdieu this means that:

> Groups invest themselves totally, with everything that opposes them to other groups, in the common words which express their social identity, i.e. their difference.[10]

In other words, the process of setting out the boundaries of linguistic differences for groups is no casual process. It is a process whereby the very identity of the groups concerned becomes intimately associated with their language use, through 'the socially charged nature of legitimate language'.[11] Linked to a social hierarchy, the capacity is clearly generated to identify not merely the language of particular groups, but to identify the language of various groups with power as defining a discourse of legitimacy, a discourse of power. This discourse of power then becomes the unmarked case – the linguistic norm, the supposedly neutral form of expression – with forms that do not follow it marked out as the marked, abnormal, negatively charged forms of language, or 'the least classifying, least marked, most common, least distinctive, least distinguishing'[12] forms of language. This process of the discourse associated with one group becoming the dominant discourse of power leads to those not possessing that discourse being:

> at the mercy of the discourses that are presented to them ... At best they are at the mercy of their own spokesmen, whose role is to provide them with the means of repossessing their own experience. The essential indeterminacy of the relationship between experience and expression is compounded by the effect of legitimacy imposition and censorship exerted by the dominant use of language, tacitly recognized, even by the spokesmen of the dominated, as the legitimate mode of expression of political opinion. The dominant language discredits and destroys the spontaneous political discourse of the dominated. It leaves them only silence or a borrowed language.[13]

In other words, those without access to this discourse of power are already marked as disadvantaged by their language use. This disadvantage is compounded by them having to use a discourse with which they do not readily identify when asserting themselves, as:

> Through the language . . . Bound up with a whole life-style, which foist themselves on anyone who seeks to participate in 'political life', a whole relation to the world is imposed.[14]

At worst it may lead to the failure of the dominated groups to represent themselves, relying rather on members of the group possessing the dominant discourse consenting to represent them and provide leadership to them, as Bourdieu notes when he says that:

> It forces recourse to spokesmen, who are themselves condemned to use the dominant language . . . or at least a routine, routinizing language which . . . constitutes the only system of defence for those who can neither play the game nor 'spoil' it, a language which never engages with reality but churns out its canonical formulae.[15]

Distinction simultaneously empowers further those already possessing power, while further dispossessing those who are already dispossessed. This book will argue that, when we look at modern English, we see distinction at work in the form of bad language. Broadly speaking, the discourse of power excludes bad language, the discourse of the disempowered includes it. Obviously, this statement is, however, something of an idealisation, as several factors may, for example, combine on any specific occasion to determine language usage. Similarly, several factors together may establish a matrix of power, as opposed to single factors generating a polar distinction between the powerful and the disempowered. Indeed, in Part 2 of this book I will explore how demographic factors may combine in such a way. For the moment, I will maintain the broad assertion made above, adding the caveat that such a statement notes what is typical and is only generally applicable when we are considering one feature in isolation. One final point I should make at this stage is that what I am discussing here is overt as opposed to covert prestige.[16] In this book I am mainly concerned with power related to overt prestige, though I accept without hesitation that in establishing an overtly prestigious form of language, a covertly prestigious form of language is entailed which may invert the matrix of power mentioned above. Research into overt and covert prestige is so well established that I feel the issue can be sidestepped in this book as there is a wealth of material that interested readers can pursue to explore this issue for themselves.[17]

To recapitulate the earlier goals and claims of this book, it will be argued that the process of forming a class distinction around swear words was undertaken in the late seventeenth/early eighteenth century by an aspiring middle class who actively sought to distinguish themselves from the lower orders by a process of 'purifying' the speech of the middle class while problematising the speech of the lower orders (see Chapters 4 and 6). Further, it will be argued that the vehicle which brought about this process of distinction was a moral panic focused on bad language in the late seventeenth century, which empowered certain members of the middle classes to act simultaneously as moral entrepreneur and *arbiter elegantium*, dictating the linguistic manners of the general population. Finally, the book will argue that the processes of disempowerment which Bourdieu suggests are entailed by such a development are observable not merely in the seventeenth century but in the present day (see Chapters 5 and 7). This brief overview of the book allows readers to see how the elements introduced in this chapter come together in order to provide a coherent account of bad language in English. The corpus is used principally to establish a series of observations related to distinctions in the use of swearing. The explanation of these distinctions is then sought through historical research, as well as the application of moral panic theory and Bourdieu's theory of distinction to texts in the period 1690–1745. The process of disempowerment is then explored further in the context of debates about language in the media in the late twentieth century. While corpus data will be instrumental in exploring the discourse of bad language in the seventeenth, eighteenth and twentieth centuries, it is the goal of this book to show that explanations for what we see in corpora often lie beyond the borders of the corpus itself – the observations we can draw from corpora, while verifiable, are not necessarily of any assistance in developing explanations, though they do frame what an acceptable explanation may look like, i.e. any explanation must match the observations drawn from the corpus. But by marrying other methodologies with the corpus method, and drawing on appropriate theories, the corpus data itself can be illuminating in the search for a wider, comprehensive account of the features of language we approach the corpus to investigate.

Corpus linguistics: the corpora used in this book

In this section, I will discuss the majority of the corpora used in this book. Two minor corpora (a corpus of seventeenth-century news texts and a corpus of German radio propaganda broadcasts) will be discussed briefly when they are introduced. One major corpus, the Lancaster Corpus of Abuse,[18] is not reviewed in this section, being reviewed instead in Chapter 2 as a prelude to an analysis of bad language in present-day English.

The Mary Whitehouse corpus (MWC)

The MWC includes the major writings of Mary Whitehouse in the period 1967–1977. This corpus covers three of her books, namely *Cleaning-up TV*, *Who Does She Think She Is?* and *Whatever Happened to Sex?*, amounting to 216,289 words in total.[19] These books, with their wide circulation, were the principal public output from the National Viewers' and Listeners'

Association (the VALA – see Chapter 5 for details) in this period, and as such I take them to be a good focus for a study of how the VALA tried to excite a moral panic in the general population of Britain.

The British National Corpus (BNC)

The BNC is a 100,000,000-word corpus of present-day British English. The corpus is split into a 90,000,000-word balanced written corpus and a 10,000,000-word corpus of orthographically transcribed spoken language. As I am using only the spoken data in this book I will limit my brief description of the BNC to its spoken section. The spoken BNC is composed of a series of spontaneous conversations recorded by members of the British public in the early 1990s. The corpus was designed to provide material from across the UK (the so-called demographically sampled subset of the corpus) and across a range of different activities (the so-called context governed subset). Demographic information about the speakers was encoded in the corpus. This demographic data was then used to balance the spoken material with regard to a number of variables, notably, for this book, age, sex and social class. The result of this balancing is that, in the corpus, the amount of speech spoken by males and females is roughly even, as is the speech produced by different age groups and social classes.

The Society for the Reformation of Manners corpus (SRMC)

The SRMC was compiled by me specifically for this study. It contains four key texts from the Society for the Reformation of Manners (SRM) amounting to 120,709 words.[20] Two texts were selected as being those which achieved the widest circulation during the period of the reformation of manners movement and which were widely cited – Yates (1699) and Walker (1711) – while two further texts were included from the end of the period of the society's activities, namely Anon. (1740) and Penn (1745).[21] The latter texts were included to permit an investigation of how, if at all, the discourse of the society shifted during its lifetime. While ideally one would like to have gathered a much larger set of texts together, the longevity of the Yates and Walker texts, and their wide distribution during the lifetime of the societies, makes them in essence texts which are representative of the society and its aims. The later texts, as noted, represent some of the final texts of the society and are included solely to allow the possibility of a diachronic approach to the writings of the society.

The Lampeter corpus

The Lampeter corpus is a diachronic corpus of English, covering the period 1640–1740. The corpus samples texts from a range of genres (economy, law, miscellaneous, politics, religion and science) over this period, taking samples at periods of roughly ten years. The corpus was constructed at the University of Chemnitz by a team led by Josef Schmied, and has been used in the diachronic study of variation in English.[22] For the purposes of this book, I will only use materials from the corpus covering the period 1690–1750, as it is in this period that I want to contrast the language of the SRM with what one might term English in general[23] (i.e. all of the genres of the Lampeter at once) and specific genres and registers of English (texts covering only one domain of Lampeter). There are 544,894 words in the Lampeter corpus in the period 1690–1750.

The Lancaster–Oslo–Bergen and Freiberg–Lancaster–Oslo–Bergen corpora (LOB and FLOB)

Both the LOB and FLOB corpora are related to an earlier corpus, the Brown University Standard Corpus of Present-day American English (i.e. the Brown corpus, see Kučera and Francis 1967). The corpus was compiled using 500 chunks of approximately 2,000 words of written texts. These texts were sampled from 15 categories. All were produced in 1961. The components of the Brown corpus are given in Table 1.1.

LOB and FLOB follow the Brown model. The Lancaster–Oslo–Bergen corpus of British English (LOB) is a British match for the Brown corpus.[24] The corpus was created using exactly the same sampling frame, with the exception that LOB aims to represent written British English used in 1961. The Freiberg–LOB corpus of British English (i.e. FLOB) represents written

Table 1.1 Text categories in the Brown corpus

Code	Text category	No. of samples	Proportion (%)
A	Press reportage	44	8.8
B	Press editorials	27	5.4
C	Press reviews	17	3.4
D	Religion	17	3.4
E	Skills, trades and hobbies	38	7.6
F	Popular lore	44	8.8
G	Biographies and essays	77	15.4
H	Miscellaneous (reports, official documents)	30	6.0
J	Science (academic prose)	80	16.0
K	General fiction	29	5.8
L	Mystery and detective fiction	24	4.8
M	Science fiction	6	1.2
N	Western and adventure fiction	29	5.8
P	Romantic fiction	29	5.8
R	Humour	9	1.8
Total		500	100.0

British English as used in 1991 using the Brown sampling frame once more.[25] LOB and FLOB, as well as being corpora which allow one to study recent change in British English, may also be used, as they are in this book, to exemplify general published written British English in the early 1960s and early 1990s respectively.

Issues

Before leaving the presentation of the corpora used in the book, it is appropriate to pause and consider a number of methodological questions arising from the use of the corpora. The first relates to claims of balance and representativeness for the specialised corpora, i.e. the MWC and the SRMC. In what way might they claim balance and representativeness? Clearly not in the same way as the BNC or Lampeter corpus can. For example, the SRMC is not particularly representative of general English in the period in which it was written. Similarly, it is not balanced with regard to general English in the period. But both of these assertions of course miss the point – it is not intended to be generally balanced and representative; it is not representing general English in the late seventeenth century. Rather, it is representing the writings of a specific group in that period. So balance and representativeness for the MWC and the SRMC should relate only to the writings of the group or writer in question, not for writers of the language in general. Yet, the focus of the specialist corpora is narrower still. The corpora in question are not trying to be representative of all of the works produced by the group in question. If that were the case, such items as handbills handed out by the Society for the Reformation of Manners to those it had had prosecuted would have to be represented.[26] But the purpose of the study of the SRMC in this book is to explore the way in which the SRM attempted to persuade society at large of its case, and more specifically how they sought to persuade society that bad language was a major problem. As such, the SRMC was constructed to focus principally on those texts which achieved very wide circulation in Britain, as one may hypothesise that it was these texts, rather than handbills handed to individuals, that had the greater impact on British society. A similar argument applies to the MWC – it is by studying the widely published works of Mary Whitehouse that we can see the effect on discourse that the VALA had, not by looking at newsletters produced for the relatively small number of subscribing members of the VALA. Yet, for both the SRM and the VALA, I would not want to claim that the more ephemeral texts they produced had no impact on society – I am sure that their effect on a micro level was notable. However, as throughout the rest of this book I am trying to focus on macro rather than micro processes with regard to attitudes to bad language, and hence the major, widely disseminated texts of the SRM and the VALA are the focus of the corpora built for this book. Balance and representativeness as issues become somewhat narrow when one has such a tightly focused research question as that under consideration here. A more fruitful way of approaching the specialised corpora constructed for this book is to think of them as corpora which are focused on a very narrow issue. For such corpora, the concepts of balance and representativeness become so specific as to be uninteresting.

A slightly more difficult issue relates to the question of the comparability of the reference and the specialised corpora, for example Lampeter with the SRMC.[27] The timeframe for the Lampeter corpus is 1640–1740. For the SRMC it is 1699 to 1745. Can one truly compare the SRMC and Lampeter with confidence when the Lampeter corpus cannot match the timeframe of the SRMC texts perfectly? There are two responses to this problem, one pragmatic, one principled. The pragmatic response is that, at times, the perfect corpora for any given study may not exist, but one may still proceed to undertake an exploration with imperfect corpora as long as one notes that, at some future point when the perfect corpora are available, researchers may wish to return to the results in order to verify, in this case, that the differences seen between the corpora were a result of a process other than language change. I encourage future researchers to do just that, as I am working with the best corpora available to me, and accept the possibility that future corpora may reveal that the differences noted in this book have everything to do with language change and nothing to do with moral panics. However, I doubt that this will happen, because of the principled point I want to make. While some features of language change rapidly – notably lexis – other features of language change much more slowly, for example, grammar. Relatively large corpora covering relatively large time periods are needed to catch grammatical change. I liken the process to normal cinematography as opposed to time-lapse cinematography. A corpus like the BNC is like a typical camera – it may be useful for capturing movements which are relatively rapid. A pair of corpora like the LOB and FLOB corpora, which are two corpora with identical sampling frames applied to English in the early 1960s and early 1990s respectively, are needed to catch much slower movements not immediately visible using a corpus such as the BNC.[28] Just as we need to use time-lapse photography to see a flower open, so we may use carefully sampled corpora with identical balance and representativeness, built to represent the same language, across a significant period of time to see slow-moving language change. My view is that the changes being looked at in this study are relatively slow moving – discourses of moral panic, I will claim, have fairly stable properties, so much so that over nearly 300 years we can see marked similarities between the panic discourse of the SRM and the VALA. Given that we are dealing with stability over time on such a scale, I think one can fairly view the slight differences in timeframe between the focused and reference corpora used in this book as being largely irrelevant.

One final issue I need to deal with is the question of variant spelling in the Early Modern period. For example, variant spelling occurs in the SRMC in the sense that certain words may be spelt differently in different texts, or even at times within the same text. Also, though at times a word form has a relatively stable spelling in the texts, the word form used is not identical to the modern English word form (e.g. *publick* v. *public*). The former type of spelling variation in particular can cause problems when exploring word frequency, as the word may be represented by many word forms, each with a separate frequency. As word frequency is an important measure used in this book, the issue of spelling variation had to be addressed. Consequently, when constructing the SRMC corpus, where spelling variation occurred, both the original word form (e.g. *govenour*) and the modern word form (e.g. *governor*) were encoded in the text. While this may not be of interest to the average reader, I should note that by the use of a mark-up language called XML I was able to encode this information in the corpus in such a way as to allow readers/analysts to see either the original spellings in the text or the modern variants, as they wished. Throughout this book, I will use the modern spelling forms encoded in the texts to construct the wordlists used in my study.

Concepts/techniques used in this book

Word frequency forms the backbone of the analyses undertaken in this book. The reason for my focus on word frequency is related to an observation made on page 6 – the discourses surrounding moral panics are obsessive, moralistic and alarmist. Each of these factors should, in principle, significantly influence the lexis of the moral panic. Moralistic and alarmist language should be signified by words with an alarmist or moralistic tone such as, perhaps, *evil*, *threat* or *danger*. My hypothesis is that these words will be used more frequently by purveyors of moral panic, and that the obsessive nature of their discourse should lead to the use of these words becoming not merely frequent, but so frequent that these words can be viewed as salient, in the sense that they distinguish texts relaying moral panics from general English, or even texts written in a similar register/genre but not conveying a moral panic. Similarly, the obsessive focus of the text on particular problems, solutions and scapegoats should mean that words denoting these elements of the moral panic will also become salient in the text. In order to explore moral panics in this way, I used the keywords function of a computer program called WordSmith[29] in order to find those words which occurred in the focused corpora significantly more frequently than in the reference corpora. As the keywords analysis is so central to the study presented in this book a brief discussion of the workings of keywords is necessary.[30]

Keywords and key-keywords

Keywords, as conceived by linguists,[31] are those words which, when a particular corpus (A) is compared to a reference corpus (B), are used significantly more or less frequently in A than in B. Note that the choice of A and

B to a large extent determines how we can interpret the results of a keyword analysis. Imagine that A is a highly specialised type of language, for example computer manuals, while B is a collection of written language similar to the written section of the BNC, i.e. a balanced and representative sample claiming to represent general English. Such a comparison will most likely show the differences between the specialised variety of English and English in general. We would expect words like *monitor, mouse* and *keyboard* to occur much more frequently in computer manuals than they generally would in written English. These are termed *positive keywords*, as they represent some of the lexis which is used more frequently by writers of this type of text, and hence may be said in a way to characterise this type of text. Similarly, words which may occur in written English quite frequently, such as *car, laugh* or *stroll* are clearly less likely to occur in computer manuals and hence may show up as *negative keywords* – lexis that is shunned by the writers of computer manuals. Positive and negative keywords may also tell us something about the nature of the discourse in the texts other than the topic area under discussion – pronouns, for example, may appear as keywords. The computer manual example will serve to illustrate this point again. It is likely that computer manuals, written to provide instructions to users, will include a higher than usual proportion of second-person singular pronouns, as *you* will be used to direct instructions to the reader. On the other hand, the other pronouns, which may be fairly evenly spread across the reference corpus, will show as negative keywords in the corpus as the computer manual texts will shun them.

Keywords are determined by WordSmith using a test for significance called the p-value,[32] which is calculated in this book on the basis of the log-likelihood score.[33] Words become keywords if they are used with a difference in frequency between corpora A and B in such a way that their frequency in A is significantly higher than B (positive keywords) or lower than B (negative keywords). In addition, the keywords themselves are ranked by the WordSmith program and given a keyness score to denote the strongest to weakest negative and positive keywords.

While comparing a specialised form of text to a general corpus of English is bound to achieve some fairly obvious results, this is not the only valid use of keyword analyses. We may, for example, wish to compare apparently similar types of texts to one another in order to identify relatively subtle differences between those texts. Consider a situation where you have access to the writings of two newspapers and you wish to see if there are any differences between the two. Setting aside the possibility of comparing radically different newspapers, let us consider what might happen if we compare two quality broadsheet newspapers, for example the *New York Times* and the *Los Angeles Times*, or *The Times* of London and the *Independent* newspaper from the UK. One would reasonably hypothesise that a number of differences could be shown between the papers concerned. It is not likely that we would see the genre specific lexis appearing as positive keywords, as happened in the fictitious comparison of the BNC and some computer manuals. Similarly, it is unlikely that the negative keywords would contain much in the way of general English in use by one newspaper but not the other. Rather, we might see lexis which betokens differences in editorial style perhaps (one newspaper may have house style rules that dictate that first person pronouns are not to be used, the other may have no such rule leading to *I* becoming a keyword) or perhaps related to differences in reporting practices (one newspaper covering a particular issue regularly in depth more than the other newspaper), or perhaps differences brought about because of the place of publication (perhaps *California* may be a key word in the comparison of the *LA Times* and the *New York Times* simply because one newspaper was published in California and reports the news from California in more depth as a consequence). So comparing texts which appear similar may be as rewarding as comparing texts which are obviously different, though the results of the analysis will most likely be somewhat different.[34]

The reason that I spent some time discussing negative and positive keywords, and their use in studying similar and different text types, is that in Part 3 of this book keyword analyses of this sort will be undertaken, and the positive and negative keywords generated by these analyses will be the main focus of the exploration of the moral panics encoded in the SRMC and the MWC. I hypothesise that the keyword list, when one compares one of the specialised corpora to its corresponding reference corpus, should be populated, in part at least, with words that identify the major roles and actors of the moral panic, as these should occur with an unusually high frequency owing to the obsessive, alarmist and moralistic nature of the moral panic.

A refinement of the keyword analysis, key-keywords, is also used in this book. Key-keywords are keywords which are key in all, or the majority, of subsections of a corpus. I use the term subsection here as the calculation of keywords is actually undertaken across individual corpus files. These may represent almost anything, e.g. a vast collection of different texts held within one file, an individual text, or a fragment of text.[35] However, assuming that the files in a corpus represent texts in some meaningful way, key-keywords are of particular use in exploring such issues as whether a keyword is key to a colony of texts (where each file is a text) or across a whole text (where each file, for example, is a chapter of a text). Key-keywords are used in Chapter 7 of this book.

Collocates, linked collocates and colligates

There is one other major form of analysis which this book will use which should be introduced here: collocational networks. In part, I will be exploring collocational networks to look for *linked keywords*, keywords which are linked by common collocates, or, as I will term them, *link collocates*. Generally, I will use collocational networks to pursue the lexical organisation of text along the lines suggested by Martin Phillips.[36]

Collocations are explored in this chapter, using the mutual information statistic as a useful heuristic to filter meaningful from non-meaningful collocates. Collocation is the process whereby words keep company with one another and thereby convey meaning via co-occurrence. The idea is not particularly new,[37] though collocates are still being analysed, refined and explored by corpus linguists.[38] For ease of discussion, some basic terminology used with reference to collocation needs to be introduced beginning with *node* and *span*. A collocate, for the purposes of this discussion, is a word which occurs with some higher than chance frequency in the context of a given word. The given word is called a *node* and the span of words either side of the node in which we search for collocates is termed the *span*. In this book, a span of five words either side of the node will be used in exploring collocation.[39] A distinction between collocation, a frequent association with content words, and *colligation*, frequent association with grammatical words, is sometimes drawn by researchers. While this distinction is noted and accepted by this work, the distinction is not particularly active in the analysis of the corpora used in this book, though where it is, the distinction will be sustained.

Collocational networks

Given a working definition of collocation, we need to consider a number of known properties of collocates. First, collocations are *directional*.[40] For example, while we might observe *red* collocating with *herring*, the association of *herring* to *red* is much stronger than the association of *red* to *herring*. In short the link between the two may be seen as more important to *herring*, which, when it occurs, is most likely to co-occur with *red*, than to *red*, which has a wide number of collocational partners, of which *herring* is one. Second, certain words attract more collocates than others. While the specific words attracting collocates may vary across a range of written contexts, given the means to investigate specific texts and corpora, we will find words which establish networks of collocation. Within these networks, the words which attract most collocates to them, or are in some sense central to that collocational network, are called *nuclear nodes*. Figure 1.2 is an example of the word POINT[41] occurring as a nuclear node in a thermodynamics textbook.[42]

In this work I will at times be using collocational networks to explore patterns of lexis surrounding certain keywords and other specific node words central to the arguments put forward in this book, e.g. SWEAR, LANGUAGE. I will focus only briefly, and rather technically, here on the extraction of such networks, as I wish to keep the focus on the uses that such networks may be put to, and how my use of them differs from that of others. Readers uninterested in the precise technique for extracting these clusters are advised to skip to page 24 at this point.[43]

The construction of collocational networks undertaken in this book

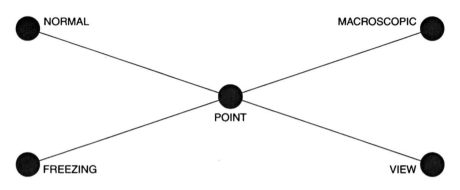

Figure 1.2 A sample collocational network.

groups words together on the basis of the strength of the association of collocates with a given node. In order to determine if the link between a candidate collocate and a node is strong enough for the two to be linked, mutual information is used.[44] Mutual information (MI) measures how often, in a given corpus, words are attracted to one another relative to their occurrence independent of one another. In relative terms, if the measure produces a positive score, the words are attracted to one another (they co-occur frequently), if the score is around zero, the two words in question have no particularly strong association, while if they yield a negative score they shun one another's company. In this study, I will include a link between two node words where the MI score exceeds 3.[45] I will indicate with an arrowhead the direction of association, where appropriate. Where no arrowheads are shown, the link can be assumed to be bidirectional. By way of illustration, Figure 1.3 shows the pattern of collocation focused around the word *swearers* in the SRMC, as explored in Chapter 6.

It should be noted that MI is not a rigorous statistic. It is certainly not a parametric test. One cannot reasonably talk about 'statistically significant' results being produced by MI. However, MI is a very useful heuristic which describes data and helps in the process of interpreting complex data sets like large corpora. It is in this spirit that MI, and the collocational networks based on this measure, are used in this book. Nonsense collocational networks, clusters and MI scores, in the sense that they defy reasonable explanation, can and do occur. However, the MI measure is helpful many times more often than it is unhelpful, and as such it provides a powerful tool to the linguist interested in studying patterns of collocation. The interactions observed, of course, require interpretation, as will be shown later, because the networks may describe a range of behaviours – such as words participating in the creation of terms or the different meanings of a word (the example given in Figure 1.2 was used by Phillips to demonstrate this property of collocational networks with reference to the word *point*).

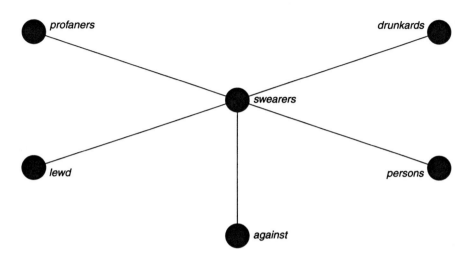

Figure 1.3 The network around *swearers* in the SRMC.

Semantic prosody

A further thing that I argue a collocational network may help to show is the *semantic prosody* of a particular word. As Stubbs (2002: 225) notes, 'there are always semantic relations between node and collocates, and among the collocates themselves.' The meaning arising from the interaction between a given node word and its collocates is referred to as *semantic prosody*, 'a form of meaning which is established through the proximity of a consistent series of collocates' (Louw 2000: 57). Semantic prosodies typically convey meanings that encode attitudes and evaluations (Louw 2000: 58). Semantic prosodies are typically negative, with relatively few of them referring to an affectively positive meaning. Semantic prosody is strongly collocational in that it transmits meaning beyond the sense of individual words, i.e. words which do not convey a negative meaning in isolation convey one when they collocate together. I will not discuss semantic prosody in more depth here, as it is used, and to an extent exemplified, in Chapters 6 and 7.

The use of the techniques

My aim in using the techniques described here is to access both the *aboutness* of the individual texts and collections of texts used in Part 3 of this book. I also wish to show the patterns of meaning being formed within a text related to certain concepts in the text. To deal with the first point, I want to be able to characterise the texts generally, in essence asking the question, 'What is this text about?' through largely automated means, as a prelude to exploring the moral panics encoded within the texts. As part of exploring the moral panics I believe to be encoded within the texts, I also wish to pursue the question of the collocational networks surrounding particular node words, accessing these networks in order to demonstrate how the meaning associated with that node is constructed. What company does a word such as *swearing* keep? How is its meaning coloured by its association with that company? Are collocational networks a means of exploring how attitudes to swearing have been formed and reinforced? It is in response to questions such as these that I will be exploring specific collocational networks (Chapter 6). I will also work with the corpus on a number of levels; I will explore the corpora at the level of the whole corpus, whole texts within a corpus and whole chapters within a corpus (see Chapter 7).[46] The overall characterisation of the aboutness of the corpora will be undertaken using a keyword analysis and exploring the links between the keywords. The exploration of the keywords will be supported by looking at the collocational networks focused around certain keywords. Each keyword, for the purposes of this book, will act as a node.

The book in outline

With an outline of the main theories to be used in this book provided, and my methodology established, we can now consider the way in which theory and methodology will come together in this book. The book is divided into three parts. Part 1 consists of Chapter 2, Part 2 consists of Chapters 3 to 5 and Part 3 consists of Chapters 6 and 7.

Part 1 is an investigation of how bad language is used in present-day English. The focus for the study is the spoken section of the British National Corpus. Using the corpus, the relationship between bad language and a number of social variables, namely age, sex and social class, is examined. Part 1 concludes by relating the differences found in the corpus to Bourdieu's theory of distinction. Having observed a number of social variables interacting with bad language in Part 1, Part 2 will set out to explore the historical context in which the distinctions apparent in the spoken BNC developed. In doing so, the chapter will explore a period before which these attitudes developed (Chapter 3), showing how bad language was not subject to widespread, state sponsored regulation, nor was it particularly associated with age, sex or social class. Chapter 4 explores the social processes whereby distinction became focused on bad language, generating the links with age, sex and social class observed in Chapter 2. In doing so, the chapter will begin to link moral panic theory and distinction, claiming that a moral panic about immorality led to a wider social movement which caused bad language to become a marker of distinction. Chapter 5 follows on from Chapter 4, moving the discussion of bad language and morality to the late twentieth century by exploring reactions to the use of bad language in the popular media in the 1960s and 1970s. In doing so, the chapter refines the theory of distinction further by relating it to a model of discourse in which purity has become equated with power, allowing for the possibility that power may be undermined by deliberate verbal impurity. In exploring this issue, the chapter focuses very much on the campaigns of Mary Whitehouse against bad language in the UK through her National Viewers' and Listeners' Association.

Part 3 reflects back on Part 2 by exploring the discourses of moral panic evident in the writings of the groups covered in Chapter 4 (explored in Chapter 6) and Chapter 5 (explored in Chapter 7). In exploring the discourses of these panics, the chapters investigate both specific rhetorical devices used to produce panic, form attitudes and assert the existence of in and out-groups in the societies being discussed.

The three sections together explore bad language use now (Part 1) the historical roots of current linguistic usage (Part 2) and discourses that have influenced that usage over time (Part 3). In terms of the use of corpora in the book, their role is crucial in Parts 1 and 3. In Part 1, it is corpus evidence which outlines the patterns of bad language use, which the historical account of the development of attitudes to bad language in Part 2 must explain. In turn, in Part 3 the discourses which are explored using data are explored in the light of the historical and social arguments presented in Part 2. Throughout, sociological theory is used to account for what I would argue is an essentially social process – the association of certain words with certain variables such as age, sex and social class. It is in using corpus data to control and direct historical, linguistic and sociological enquiry that I hope this book can prove to be thought-provoking.

Part 1
How Brits swear[47]

2 'So you recorded swearing'

Bad language in present-day English[48]

Bad language as a marker of distinction

Bad language words (henceforth BLWs) are a marker of distinction in English. As will be shown, distinction, BLWs and a range of sociolinguistic variables interact in ways which are at times predictable. Yet, at other times, they are quite unexpected. This chapter will explore those patterns of interaction. Before doing so, however, I feel I should address my assertion that BLWs are a marker of distinction as opposed to simply being markers of difference. I accept that one might normally express observations such as those that will be made in this chapter in terms of difference. Yet in the case of BLWs I argue that what we are in fact looking at is a process of distinction – the difference is directly related to prestige. BLW use is one of a number of linguistic variables we may consider when we discuss non-prestige forms of language. Hence the presence or absence of BLW use in language is a marker of distinction, with the relative absence of BLW use being a marker of a more prestigious, more refined version of the language. I will leave this defence of my approach to BLW use being based on distinction here for the moment – the conclusion to this chapter, Chapter 4 and Chapter 5 return to this issue. The conclusion of this chapter refines the notion of distinction in the light of the findings here. Chapters 4 and 5 review two discourses about BLW which very clearly make the point that BLW is linked to prestige.

In this chapter I will look at BLWs in English, as used in everyday speech, in order to explore the ways in which distinction relates to it. In doing so, I will explore the behaviour of single BLWs, groups of BLWs and types of BLWs. We will see how those words are related to specific groups, or may be indicative of interactions between specific groups. However, before exploring these issues, let me present the data used in this chapter.

The Lancaster Corpus of Abuse

The work in this chapter is based on the Lancaster Corpus of Abuse (LCA) which in turn is based on the BNC spoken corpus. The LCA is a problem oriented corpus based on data extracted from the BNC spoken corpus.[49] The corpus contains only those examples of BLW usage where the age, sex and social class of the speaker are known.[50] Within the corpus, BLWs have been annotated using a scheme developed to encode a range of information relevant to the linguistic study of such terms. In this chapter, when I am looking at these features – notably categories of BLW use and gender of the target of a BLW – I use the LCA. Otherwise I use the whole BNC spoken section in order to increase the volume of examples retrieved.

In deciding what words I wanted to include within the corpus, I was partly guided by claims within the literature, partly by my own intuition, partly by serendipitous discovery and partly by words I encountered within the corpus which fitted the classification system developed. This later point will be returned to shortly. To give examples of each of the first three types of words, I have used the corpus to explore claims made by researchers such as Hughes (1998) in his work on swearing in English.[51] Hence, words explored by Hughes were included in the corpus. Yet I knew, on the basis of my own knowledge of bad language, that there were many examples of bad language not addressed in the literature. I then expanded the coverage of the LCA (2.0) on the basis of my intuition. Beyond this, however, when I examined the corpus data from time to time I would come across new examples of bad language. Sometimes these words were familiar to me, but I had simply forgotten them (e.g. *pissy*). However, sometimes the words/phrases were entirely new to me and their discovery by me in the corpus was entirely accidental (e.g. *battyman* as an abusive term to refer to male homosexuals) and sometimes they were relatively novel terms formed, for example, as a result of word play (e.g. *Cuntona* occurs in the BNC as an insulting pun on *Cantona*, the surname of a French footballer).

The LCA inherits the balance of its parent corpus, the BNC, which is balanced for age, sex and social class. This is fortunate, as these are the three variables with which this chapter is principally concerned.

The BLWs covered by the LCA can broadly be grouped under the following main headings – swear words (e.g. FUCK, PISS, SHIT), animal terms of abuse (e.g. PIG, COW, BITCH), sexist terms of abuse (e.g. BITCH, WHORE, SLUT), intellect-based terms of abuse (e.g. IDIOT, PRAT, IMBECILE), racist terms of abuse (e.g. PAKI, NIGGER, CHINK) and homophobic terms of abuse (e.g. QUEER). Obviously, there is an interplay between these broad categories – for example, animal terms of abuse may also be sexist abuse forms (e.g. *cow*). However, for the purposes of describing the contents of the corpus, this broad classification will suffice.[52]

All told, there are 8,284 separate examples in the LCA. The corpus also contains annotations, as in order to retrieve information from the LCA in a speedy and systematic way,' I needed to develop a set of annotations geared to the study of BLWs. In the following section the development of this system will be outlined.

The annotation scheme

The examples in the LCA are all annotated so that the relevant metadata encoded in the BNC is retained by the example in the LCA. So, for example, if an utterance in the BNC was spoken by a male, aged 0–15, of social class DE, this information is retained by the LCA. Note that in building the LCA I was only interested in examples for which all of the relevant metadata was available. For example, where the age, sex or social class of a speaker of a BLW was unknown in the BNC, this data was not included in the LCA, as my purpose in building the LCA was to develop as rich a set of annotated data related to BLWs as was possible. Note, however, that in the study of BLWs related to the age, sex and social class of speakers in this chapter, the whole BNC is once again used to maximise the number of examples recovered, so the restrictions imposed on the LCA are only relevant to a subset of the features explored in this chapter.

One major limitation imposed on the LCA was inherited from the BNC. As well as studying who spoke an instance of BLW use, I was equally interested in knowing who they had been speaking to. However, with the spoken BNC it is impossible most of the time to discover who the hearer/hearers of any given utterance was/were. Similarly, it can be very difficult on occasion to determine the gender, age and social class of the person or object a specific example of BLW use is directed at. Hence while the LCA represents a richly annotated corpus for the study of BLWs, the corpus does not represent the ideal resource with which to investigate BLWs. It does, however, represent the best alternative given the resources available to construct it.

While the LCA owes a great deal of its annotation to the BNC, as it simply inherited annotations from that corpus, additional annotations were introduced to the LCA data, namely gender of target, animacy, metalinguistic usage and BLW type. I will describe each of these briefly. Where it was possible to determine the gender of the person at whom any example of abusive language has been directed, that was annotated. The identification of such examples relied on a close reading of the context of the utterance, with clues, particularly gender marked pronouns, being very important in the process of determining the gender of the person at whom the bad language was directed. Similarly, information on the animacy of the object/person at whom the bad language was directed was annotated in the corpus – again this required a human analyst to read the text to determine the object/person in question. Where it was possible to identify at who/what the example of bad language was directed, the animacy of that object/person was then noted. Metalinguistic usage was also noted – not all examples of bad language in the BNC constitute the actual use of bad language. On occasion people are merely discussing their favourite swear word, for example. By considering each example in the corpus, such metalinguistic uses of bad language were identified. Finally, a scheme which categorised the type of bad language in use in each example was developed. I will not discuss this classification scheme in detail here as it has been the subject of discussion in a number of other publications.[53] However, suffice it to say that the scheme itself has undergone a number of changes since its inception and that some categories, especially those related to metaphoric usage, are certainly susceptible to further development. With that said, the scheme itself proved robust when it was manually applied to the corpus, and as such seems to provide a credible basis for the categorisation and differentiation of the uses of BLWs. Table 2.1 outlines the bad language categorisation scheme, while Table 2.2 shows the full range of annotations applied to each example of bad language in the LCA.

A brief discussion of Table 2.1 is necessary. There is, quite clearly, a link between morphosyntax and the classification scheme given. At times, a given word is classified partly because of its part of speech, e.g. when a word is acting as an adverbial booster it receives one label, when the same word form is acting as a premodifying adjectival intensifier it receives another label. One cannot, however, simply replace the labels with part-of-speech categories. For example, Curse, Dest, Gen and Literal are all examples where, for the word FUCK, the word is most likely to be a verb, as shown in the examples given in the table for this word. Yet in each case the use of the words, in functional terms, clearly differs. In Curse there is a clear insult intended, with a very clear target for the word. With Dest, while once again the intention to some degree is to insult, there is also an imperative involved, typically with a demand being made that the target go away. In a Gen utterance, FUCK is used

Table 2.1 The categorisation of bad language

Code	Description
PredNeg	Predicative negative adjective: 'the film is **shit**'
AdvB	Adverbial booster: '**Fucking** marvellous' '**Fucking** awful'
Curse	Cursing expletive: '**Fuck** You!/Me!/Him!/It!'
Dest	Destinational usage: '**Fuck** off!' 'He **fucked** off'
EmphAdv	Emphatic adverb/adjective: 'He **fucking** did it' 'in the **fucking** car'
Figurtv	Figurative extension of literal meaning: 'to **fuck** about'
Gen	General expletive '(Oh) **Fuck!**'
Idiom	Idiomatic 'set phrase': '**fuck** all' 'give a **fuck**'
Literal	Literal usage denoting taboo referent: 'We **fucked**'
Image	Imagery based on literal meaning: 'kick **shit** out of'
PremNeg	Premodifying intensifying negative adjective: 'the **fucking** idiot'
Pron	'Pronominal' form with undefined referent: 'got **shit** to do'
Personal	Personal insult referring to defined entity: 'You **fuck!**'/'That **fuck**'
Reclaimed	'Reclaimed' usage – no negative intent, e.g. **Niggers/Niggaz** as used by African American rappers
Oath	Religious oath used for emphasis: 'by God'
Unc	Unclassifiable due to insufficient context

Table 2.2 Categories of annotation

Field	Feature marked	Possible values
1	Gender of speaker	M = male, F = female, X = unknown
2	Social class of speaker	As per social class categories of BNC (see Aston and Burnard 1998)
3	Age of speaker	As per age categories of BNC (see Aston and Burnard 1998)
4	Category of insult	As per Table 2.1
5	Gender of hearer	As per gender of speaker
6	Person of target	1 = first person, 2 = second person, 3 = third person, X = unknown
7	Metalinguistic usage	0 = no, 1 = yes
8	Animacy of target	+ = animate, − = non-animate, X = unknown
9	Gender of target	As per gender of speaker
10	Number of target	1 = singular, 2 = plural, X = unknown
11	Quotation	Q = quotation, N = non-quotation, X = unknown

as an expression of general anger, annoyance or frustration. In the case of Literal, there is no clear intention to insult, merely an intent to describe an act of coitus. Parts of speech are clearly important to the categorisation scheme, but the scheme itself is not simply a relabelling of parts of speech. Also, and interestingly, just because a particular word covered in the LCA has a part of speech connected with a category does not mean to say that the word will appear in that category. For example, consider SHIT and FUCK. Both may clearly be nouns (*the fuck I had last night was marvellous, I have just had a shit*) or verbs (*I was shitting when the cat came in, I fucked him*). Morphosyntactically the words are similar. However, their distribution across the bad language categories differs – SHIT occurs only in categories PredNeg, AdvB, Figurtv, Gen, Idiom, Literal, Image, PremNeg, Pron and Personal. FUCK occurs in a larger number of categories – AdvB, Curse, Dest, EmphAdv, Figurtv, Gen, Idiom, Literal, PremNeg, Pron, Personal. While morphosyntactically similar, the words respond to these categories in different ways – FUCK has a much broader set of functions than SHIT. Yet there are some categories in which SHIT can be placed which do not apply to FUCK (e.g. PredNeg) and some categories FUCK can be placed in which do not apply to SHIT (e.g. Dest). It should also be noted that the distribution of examples across these categories is different – for example, EmphAdv accounts for most of the occurrences of FUCK in the LCA (55 per cent), while for SHIT most of its occurrences (44.6 per cent) occur in category Gen. BLWs do not act the same just because they share similar parts of speech. The range of classifications the word may express can differ, and their affinities for different categories in quantitative terms may differ radically, even where two words can appear in the same category. Given that the categories seem at least to display discriminating power, I will not seek to justify them further here.

Before proceeding to explore the relationship of bad language to distinction, I will note once more that my focus here will be on the spoken language. Bad language in written English is still the subject of censorship. Hence, for any feature we observe – or fail to observe – in a written corpus, it is difficult to know whether it is an artefact of censorship or not. While there are limitations placed on speech also, these tend to be social rather than legal in nature, and hence the study of bad language in a corpus of spontaneous spoken English, such as that in the BNC, provides a much more secure basis for the study of bad language, as opposed to language which is subject to overt censorship.

Sex

One might imagine that males use bad language more than females. Indeed it has been suggested in the past – especially in research in the 1970s – that swearing was a behaviour engaged in more frequently by males than by females,[54] though recent research has retreated from that position to suggest that frequency for both sexes may vary markedly depending on context and the gender of the hearer/hearers.[55] However, it is still, in my opinion, a widely held folk belief in Britain that men swear more often than women. This is not the case. When all of the words in the LCA are considered, it is equally likely that bad language will be used by a male as by a female.[56] A possible means of invalidating this finding, and to prove that males do indeed use BLWs more than females, would be to discover that a very frequent BLW used almost exclusively by males had been excluded from the LCA. This is clearly not the case. Another possible explanation is that a great number of low-frequency BLWs exclusively used by males had been omitted. Given the wide range of words included in the LCA, this also seems unlikely. A more likely explanation begins to emerge if we look at the distribution of BLWs between males and females. If we compare the BLW word forms used by males and females, we discover that there are a set of words significantly overused by males and a set of words significantly overused by females. If we look only at those words where a highly significant difference in use by males and females occurs (i.e. where there is a one-in-one-hundred chance or less that the result we have observed is attributable to chance) then 15 words emerge as being those which distinguish male and female swearing – *fucking, fuck, jesus, cunt* and *fucker* are, in descending order of significance, more typical of males; *god, bloody, pig, hell, bugger, bitch, pissed, arsed, shit*[57] and *pissy* are, once again in descending order of significance, more typical of females. The results are shown in Table 2.3.[58]

So, while BLWs as a set may not differentiate males from females, the frequency of use of individual BLWs clearly does mark males and females apart. The words themselves suggest, to my intuition, another way in which males and females may differ. May it be the case that males have a preference for 'stronger' word forms while females have a preference for 'weaker' word

Table 2.3 Words preferred by males and females in the BNC ranked by LL value

Word	Frequency of use by females per 1,000,000 words	Frequency of use by males per 1,000,000 words	Overuse by	Log-likelihood (LL) value
god	459.38	172.33	Females	549.09
fucking	99.77	284.10	Males	350.83
bloody	526.71	277.80	Females	314.15
fuck	32.75	68.28	Males	48.98
pig	11.32	1.42	Females	36.55
hell	146.29	114.21	Females	15.69
bugger	39.48	25.00	Females	13.09
bitch	17.14	8.54	Females	11.82
pissed	24.18	13.82	Females	11.45
jesus	9.79	18.70	Males	10.88
arsed	2.45	0.20	Females	9.44
cunt	5.51	11.18	Males	7.54
fucker	0.61	3.25	Males	7.41
shit	80.19	63.81	Females	7.38
pissy	1.22	0.00	Females	7.35

forms, i.e. those less likely to cause offence? It seems to me that the male marked words are more offensive, more potent, than the female marked words. However, in order to explore this hypothesis I need something more than my intuitions – I need access to something like a Richter scale for BLWs. It was beyond the scope of my work to conduct a large-scale survey to determine the strength of particular BLWs. Fortunately there was no need to do so, as such reviews have been commissioned by various media watchdogs in the UK. I have combined the results of two such surveys in order to provide a five-part scale of offence with which to classify the use of BLWs.[59] The scale itself is borrowed from one of the sources that have contributed to its construction, the British Board of Film Classification. The scale is shown in Table 2.4.

Using this scale it is possible to revisit Table 2.3 to explore the relationship between the strength of the words and such matters as gendered direction and speaker sex. In Table 2.5[60] each word is followed by a number in parentheses which indicate its position in the LL-score ranked table shown in Table 2.3.

So, BLWs are a marker of distinction between males and females, but the distinction is marked quantitatively with a small set of word forms and is more generally marked qualitatively, with males drawing more typically from a stronger set of words than females. One further way in which male and female BLW use may differ is with reference to the types of BLWs discussed in the previous section. Are there categories of BLW use that are more markedly male or female? In order to explore this I contrasted the use

Table 2.4 A scale of offence

Categorisation	Words in the category
Very mild	*bird, bloody, crap, damn, god, hell, hussy, idiot, pig, pillock, sod, son-of-a-bitch, tart*
Mild	*arse, balls, bitch, bugger, christ, cow, dickhead, git, jesus, jew, moron, pissed off, screw, shit, slag, slut, sod, tit, tits, tosser*
Moderate	*arsehole, bastard, bollocks, gay, nigger, piss, paki, poofter, prick, shag, spastic, twat, wanker, whore*
Strong	*fuck*
Very strong	*cunt, motherfucker*

Table 2.5 Table 2.3 revisited – BLWs typical of males and females mapped onto the scale of offence

Shock	Male	Female
Very mild		*god* (1), *bloody* (2), *pig* (3), *hell* (4)
Mild	*jesus* (3)	*bugger* (5), *bitch* (6), *pissed* (7), *arsed* (8), *shit* (9)
Moderate		
Strong	*fucking* (1), *fuck* (2), *fucker* (5)	
Very strong	*cunt* (4)	

of the different types of BLWs by males and females. Table 2.6 shows those categories which are overused by either males or females.

It is interesting to note that Gen, a category which is not associated with abuse, is a more typically female than male category. Premodifying intensification and literal usage are also more typical of females than males. Again, neither is linked directly to personal abuse. The typically male usages are also, interestingly, not linked to abuse as such – they are both associated with intensification. So in terms of categories of swearing, it appears that only two styles of intensification – AdvB and EmphAdv – are markedly male. Note that the explanation for this may be linked to the male marked words. *Fucking* is the word which is most clearly male marked in the data (see Table 2.3). This word is only used by females 226 times in the LCA, 19 times as an AdvB and 154 times as an EmphAdv. By contrast the word is used 982 times by males, 107 times as an AdvB and 683 times as an EmphAdv. Given that there are in total 317 examples of BLWs in category AdvB and 1,953 examples of EmphAdv in the corpus, it is reasonable to say that the word *fucking* is a strongly male marked word, used mainly to

Table 2.6 Categories of BLW use more typical of males and females ranked by LL value

Type of word	Frequency of use by males	Frequency of use by females	Overuse by	Log-likelihood (LL) value
Gen	799	1,250	Females	100.09
EmphAdv	1,131	822	Males	49.10
AdvB	202	115	Males	24.19
PremNeg	413	517	Females	11.65
Idiom	58	90	Females	6.97

produce AdvB and EmphAdv effects. Given the ratio of all examples of AdvB and EmphAdv to those produced using the word *fucking* by males, AdvB and EmphAdv in turn become typical of male speech.

The PremNeg category also bears some discussion, however, as it is a category within which *fucking* can and does occur. Might it be the case that the word *fucking* is a favourite form of female intensification and females reserve their use of the word *fucking* for the PremNeg form of intensification? The answer to this question is no – while males will often use *fucking* to realise PremNeg, females shun the word in the PremNeg category in favour of *bloody*. In the LCA, males use *fucking* as a PremNeg 158 times, in contrast to females who use it only 48 times. Yet females use *bloody* 422 times as a PremNeg, as opposed to males who use it only 126 times. *Bloody* is the word most typical of female intensification. Interestingly, the word does appear as both an AdvB and an EmphAdv, but is not used by males and females differently in a way that is statistically significant (AdvB 75 and 76 times respectively, EmphAdv 426 and 650 times respectively). It is only in the PremNeg category that a statistically significant difference emerges. So *bloody* as a typically female word (see Table 2.3) and PremNeg as a typically female intensification strategy seem to be choices which are complementary to those of males, who prefer *fucking* and AdvB/EmphAdv type intensification. As such, intensification is an area in which there is a marked distinction between males and females both in terms of lexical choice and BLW category choice.

Yet speaker sex is not the only gender variable in the LCA. How do speakers respond to speakers of the same, or different, sex? Do males act, as one would imagine that gentlemen may, to avoid BLW use in the presence of ladies? Do they refrain from directing BLWs at ladies? With regard to women, do we find that women are less likely to use BLWs in the presence of other women? Do they also prefer not to direct BLWs at other women? The LCA can shed some light on these questions, though not really on the hearer-related questions – as noted, deriving hearer gender from the BNC is difficult. So answering the questions about whether BLW use will take place in the presence of people of a certain sex is impossible with BNC derived data. It is possible to study the gender of the direction of BLW use, however. If one limits one's questions to examples where there is a clear direction to the BLW use, one is able to explore whether males direct BLWs at males more often than females, whether females direct BLWs more often at males than females, etc. When one explores these issues in the LCA, one observation can be made immediately: BLWs are directed at males more often than females.[61] While this shows us something about language directed at males, it shows us little about the patterns of interactions behind that general pattern. Who is it that is swearing at males more than females? Other males? Females? In order to explore these questions I constructed the matrix shown in Table 2.7. This table shows how often one gender directs BLWs at either gender in the LCA.

All of the pairwise comparisons one may want to make in Table 2.7 are significant. Males direct BLWs at a male target far more often than they do at a female. Exactly the reverse is true of women – they are more likely to direct BLWs at other women. At this point the question of hearer becomes relevant again. Is it the case that women use BLWs more in the presence of other women, but suppress them in male company so as to appear more 'ladylike'? While this is certainly a possibility, the inability to annotate hearer information in the corpus precludes the exploration of this hypothesis here. However, what can be seen very clearly are preferences for an intragender direction of BLWs for both sexes. This result only holds if we treat all BLWs as identical, however. If we assume that some BLWs may prefer intragender direction, while others prefer intergender direction, and study gendered direction at the word level, we may discover not only that certain words do prefer intergender direction, but also that certain words are exclusively directed at one sex rather than the other. Tables 2.8 and 2.9 explore these questions.

As can be seen from Tables 2.8 and 2.9, for both sexes there is some degree of differentiation of the use of BLWs for targets of different sexes with, for example, the words *cow, bitch, bloody, fucking, slag, tart, tit, tits* and *whore* showing a pronounced bias for being directed at females by females and *god, bastard, gay, christ, git* and *cunt* being words which, when used by females, show a pronounced bias towards being directed at males. The words themselves seem to display some evidence of being directed quite differently by males and females. For example, the word *cunt* is directed exclusively at males by females. It is a pure intergender BLW for females. This is not true

Table 2.7 Patterns of male/female-directed BLW use

	Male directed	Female directed	LL score
Male speaker	702	156	375.82
Female speaker	392	497	12.43
LL score	89.06	187.2	

Table 2.8 Words more likely to be directed by females at either males or females ranked by LL score

Word	Female targets	Male targets	Preferred target	LL score
cow	25	0	Female	34.66
god	16	55	Male	22.66
bastard	2	24	Male	21.94
bitch	26	3	Female	20.91
bloody	153	85	Female	19.70
gay	0	12	Male	16.64
fucking	58	24	Female	14.53
christ	0	10	Male	13.86
git	0	9	Male	12.48
slag	9	0	Female	12.48
cunt	0	8	Male	11.09
tart	8	0	Female	11.09
tit	6	0	Female	8.32
tits	6	0	Females	8.32
whore	6	0	Female	8.32

Table 2.9 Words more likely to be directed by males at either males or females ranked by LL score

Word	Female target	Male target	Preferred target	LL score
fucking	37	254	Males	181.71
god	1	35	Males	40.77
bloody	25	89	Males	38.11
fuck	1	33	Males	38.11
pissed	0	27	Males	37.43
bastard	2	30	Males	29.40
wanker	0	13	Males	18.02
cunt	1	15	Males	14.70
arse	5	25	Males	14.56
fucked	0	10	Males	13.86
shit	3	19	Males	12.97
piss	2	16	Males	12.40
git	1	13	Males	12.20
bird	7	0	Females	9.70
christ	0	7	Males	9.70
gay	0	7	Males	9.70
sod	1	10	Males	8.55
arsehole	0	6	Males	8.32
prick	0	6	Males	8.32
cow	9	1	Females	7.36
idiot	1	9	Males	7.36

for males, who, while showing a strong preference for directing the word at males, do also direct it at females. *Cow* is a pure intragender word for females; this does not appear to be the case for males. So the question of whether or not certain words may be directed at one sex or another may very well depend on the speaker. However, there is doubtless another set of words in the LCA which have purely male and female targets, irrespective of the gender of the speaker. These are listed in Table 2.10.[62] The figures in parentheses indicate the number of occasions in the LCA in which the word is directed at either a male or female, as appropriate.

In very few instances in the table are the figures large enough to allow one to generate a claim of statistical significance. Nonetheless, it is interesting to note that there do appear to be some words which are exclusively male directed and exclusively female directed irrespective of the gender of the speaker. This is certainly the case for words like *whore*, for example, which is directed at females by females six times and by males at females twice. Similarly, *gay* is directed exclusively at males, seven times by men, 12 times by women.[63] Note that the *gay* example is an interesting one – it has taken on the role of being a BLW applied exclusively to males, while this need not be the case, as the term can cover males and females. Also, it has retained that gender-exclusive direction even though other words which one might assume would exhibit such a gender exclusive direction, such as *bitch*, do not exhibit such exclusivity.[64]

So, it seems to be the case that there is a set of BLWs which are used with an exclusive gender direction by male speakers but not female speakers (e.g. *arsehole*).[65] Similarly there is a set of BLWs used with an exclusive gender direction by female speakers but not males (e.g. *cow*). There is a third set of words which are exclusively directed at a particular gender by a speaker irrespective of the sex of the speaker (e.g. *gay*). Over and above that, there are words which show a strong gender targeting/production preference for/by males or females but which are not gender exclusive (e.g. *bloody* tends to be targeted at females by females, *bastard* tends to be directed at males by males).

Given that there are at least three types of words where some degree of gender exclusivity in direction applies, an obvious question one should ask is whether there is anything that typifies the words targeted at either gender.

Table 2.10 BLWs directed solely at males and females ranked by frequency of usage

Female-only direction
slag (12), bird (10), tart (10), tits (9), whore (8), tit (7), birds (3), hussy (3), whores (3), bitches (2), slagged (2), tarty (2)

Male-only direction
gay (19), christ (17), wanker (16), prick (7), pillock (4), poofter (4), fucker (3), moron (3), pissing (3), pissy (2)

Given that speaker sex is an important variable for two of these sets of words, and that sex is an important variable in dictating the direction of the words, gender seems, once more, an interesting variable to explore. May it be that, in some qualitative sense, the BLWs in the three sets vary? One obvious way in which they may vary is in the strength of the words. Are males and females as harsh in their use of gender exclusive/biased BLWs? Do males use weaker BLWs when directing them towards females rather than males? A host of questions may be related to the question of gender, direction of BLW, speaker and strength of the language employed.

Tables 2.11 and 2.12 also suggest that intragender BLW use is more frequent generally than intergender BLW use. They also make it fairly obvious, once more, that stronger BLWs are more often directed at males than females. May it simply be the case that, when it comes to gender exclusive/biased BLWs, this is true, but for all of the other BLWs it is not, meaning that, overall, it is not the case that there is any differentiation in the strength of BLWs directed at males and females? This question was explored to some extent in Table 2.5, but is worth revisiting. In order to explore this question further I assigned a value to each of the BLWs appearing in Table 2.10, with the words in the mildest category assigned an offence strength of one, with the offence strength increasing by category to a

Table 2.11 Table 2.8 revisited – BLWs typical of females used either of males or females mapped onto the scale of offence

Shock	Male target	Female target
Very mild	god (55)	bloody (153), tart (8)
Mild	christ (10), git (9)	cow (25), slag (9), tit (6), tits (6)
Moderate	bastard (24), gay (12)	bitch (26), whore (6)
Strong		fucking (58)
Very strong	cunt (8)	

Table 2.12 Table 2.9 revisited – BLWs typical of males used either of males or females mapped onto the scale of offence

Shock	Male target	Female target
Very mild	god (35), bloody (89), idiot (9)	bird (7)
Mild	pissed off (27), arse (25), shit (19), git (13), christ (7), sod (10)	cow (9)
Moderate	bastard (30), wanker (13), piss off (16), gay (7), arsehole (6), prick (6)	
Strong	fucking (254), fuck (33), fucked (10)	
Very strong	cunt (15)	

maximum of five for a word such as *cunt*.[66] Then, the number of times each word was directed at males was multiplied by the strength of the word. This was repeated for all words and the results added together and divided by the total number of words under consideration to yield an average strength of a BLW directed at a male by a male. The process was then repeated with all combinations of male/female direction. The result is that females target females with an average BLW strength of 1.956 and males with an average BLW strength of 2.042. Males target females with an average BLW strength of 1.562 and males with a BLW strength of 2.779.[67] So, while the frequency of BLW is higher in intragender BLW use, in terms of strength males have stronger BLWs targeted at them by speakers of both sexes. While females may direct BLWs at females more frequently, when they direct them at males, they select stronger BLWs than when they are directing them at females. Males, on the other hand, both direct BLWs less frequently at females than males and use weaker BLWs when directing BLWs at females rather than males.

May the pattern change if we look at BLWs independent of target, i.e. include non-targeted BLWs (e.g. Gen types)? The average strength of a BLW spoken by a female, irrespective of target, is 1.48. For males it is 2.23.[68] It is apparent that not only do females generally use 'weaker' BLWs, they also have weaker BLWs directed at them. Males, on the other hand, use stronger BLWs on average and have stronger BLWs directed at them, though when directing BLWs at females, as we have seen, they use weaker BLWs than females would.[69]

Before leaving the issue of strength, may it also be the case that the affinities of the different types of BLW use to the different sexes is related to the association of these categories with stronger or weaker forms of BLW use? This is indeed the case. Table 2.13 gives a rank ordered scale of the average strength used in each BLW category.

This table deserves some discussion. One possible response to the finding is to note, for example, that most examples of the word FUCK occur in the Curse and Dest categories. As FUCK has a high strength, the category has a high strength. However, this is overlooking the versatility of FUCK and other BLWs. There are a wide range of words which can be used to realise a Curse-type BLW expression, or a Dest type. For example, *bugger* can also be a Curse. Yet there are almost twice as many (49 v. 29 examples) of *fuck* as a Curse compared to *bugger* as a Curse. There is a clear choice by speakers to select the stronger word when producing an expression which would fall into this category. Similarly, for category Personal, both *bugger* and *fuck* are possible choices when realising a Personal type utterance. Yet in this category *bugger* is more frequent than *fuck* (194 v. 8 examples). There is evidence that some categories select the stronger words while others select weaker words. A good example of this is category Gen – the BLWs (in descending order of frequency, with the frequency of the appearance of this word following the word in parentheses) in the Gen category are as follows:

Table 2.13 Average strength of BLWs in each category

Category	Frequency in LCA	Average strength of word in the category
Dest	110	3.37
Curse	105	3.10
Reclaimed	22	3.00
Personal	756	2.48
Literal	144	2.41
EmphAdv	1,948	2.29
AdvB	312	2.22
Figurtv	384	2.01
Image	108	1.94
Pron	36	1.79
PremNeg	828	1.69
Idiom	453	1.52
PredNeg	101	1.37
Gen	2,048	1.29
Oath	53	1.01

god (1,288), *hell* (281), *shit* (159), *christ* (109), *jesus* (92), *fuck* (70), *damn* (16), *bugger* (11), *crap* (8), *gods* (2), *piss* (2), *shite* (2), *bloody* (1). Other than *fuck*, there is not a single word in the Gen category with a strength higher than 2.[70] Gen, as a category, seems to select milder words. Given that many of the words which mark out differences between males and females are linked to these categories (e.g. *god* as a weak word preferred by females, strongly associated with Gen-type BLW use) a fuller picture emerges of the differences between male and female BLW use, with females using weaker words in consequence of using weaker categories of BLW use (or, conversely, choosing weaker categories of BLW use because they wish to use the weaker words).

Sex as a variable will be revisited throughout this chapter. This initial investigation of gender-based differences is interesting in that it demonstrates the relative subtlety of the differences in BLWs between males and females. It also demonstrates the utility of using the LCA for such an investigation. Let us now explore another factor: age.

Age

Again, the literature would lead one to believe that age is an important variable in the use of BLWs. For example, Cheshire (1982: 101) claimed that swearing has a particular value for teenagers, as it is a 'major symbol of vernacular identity' for this age group. Hence one would expect to find more swearing in that group. This is indeed the case. When one looks at all of the BLWs in the LCA, there is a positive correlation between age and the production of BLWs, though the pattern is not quite as straightforward as it at first appears. In rank terms, using the same age intervals as those in the spoken section of the British National Corpus, the profile of BLW use shown in Figure 2.1 emerges.

This figure shows that BLW use increases into the age range U25 and thereafter generally steadily declines.[71] This result holds for both males and females. This graph certainly lends some support to the hypothesis that adolescents are more likely to use BLWs, perhaps for the reasons that Cheshire outlined. While it would be nice to have a corpus in which actual ages, rather than ages within a band, were recorded so that the U15 and U25 categories could be further broken down, it is far from implausible to suggest that there could well be a hidden peak in BLW use in this graph in the adolescent age range. This peak may be responsible for the high volume of U15 data and may largely account for the peak in the U25 data. While this must remain speculative, given that the hypothesis is in line with the predictions and findings of others, I would venture to say that this hidden peak is almost certainly present in this data.

Hidden peaks aside, some questions may still be asked of these results. May the results be a side-effect of the omission of one or more very frequent BLWs used by the older speakers? There is no evidence for this in my exploration of the BNC and the LCA. The only possible grounds on which such a result could rest relates, in my view, to such matters as euphemisms or very, very mild realisations of BLW categories (e.g. *dear* in 'Oh dear!'). It may be the case that the older speakers produce more very weak BLW utterances, avoiding the direct use of BLWs. So, for example, they may say 'oh fudge' or 'oh flip' rather than 'oh fuck'. As my study does not cover euphemism, I have not recorded or explored such cases. To do so would require a very labour intensive, manual exploration of the BNC. However, in

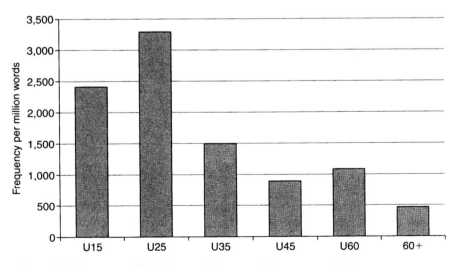

Figure 2.1 Frequency of BLWs per million words in groups of different ages.

such an exploration, the categories developed in this study may be of help –
most of them are associated with fairly fixed frameworks which help to generate an utterance of a certain category. So, for example, 'Oh' followed by a
BLW typically generates a Gen.[72] If we find other words other than a BLW
in such a context, we also have the potential for a Gen, e.g. 'oh flip', 'oh
sugar', 'oh fiddlesticks'. In order to check the potential impact of such omis-
sions on my results, I explored the pattern 'Oh+*any word*+!' in the spoken
BNC.[73] The results do not indicate that large numbers of Gen types were
missed by the LCA. Those that were missed for this pattern would not have
boosted the frequency of Gen types for the older speakers. In fact, it would
have done quite the reverse. The search gave rise to five Gen types for males
under 15 formed with the words, *sugar*, *dear*, *boy*, *blimey* and *golly*. For
females, two new Gen types were spotted, both produced by under-15-year-
olds and both formed with *dear*. From this, admittedly limited study, there
is no evidence that a vast swathe of BLW-like events are not represented in
the LCA, and there is no evidence that this leads to the frequency of
BLWs produced by older speakers being under-reported, though there is the
scantiest indication that BLW-like utterances by the under-15s may be
under-reported.

The next obvious question one may ask of the data is will the order
reported here change if we take the strength of the BLWs produced by
speakers of different ages into account? The answer is no; when one calculates the average strength of a BLW produced by speakers in the different
age groups, the results powerfully reinforce the negative correlation of age
with swearing. The results are: U15 – 2.24, U25 – 2.31, U35 – 2.16, U45 –
1.31, U60 – 1.55 and 60+ 1.17. While the correlation with age is, once
again, not perfect, the correlation is nonetheless noticeable and generally
negative.

Given that there is a diachronic dimension to comparing speakers of different ages, one does need to consider whether one is observing language
change, or whether the snapshot provided by the BNC is typical of BLW use
in any era. This is a difficult question to address given the corpus resources
available. If in the future an equivalent to the spoken BNC is produced, it
may be possible to explore changing patterns of BLW use over time. As it
stands, however, this is not possible at the moment. On the other hand,
given that the literature on BLW use argues that the correlation observed
here should indeed be observed, I will assume, until evidence to the contrary
presents itself, that what is observed here is what researchers have expected
to see for some time – a correlation between age and BLW use, with BLW
use declining as speakers become more conservative with age.

Before leaving the discussion of age, it is worth considering whether the
different age groups select from the BLW categories differently, and
whether the particular age groups have particular preferences for certain
BLW categories. With respect to the question of whether the age groups
vary in their BLW category choice, the answer is yes.[74] The results of an

exploration of which age group is the most, and which is the least, frequent user of each type of BLW use are given in Table 2.14.

The results for the 60+ category is worth discussing – the evidence is that, pretty much across the board, this group uses BLWs least and avoids the largest number of BLWs as a consequence. In the case of Reclaimed, although this group uses the largest proportion of all recorded examples of this category other than the U15 age group, this result should be treated with caution as Reclaimed is the least frequent category in the LCA (see Table 2.13) – there are only five recorded examples of the 60+ group using a Reclaimed in the corpus. With reference to Oath, this is the weakest category of BLW use. Hence its relatively more frequent use by the U60 (and 60+) group is explicable purely in terms of them using these weaker BLW forms. Note that the avoidance of this category by the U25 group is explicable on the same grounds, as is the attraction of the U15 groups to stronger BLW categories on the whole. The U15 and U25 groups are attracted to much stronger BLWs (notably those forming Dest and Personal types). They correspondingly avoid the weaker BLW categories, leading to their avoidance of Oath types. Table 2.14 in conjunction with Table 2.13 clearly suggests a relationship between BLW category strength and age.

Within the age groups, this is reinforced slightly. In Table 2.15, the top four ranking categories for each age group are given. Following each type in the table is a figure indicating its rank in the strength of BLW table (with 1 being strongest, see Table 2.13).

For each age group the picture is remarkably similar – they use EmphAdv, Gen, Personal and PremNeg types most frequently, except the

Table 2.14 The most frequent and least frequent users of particular BLW categories, categories ranked by strength from highest to lowest

Category	Highest use	Lowest use
Dest	U25	60+
Curse	U35/U60	60+
Reclaimed	U15	U35/U45
Personal	U15	60+
Literal	U15	60+
EmphAdv	U60	60+
AdvB	U35	60+
Figurtv	U25	60+
Image	U25	60+
Pron	U15	60+
PremNeg	U60	60+
Idiom	U60	60+
PredNeg	U15	60+
Gen	U25	60+
Oath	U60	U25

Table 2.15 The top-four BLW categories for each age group

Rank	Type U15	Type U25	Type U35	Type U45	Type U60	Type 60+
1	Gen (14)	Gen (14)	EmphAdv (6)	Gen (14)	EmphAdv (6)	EmphAdv (6)
2	Personal (4)	EmphAdv (6)	Gen (14)	EmphAdv (6)	Gen (14)	Gen (14)
3	EmphAdv (6)	Personal (4)	Personal (4)	PremNeg (11)	PremNeg (11)	PremNeg (11)
4	PremNeg (11)	PremNeg (11)	PremNeg (11)	Personal (4)	Personal (4)	Idiom (12)

60+ age group, where Personal does not feature in the top four, being usurped by the much weaker Idiom type. While the ordering of EmphAdv, Gen, Personal and PremNeg varies somewhat by age group, it is clearly in the 60+ age group that the major change occurs. However, looking across the table, one might claim again that age and strength interact – Personal, the strongest category in the table, declines steadily in the rank ordering as the speakers grow older, with the rank profile being 2, 3, 3, 4, 4 before the Personal type exits the top four in the 60+ column. So, with specific reference to the Personal type, we might suggest that, once again, Table 2.15 furnishes evidence that age and strength of BLW use is correlated.

An obvious problem, however, is that within each age category are respondents who differ in a number of potentially important ways, e.g. sex and social class. While I have already made some observations about sex, I have yet to consider social class. In the next section I will, therefore, consider social class as a variable before returning to the question of how age, sex and social class may interact.

Social class

What of social class and BLW use? Does BLW use simply decline as we look higher up the social hierarchy? When tested, the differences in the use of BLWs by different social classes is indeed significantly different.[75]

Does this clear distinction between the classes shown in Figure 2.2 also hold for strength of BLW use – do the lower social classes select stronger BLWs, while the higher social classes select weaker ones? When one calculates the average strength of BLW for each social class, a different picture

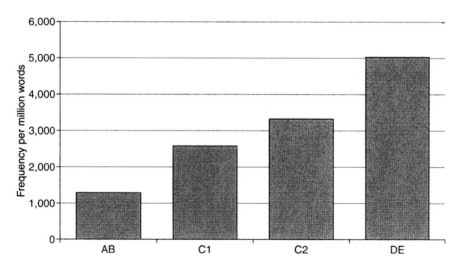

Figure 2.2 Frequency of BLWs per million words of speech produced by different social classes.

emerges: ABs use slightly stronger words than C1s. The average strength of BLW used by each social class is as follows: AB – 1.81, C1 – 1.76, C2 – 2.16 and DE 2.47. In short, the rank order changes slightly from that produced by frequency alone and it no longer aligns itself neatly with the social class hierarchy, with the rank order being DE > C2 > AB > C1. While AB speakers use BLWs less frequently than C1 speakers, on average they use BLWs with a greater strength than C1s. This could be evidence of hypercorrection[76] by C1 speakers: in attempting to copy the linguistic habits of the AB social class, the lower-middle-class speakers exaggerate what they view to be a feature of AB speech, i.e. the avoidance of strong BLWs. However, they do it to such a degree that they avoid strong BLWs more than the ABs do. While I will not discuss this hypothesis further here, it certainly provides an explanation for many of the differences between C1 and AB speech presented in the rest of this chapter.

What of the type of BLW use undertaken? In terms of proportionate contribution to each category of BLW use, social class DE is attracted fairly uniformly to all forms of BLW usage except for PredNeg, Literal and Pron type BLW use.[77] Speakers of social class AB are the most frequent users of these categories of BLWs. At the other end of the spectrum, as we would expect from the results presented in this section so far, C1 speakers are the opposite of DEs: they are infrequent users of almost every category of BLW use. There are, however, two exceptions. C2s shun PredNeg types more than C1s, and C2s shun Gen types more than C1s. The result with the PredNeg types is particularly interesting. With this type of BLW we see a marked change of behaviour for the C1s, which may be caused by the preference of ABs for that category, i.e. it may be the case that this category of BLW use is attractive to the C1s because it is strongly associated with a higher social grouping. However, there is another, possibly complementary, explanation for the use of PredNegs and Gens by the C1s – they are two BLW categories associated with weaker BLWs, as explored in pages 42–43 of this chapter. The use of As and Gs by the C1s may simply be a reflection of their use of weaker BLWs selected by weaker BLW categories. Similarly, when one considers the behaviour of the ABs, their use of As may be a reflection of the relatively weak nature of this category. The same is clearly less true for Pron and apparently not true at all of Literal-type BLW use. However, with reference to Literal usage, a question which cannot be explored here, as it was not explored in the studies on which the strength of the BLW scale was based, is whether when BLWs have a literal meaning they are less offensive than when they are being used, for example, to form a personal insult. For example, is the use of FUCK in 'I fucked her' less offensive than its use in 'I cannot stand that fucking Dean'? If this were true, then there would be a much more persuasive case for the usurpation of the dominance of the DEs in certain BLW use categories by ABs being related to the strength of the word involved. However, on the basis of current evidence this must remain speculation.

What if, rather than looking across the classes, one focuses on each class to see which categories of BLW each class favours and which it shuns? Broadly speaking, all of the social classes use BLWs of different categories in broadly similar proportions. There is relatively little variation as one moves from one social class to another with regard to how frequently they choose each category to express a BLW. Yet there are differences. If we focus on the top four categories of BLW use per social class this becomes apparent. For DE and C2 speakers they are identical: EmphAdv > Gen > PremNeg > Personal. For AB and C1 speakers, the same four categories also represent the top four, but the order differs: for AB and C1 speakers, the top two categories are Gen > EmphAdv. For ABs these are followed by Personal > PremNeg, while for C1s the patterning of the C2/DE group reasserts itself to produce PremNeg > Personal. In short, C2 and DE are identical, C1 is very similar to C2/DE, and for ABs there is not a single BLW type ranked the same as for C2s and DEs in the top four. As a further argument for social assimilation, the case is persuasive. AB is different from C2/DE speech, yet C1 speech positions itself between AB and C2/DE speech, at least with reference to BLW use.

Looking at the top four most frequent BLWs for each class reveals a very similar pattern across the classes once again. The top four BLWs (lemmatised, in rank order) are: for ABs GOD > BLOODY > FUCK > HELL, for C1s GOD > BLOODY > FUCK > HELL, for C2s BLOODY > FUCK > GOD > HELL and for DEs FUCK > BLOODY > GOD > HELL. Once again, the ABs and C1s are identical, with frequency being roughly in inverse proportion to strength of BLW. Yet as we move through the social classes, this correlation reverses itself and the top four changes so that the rough correlation between frequency and strength of BLW become inverted, i.e. the more frequent the word, the higher its strength. Overall, the patterning, and the changes to the patterning as one moves through the social classes, reinforce the findings based on category of BLW use, though in this case the similarity of C1 to AB speech is much more compelling.

As well as BLW type interacting with class, gender may also interact with social class and BLW use. One way in which it may do so relates to the likelihood of a BLW being directed at a particular gender. It is plausible that the BLWs directed at one gender or another by speakers may vary by social class. Intuitively, one might expect that, as one goes up the scale of social class, the likelihood of BLWs being targeted at females may decrease, as this language would increasingly be viewed as something which it was not fitting to use in the presence of or with reference to a woman. When this intuition is explored using the LCA it is proved to be partly wrong: there is a difference in the targeting of males and females with BLWs, but it varies in ways which are more akin to the overall pattern of variation for BLWs and class. When we look at the rank ordering of BLWs targeted at males, the rank ordering is thus (the occurrences per million tokens directed at males by that particular social class are given in parentheses): DE (2,567.36) > C2 (852.17) > AB (671.85) > C1 (284.54). The pattern is exactly the same as the overall pattern for the selection of BLWs of a greater strength by the different social classes. More surprising is the result of the exploration of female directed BLW usage, the rank ordering is: DE (1,260.99) > AB (499.69) > C2 (195.54) > C1 (106.11). When these results are compared pair-wise within each social class, it is still the case that each social class differs in its approach to BLW use directed towards males and females, directing significantly fewer BLWs at females than males.[78] However, the rank ordering clearly shows us that for the AB class this trend is less pronounced to the degree that, when considered as a proportion of all BLWs targeted at either sex, ABs are the third largest users of BLWs targeted at males, but the second largest users of BLWs targeted at females.

So while class relates to BLW use in ways in which we might expect (frequency of usage being inverse to height of social class) there is evidence to suggest that class also interacts as a variable with BLW use in ways we would not expect, with the highest social class in the BNC, AB, sometimes bucking the trend the other social classes conform to by using more and stronger BLWs directed more indiscriminately at both males and females. Yet what of the variables in combination? May age, sex and social class interact? This question is explored in the following section.

Combining factors[79]

At this stage in the study, it would be useful to look at how the age, sex and social class variables interact in the BNC. This, however, is not possible with all of the BLWs studied so far. The reason for this relates to what happens to the available data in the BNC when we combine these factors: the corpus becomes very unbalanced. When we study one factor alone in the BNC, there is plenty of data in the corpus to populate the different categories. However, when we combine the factors, some categories have scarcely any examples in them at all. Take the example of the speakers of a specific age, sex and social class in the BNC who use very few BLWs (as recorded in the LCA): male AB speakers aged 25–34, male C1 speakers aged 15–24 and female DE speakers aged 0–14. The identification of these three groups as infrequent BLW users seems to challenge some of the general results presented in the previous sections – we appear to have found three groups who hardly use BLWs at all even though they are in age groups, and often in social classes, in which we would expect relatively frequent BLW usage.[80] But in fact the answer to this conundrum is rather simple – there is hardly any data for those speakers in the BNC. Table 2.16 shows how many words are uttered by speakers from these groups in the spoken section of the BNC.[81]

The apparent avoidance of BLWs by these groups is illusory – there is simply a lack of data for these groups. Yet even where there is apparently

Table 2.16 The number of words spoken by three categories of speaker in the spoken BNC

Group	Total words uttered by the group in the spoken BNC
Male AB speakers aged 25–34	2,259
Male C1 speakers aged 15–24	3,796
Female DE speakers aged 0–14	812

plentiful data, the number of groups created by combining factors together can spread the existing data so thinly that it ceases to be useful. Take the word *bastard* for example. There are 31 examples of the word in the LCA. However, when we combine age, sex and social class, the result is 48 categories ($2 \times 4 \times 6$). There are more categories than examples leading, not surprisingly, to 25 of the categories being empty when the examples of *bastard* are assigned to them. Hardly the basis for an illuminating investigation of the interaction of age, sex, social class and BLWs. While disappointing, this does serve to show that, even in a large corpus such as the BNC spoken section, data sparsity can be a very real problem.[82]

Nonetheless it is possible to look at some of the interactions of age, social class and sex with reference to a number of high-frequency words, namely *bloody*, *fucking* and *shit*. In order to do this the frequency counts of these words were subjected to a further statistical test: log-linear modelling. In the first phase of this test, the model tested to see whether the words varied within each variable, i.e. it sought to verify the findings presented so far. The model verified those findings, indicating that the differences for the different subcategories of age, sex and social class gave rise to significant differences of use by the different speakers in the subcategories.[83] This result, while useful as it corroborated the findings presented so far, did not look at the interaction of the variables. The next stage of the test was to look at whether pairs of variables generated subcategories across which the use of these words varied significantly. When looking at age and class, gender and age, and gender and class, the model returned a significant result each time, indicating that there was an interaction between the variables which influenced the frequency of the use of the three words under investigation. Before considering what the nature of that relationship is, however, the issue of data sparsity becomes relevant once more. While gender and class together generate a relatively limited set of categories (i.e. number of categories of sex multiplied by the number of categories for class, $2 \times 4 = 8$) the number of categories increase when we consider gender and age ($2 \times 6 = 12$) and becomes large when we consider age and class ($4 \times 6 = 24$). While there is sufficient data to reliably test the interaction of gender and class and gender and age, the number of categories generated by age and class is too great – the results become unreliable.[84] This means that, unfortunately, any results in this category can best be described as indicative only – they are certainly not something one would want to rely on. Unsurprisingly, therefore, even with these frequent words we are not able to study the interaction of all three variables as the number of categories (48) that this produces is far too great. It should be noted, though, that when this model is tested, the interaction of all three is significant, but the model is once again so sparsely populated that it would be wisest to discard the result. However, we can reliably test the interaction of gender and age and gender and class. As these have proved to be significant, the following sub-sections will explore the nature of these two relationships.

Age and sex

The log-linear model is very useful when identifying if a relationship exists between two variables. It does not, in itself, indicate very clearly exactly what the nature of the relationship is. To discover that, we need to return to the raw data and look at the pattern of interaction set up by the two variables. This is easily done – we simply need to look at the distribution of the uses of the three words across the eight categories generated by the interaction of age and sex. Table 2.17 shows the interaction between these two variables.

What is apparent from the table is that the single behaviours – gender differentiation being apparent for certain BLWs, and BLW use peaking in the U25 age group and declining thereafter – generally hold in this table. There are exceptions to the general pattern, however, with most of the exceptions being related to the word *bloody*. In males, the use of *bloody* peaks later – in the U35 category – and its decline thereafter is far from marked, with the frequency rising again from the U60 category onwards. For females, there is an early peak in the U25 category, but once again a second

Table 2.17 The interaction of age and sex, frequencies given as normalised counts per million words

Word	U15	U25	U35	U45	U60	60+
Male						
bloody	87.85	154.82	416.94	305.73	362.50	372.75
fucking	111.64	903.46	875.43	33.56	191.24	6.55
shit	118.06	168.97	126.62	50.09	18.98	9.70
Female						
bloody	27.95	348.99	342.30	157.57	552.81	121.49
fucking	43.39	149.99	70.23	10.04	120.28	0.00
shit	37.64	208.64	7.74	9.16	26.96	1.19
Total	426.53	1,934.88	1,839.26	566.16	1,272.77	511.69

peak, and in this case the highest peak of usage, occurs in the U60 category. In both cases, the peaks for *bloody* usage by females far exceed those for the males. The word *fucking* also gives rise to a double peak, for both males and females in the U25 and U60 categories, but in this case the male peaks exceed the female peaks. The word *shit* shows a double peak for females only, once again in the U25 and U60 categories.

If there were a much larger data set in which one could view this twin peak patterning for *bloody* against the patterns achieved for other words, a number of hypotheses could be explored to explain the usage of the word. In the absence of that data set, I will permit myself a little intuitive speculation. Given that the general pattern of BLW use with age is a decline in usage beyond U25 – a pattern attested here only with reference to the word *shit* used by males – how can the double peaks for *bloody* and *fucking* be explained? The higher peaks for *bloody* when used by females as opposed to males is easily explained – as shown on page 35, *bloody* is a BLW used more heavily by females than males, hence its relative over-use here is quite understandable. What is more difficult to explain is why the second peak occurs. My hypothesis would be that there is a narrowing in the BLW lexicon with age. While BLWs as a group may be used less frequently with age, the number of BLWs called on shrinks more swiftly so that, almost paradoxically, the selection of a specific BLW in the age range U60 may peak temporarily as the range of words used to realise a BLW utterance shrinks more markedly than the rate of decline of BLW usage. This gives rise to a series of local peaks in BLW usage for certain words in the U60 age range which are flattened as age increases and BLW use declines further, meaning that, even for the few BLW words still used by the speaker, their rate of BLW usage is now so low that the frequencies of the surviving BLWs are reducing again. To thoroughly test this hypothesis would, of course, require a much larger corpus than the one I have available. However, some persuasive evidence can be provided from the BNC if one maps the usage of different BLW word forms (types) against age. The results show a very familiar pattern – the number of different word forms related to BLW usage peaks in the age range U25 and declines thereafter. The results are shown in Table 2.18.

Table 2.18, while in no way proving my hypothesis, certainly lends it support. There is a marked reduction in the number of types of BLWs used by the U60 age group, with a further marked reduction in the 60+ age group. Hence the hypothesis that the shrinking BLW lexicon of the U60s

Table 2.18 The number of different word forms used to realise BLW use by the different age groups in the LCA

	U15	*U25*	*U35*	*U45*	*U60*	*60+*
Word count	71	75	58	51	43	29

causes a peak in usage for some of their remaining BLWs is certainly plausible.[85] Yet much more work is needed before that hypothesis can be stated with anything approaching certainty.[86] Given that such work is well beyond the scope of a sole scholar, I leave this hypothesis to others to investigate further.

Before leaving the discussion of age and sex, however, it is worth considering the claims made about age and sex by other researchers, using smaller data sets. One major problem with these studies, such as Eiskovits (1998), is that they have tended to treat words as a lumpen mass and have looked to see how gender relates to that mass of words. As shown in this chapter, and this section, words which might be lumped together, e.g. BLWs, may respond to factors such as gender and age very differently. Hence when Eiskovits studied non-standard features, the results may have over-generalised how gender and non-standard language relate to one another. For example, Eiskovits studies non-standard grammar and swearing.[87] Her conclusion was that girls modify their speech in the direction of the standard as they moved out of adolescence while boys increased their use of non-standard features such as swearing. However, as can be seen from the data in this section, this may not be true of certain word forms. Nor may it be true in general when attested language use, rather than reports of language use, which Eiskovits relied on for her comments on swearing, is considered. One might modify what researchers such as Eiskovits claim to say that, as males and females move out of adolescence, their use of BLWs becomes more gender differentiated, with frequency of use of these words generally declining over time, as all BLW usage declines. But if the findings presented in this chapter so far show anything, they certainly show that grouping words, while useful, should always be balanced by the study of words in isolation when considering how words and sociolinguistic variables interact.

Sex and social class

Table 2.19 shows the interaction between the variables sex and social class.

A general trend is obvious from the table – female BLW use meets the expectations we have for speakers of different social classes more readily than male BLW use does. The rank of BLW use is in an inverse relationship with social class for females: the higher the social class, the lower the usage of BLWs. While the frequency profile of BLW usage for females is AB < C1 < C2 < DE for all of the words in Table 2.19, this pattern is much more confused for males, and varies somewhat by word. For *bloody* it is AB < C2 < DE < C1. For *fucking* it is C1 < AB < C2 < DE. Finally, for *shit* it is AB < C2 < DE < C1. The results look curious indeed. Only in the case of *fucking* is the patterning anything like that for females. However, the anomaly in the *fucking* ranking can be explained: ABs have a preference for stronger BLWs, as shown on pages 50–51. In fact, the frequency ranking by social class for males saying *fucking* matches that perfectly for BLW usage strength

Table 2.19 The distribution of three BLWs by age and social class, frequencies given as normalised counts per million words

Word	Female				Male			
	AB	C1	C2	DE	AB	C1	C2	DE
bloody	69.41	323.31	441.65	716.75	282.85	565.88	422.63	429.23
fucking	4.45	60.77	86.42	242.30	122.75	94.72	824.39	1,080.01
shit	43.06	66.86	68.68	112.74	66.99	162.58	126.22	136.63
Total	116.91	450.94	596.74	1,071.78	472.58	823.18	1,373.24	1,645.88

by the social classes – in short this strong word reflects the overall pattern for strength of BLW usage by the social classes. It also suggests that, if more data were available, we may have found that the ABs who bucked the trend to use stronger BLWs than C1s (page 51) were generally male. That, however, must remain speculation. An explanation may also be put forward for the apparently anomalous results for *bloody* and *shit*. First, both are weak BLWs – the males in question, with a preference for stronger BLWs, may have simply avoided these words. Also, those social groups attracted to the stronger BLWs (AB, C2 and DE social classes) should avoid these words while the social class that prefers to select the weakest BLWs on average (C1) selects these weaker forms most frequently. In doing so, we may also suggest another reason that these words may be shunned by males in particular – they are words that have been shown to be typical of female BLW use (see page 35); males are avoiding these BLWs not simply because they are weak, they are avoiding them because they are typical of females. The strongest argument for this position may be made with reference to *bloody*. The word *bloody* is used with decreasing frequency by males of social classes C2 and DE, so much so that females of social classes C2 and DE use the word *bloody* more frequently than males of the same social class, the only time that female BLW use is more frequent than male BLW use in the same social class in Table 2.19. Table 2.19 shows a clearer picture of the use of *bloody* than was provided on page 35 – it is in fact more indicative of female C2/DE speech in particular rather than female speech in general. One could argue that the word appears to be so indicative of female speech in those social classes that male C2 and DE speakers shun it, causing the word to buck the usual trend of (1) increasing usage of a BLW as social class approaches DE and (2) greater BLW use in this table by males rather than females.

Distinction and bad language

The analysis of the BNC undertaken in this chapter has certainly shown that distinction and bad language are linked. The use or lack of use of BLWs is a fault line along which age, sex and social class may be differentiated. This fault line, in turn, gives rise to inferences when speakers of English use, or fail to use, bad language, as was suggested at the beginning of this book. Yet distinction, as conceived by Bourdieu, is a social process. Distinctions are generated by groups in society. These distinctions relate features such as age, sex and social class to power. Is this the case with swearing, or may it be that women swear less than men by nature, i.e. they are genetically predisposed to produce fewer BLWs than males? Similarly are the young and the poor/powerless more inclined, genetically, to use BLWs more often than the old and powerful? I believe that Bourdieu's theory provides a better explanation than genetics here – I view it as far-fetched to assume that genetics has very much to do with the differences presented in this chapter. Yet if the argument is that a social process generated these distinctions and aligned BLW use with power (with the language of power being characterised by a relative lack of BLW use) then a problem presents itself: when and how were these distinctions created? The next section of this book will look at these questions. In the next chapter I will look at a time before the modern distinctions were naturalised in every day speech. In the chapter following that, I will look at the process which established the distinctions observed here. Finally, in Chapter 5, I will explore how, after being established for some centuries, these distinctions were defended and maintained in the face of an attempt to undermine them and, by extension, the power structures which those distinctions have come to support.

Part 2

Censors, zealots and four-letter assaults on authority

3   Early modern censorship of bad language

Introduction

The previous chapter, in which I looked at BLWs (bad language words) in the late twentieth century, focused largely on swear words. While in this chapter I will, once again, discuss bad language, the term will mask a certain confusion. What was termed swearing in the sixteenth and seventeenth centuries was actually quite different from modern swearing, as the word *swearing* was related to the swearing of oaths. The swearing of oaths in itself, however, did constitute bad language. Yet while profligate swearing in the seventeenth century may have been a cause of offence, it was distinct from obscene language, which was much closer to what one may term modern swearing. Also, while both potentially offensive, obscene language and swearing were not the only causes of potential linguistic offence in this period. Blasphemy, as will be discussed in this chapter, was an important source of offence, too. So, unless the discussion is of a specific form of bad language, in this chapter the term 'bad language' will be used to encompass all forms of speech and writing found to be morally offensive in this period.

Bad language certainly caused some offence in England for some time prior to the seventeenth century. Indeed, at least as early as the fourteenth century, attempts were made in England to introduce a law against swearing.[88] However, before the sixteenth century, the practical censorship of bad language was very difficult. This may seem strange to say, yet it is true, because up to the point where mass literacy and printing became possible, linguistic censorship was bound to prove difficult. The censorship of speech produced in private has proved to be difficult whenever it has been attempted.[89] It is hardly surprising, therefore, that swearing has proved incredibly resilient in its spoken form. If this were not the case, we would be left with some difficult explanations to provide. For example, if we take the printed word as our sole source of evidence, we may well conclude that swearing was almost extinct in the nineteenth century. Yet this near extinction clearly did not happen. Apart from passing references to the habit by writers in that century, we know that major changes in swearing in English took place in the nineteenth century, with DAMN falling out of favour and

FUCK undergoing a surge in popularity. As FUCK surged in popularity, its meaning diversified and the word form was subject to a wider range of morphological processes, resulting in the word appearing with a greater range of parts of speech.[90] In short, censorship hardly stifled the development of bad language. In spite of all of the attempts of moral entrepreneurs and government bills, bad language has survived censorship in all of its forms.

Attitudes to the use of BLWs was different in the early seventeenth century.[91] A striking example of this comes from the following historical event. On his accession, James I was faced with a number of theological problems. His response was to call a conference of learned divines to discuss a range of such issues contained in the so-called Millenary Petition. The conference was held for three days at Hampton Court, starting on 14 January 1604. The aim of the meeting was to provide a forum for the debate of the issues outlined in the Millenary Petition so that James could arbitrate and find a solution. During the debates, James, in response to an argument presented by the Bishop of Peterborough, dismissed Peterborough with the phrase, 'A turd for this argument'.[92] If we transplant this debate to the twenty-first century, the effect would be shocking. When Princess Anne used the term 'naff off', the press coverage of it was intense and disapproving. If Elizabeth II, at a public meeting of great importance, dismissed the words of a cleric on the grounds that the argument was 'not worth a turd', the newspapers would report little else for some time to come. Yet in the seventeenth century the king's choice of words in his pursuit of an argument, while they proved an unexpected rhetorical device for the collected divines, caused no particular scandal or controversy. On the contrary, the meeting at Hampton Court was thought to be a great success, at least initially. After the meeting, the Bishop of Durham wrote to the Archbishop of York saying that he found James to be 'a king and priest in one person to propose, discuss, and determine so many important matters so soundly as I never look to see or hear the like again'.[93] James' language did not cause the distraction it would undoubtedly cause today.

While the example given above is admittedly limited in scope, it does show quite clearly that the attitudes to bad language prevalent in seventeenth-century England bear little relation to those held in twenty-first-century England. Consequently, when considering the censorship of bad language in the seventeenth century, we should be wary of jumping to conclusions. What may seem like the obvious reason for a specific act of censorship, or even a censorious Act of Parliament, may be nothing more than a twenty-first-century attitude mistakenly transplanted to a seventeenth-century context. The explanation for any act of censorship in the seventeenth century has to draw its evidence from that era, and make sense in the social and political context of that era. Consequently it is the dynamic sociopolitical context of the seventeenth century which is the principal focus of this chapter. While the period covered in this chapter, from the reign of Elizabeth I to the Restoration, covers four monarchs and the interregnum of the Commonwealth, the attitude to censorship in the reign of each monarch, and during the Commonwealth, was remarkably consistent in spite of the evolving political and social context. The public expression of dangerous political opinions and heretical religious views were censored; little else was. While changes of regime brought about changes in emphasis, and individual censors could at times appear to undertake acts of linguistic censorship based on their personal morality, censorship in this period had almost nothing to do with a genuine attempt to suppress bad language. When such censorship was apparently undertaken, either in a single case or through the introduction of an Act of Parliament, the reality was that such censorship usually served political or economic ends. The inconsistencies in censorship practices and in the applications of laws such as the 1650 Blasphemy Act become too overwhelming if we attempt to reach any other conclusion. The censorship of bad language in the early modern period was a smoke screen behind which the suppression of groups and views that represented a danger to the state or printing establishment was undertaken. In justifying this claim this chapter will look at a number of case studies, including the publication of obscene hymns, the censorship of obscenity in stage plays, radical protestant sects who promoted the use of bad language, and obscenity in newspapers in the 1650s. However, before one can begin to make sense of any acts of censorship in this period, one needs to understand the mechanisms and nature of that censorship. The regime of censorship that prevailed in England during the first half of the seventeenth century was established in the late sixteenth century by Elizabeth I.

Elizabeth I

Printing became increasingly widespread during the sixteenth century, providing texts for an increasingly literate population.[94] In response to this, Elizabeth I established a framework for the censorship of printed works that endured through to the Civil War. Elizabeth's goal in developing this framework was political – the publication of propaganda which sought to undermine the Elizabethan religious settlement had to be prevented. However, the printing press, while causing a problem in that it could be used for the mass production of dangerous texts, also provided an effective means of censorship. The presses could be limited and controlled, providing an opportunity to suppress undesirable texts. This is the route that Elizabethan censorship took. In doing so, it was building on a previous, unsuccessful, attempt to establish the censorship of the printed word. A monopoly – and hence control – of printing had been granted to the Stationers' Company, formed in 1557. However, the monopoly was frequently breached and consequently the promise of press control failed to materialise. In response, the monopoly was underpinned by a regime of censorship instituted in 1586 by a decree of the Star Chamber. This passed censorship of all published work into the hands of the Church Court of High Commission, which was controlled by the Archbishop of Canterbury and the Bishop of London.[95] The monarch, however, remained the ultimate authority in all censorship cases. The Stationers retained their monopoly, but the act of breaking that monopoly was now much more serious, as one would also have to circumvent the state censorship system in order to circumvent the monopoly, as the Court of High Commission licensed texts from the Stationers' Company. So the Stationers themselves probably not merely welcomed, but promoted, the Star Chamber decrees. While the government was undoubtedly interested in the effective control of printed matter for political reasons, the Stationers saw their monopoly as being under threat from unlicensed printers. The political goals of the government and the economic goals of the Stationers' Company were both achieved through the Star Chamber decrees. As well as controlling the presses and enriching the Stationers, the Star Chamber decrees added to the existing censorship system, since in spite of the role of the Church Court of High Commission in censorship, the members of the Stationers' Company continued to constitute a formidable power for censorship in their own right.[96]

As well as serving the needs of the state and the Stationers, introducing the Church Court of High Commission into the censorship of written English was logical. Before the printing press, the pulpit was one of the best forms of mass communication,[97] and the Church Court of High Commission had long exercised control over the pulpit.[98] The addition of a second level of censorship of printed materials in the form of an established and successful mechanism for the regulation of the mass media – the Church Court of High Commission – was clearly quite a logical step to take.

The Church and the Stationers together could in principle censor the experience of the English language in a much more pervasive way than had ever been possible before. In the age of the scribe and limited literacy there was no mass experience of language through the printed medium. With the invention of the printing press, a process began whereby not only did the means of the production and dissemination of the written word become much more widespread, but literacy also slowly became democratised. As the experience of the written word was democratised, it became possible for censorship to affect an ever larger proportion of the population. While a censor could not be present to monitor the speech of any given individual, in any place, at any time of the day, this could in effect be achieved with the printed word. While a preacher may provide an approved speech from a pulpit at an appointed time, approved texts could be perused at any time of the day or night by the literate.[99] As long as language was consistently censored at source, then, barring illicit presses and smuggled work, any representation of language in print that any literate person came across would be a representation of censored English.

The existence of this two-tiered censorship system may in turn have effectively added a third level of censorship, as it probably simply discouraged many writers from producing materials they thought would be censored.[100] However, it must be remembered that the control of specific types of language was not a focus of the Star Chamber decree. The introduction of state-sponsored censorship operating via a print monopoly was motivated by economics and politics rather than morality.[101] One must resist any temptation to paint the Star Chamber decrees as a step towards linguistic censorship in particular. While the system of censorship could have been used to control the representation of the English language, there is no clear evidence that it was used to do so in Elizabethan England.

The other temptation that must be resisted is to assume that this system led to every printed word being scrutinised and licensed by the Stationers and Court of High Commission. The Court of High Commission in Elizabeth's reign did not even license a majority of printed works – in the 1590s, only 44 per cent of printed works were authorised.[102] In the reign of Elizabeth, the role of the Court of High Commission seemed to be to act as a place to secure permission to print potentially dangerous works, or as a place for the state to pursue the suppression of unlicensed works which caused offence.

While it is conceivable that the censorship of bad language may have occurred on either of the first two levels of censorship, there is no clear evidence of this. Censorship in the Elizabethan age was most centrally interested in the repression of religious groupings such as the Puritans and Catholics who, in different ways, represented a threat to the state as conceived by Elizabeth.[103] It is hardly surprising, therefore, that Elizabethan censorship was preoccupied with religious texts such as the *Martin Marprelate Tracts*,[104] which sought to undermine the Elizabethan religious settlement. The Puritans themselves were aware that they were a target of Elizabethan censorship, and used opportunities that presented themselves in Parliament to block censorship measures which may have worsened the situation for them, especially bills aimed at closing clandestine Puritan presses.[105] While various groups and ideas were subject to censorship, at no point did the Elizabethan state focus on bad language specifically. The only group clearly agitating for the censorship of bad language in the Elizabethan age was the Puritans. They found swearing, blasphemy and oaths offensive and sought to introduce legislation to control them. There is evidence that, as early as 1584, they were considering promoting legislation to enforce linguistic censorship; in an anonymous Puritan speech prepared for the 1584 session of Parliament, there was an unsuccessful call for the control of 'Idell pamphletts & dire leud & wantn discourse of love of all languages leud'.[106] But such efforts were not likely to succeed for two reasons. First, this was not a subject of concern for the Elizabethan state. Second, the group for which the subject was a matter of concern was alienated from the establishment to such a degree that they were actively censored themselves. Minimally one would say that it was deeply unlikely that the government would act at the behest of such a group. Perhaps more importantly, one may say that if the government had done so it may have implied an accommodation with the group that simply did not exist.

Nonetheless, the Puritans did have a role to play in Elizabethan censorship which may have caused bad language to be censored, even if they could not force through Acts of Parliament outlawing it themselves. Many prominent members of the Stationers' Company were Puritans.[107] As the company was the second tier of censorship in the Elizabethan state, and the one through which all works other than those produced on illegal presses had, in principle, to pass, Puritan printers controlled the printing presses in the sense that they owned many of them under a royal monopoly. If one could not have acts for linguistic censorship passed by Parliament, nor control the Church Court of High Commission or the position of Master of the Revels, controlling a good number of the official presses was a means by which linguistic censorship could be exercised. If the censoring of bad language did occur in the Elizabethan era, it was most likely undertaken clandestinely by Puritan printers.

James I

With the accession of James to the English throne, the political landscape changed significantly[108] in two ways: the regulation of printing increased markedly and there was a rapprochement between the Crown and the Puritans.

The period of James' rule sees a marked increase in the practice of licensing printed works. Whereas in the 1590s only some 44 per cent of published works were officially licensed, by the 1620s this figure almost doubled, reaching 84 per cent of published works.[109] The increase in licensing probably had three origins. First, James was much more interested in censorship than Elizabeth had been. Indeed, one of his earliest acts as King was to warn publishers that he intended to strengthen the licensing system to prevent 'indiscreet publishing in print of divers book containing and divulging matters of much offence'.[110] James was aware that censorship constituted a political act, and from time to time would make a public performance of his personal disapproval of certain works by having them incinerated in public book-burning ceremonies.[111] Second, James' action may in part be explained by the fact that as King in Scotland he had been the sole source of printing licences. James had been the censor in Scotland and brought his Scottish experience to England with him. This led him to both encourage further censorship and, at times, initiate censorship himself.[112] Finally, it is also arguable that the system of censorship slowly established itself as an acceptable practice in the period from its introduction in 1586 to the 1620s, as there is a steady increase in the percentage of books registered from the 1580s to the 1620s.

In spite of the increased volume of licensing, in many respects Jacobean censorship is very similar to Elizabethan censorship. Its aim is political, though the political problems that James faced meant that the targets of censorship changed. There is one significant difference between Elizabethan and Jacobean censorship, however, as James introduced a law clearly encompassing bad language: the 1606 Act to Restrain the Abuses of Players. In order to understand the background to this act, it is necessary to consider the second major change to the political landscape occasioned by James' accession – the rapprochement between the Crown and the Puritans.

James, as noted previously, tried early in his reign to deal with the theological problems that had refused to go away during the reign of Elizabeth. While Catholicism remained the principal source of concern for the state, especially in the wake of the supposed Catholic Gunpowder Plot of 1605[113] and the vilification of James by the Catholic Church following the publication of James' book, *A Premonition*,[114] there were clear signs that James sought a rapprochement with Puritanism. That does not mean to say he embraced Puritan radicals. James' accommodation was based on winning over moderate Puritans. James appointed within the Church on a largely meritocratic basis, with Anglicans as well as moderate Puritans finding favour, so with the ascent of James to the throne the influence of the Puritans broke through to the upper tier of censorship. It was in this context that the 1606 Act to Restrain the Abuses of Players came into force.

In the late sixteenth and early seventeenth century, the play constituted a relatively new form of language written to be spoken, and the stage constituted a form of mass communication. As noted in the discussion of sermons, the government could and did exercise control over language written to be spoken. In the early seventeenth century it decided to do so again with respect to the play. An additional, though not necessarily separate, instrument of censorship was established to deal with the censorship of language in plays. This process began in 1589, when the Privy Council ordered the Master of the Revels, Edmond Tilney, to act in consort with nominees of the Mayor of London and the Archbishop of Canterbury to establish a commission to censor all plays performed in and around London.[115] In the early Jacobean period, the Act to Restrain the Abuses of Players codified the need for the Master to censor blasphemous language in plays. In this year the role of the Master also extended to print, when the Master of the Revels took over the task of licensing plays intended for the press from the Church Court of High Commission.[116] The Master did not have sole responsibility for the censorship of plays, however; after 1606 there were occasions when the Church Court of High Commission intervened to censor material which the Master of the Revels had allowed.[117] Similarly, the monarch continued to act as a final court of appeal in censorship cases[118] and from time to time intervened, for example, to insist that censorship take place.[119] Yet, generally speaking, from 1606 the Church Court of High Commission dealt exclusively with non-dramatic printed matter while the Master of the Revels dealt with dramatic printed matter.

In censoring the stage, one could claim that the Jacobean government was responding to complaints from the Puritans about the public use of bad language. The government in turn exploited this moral panic to censor materials it found offensive not on moral, but on political grounds. The Stationers' Company also exploited this moral panic to object to material on moral grounds, when their true concern was economic. A good example of this is their attack on George Wither.

Obscene and carnal hymns

In 1622 George Wither had a book entitled *Cantata Sacra or the Holy Psalms* published.[120] The book had been printed under licence, and it was duly registered in the Stationers' Register. The book proved to be popular, and Wither applied to James himself for recognition of his patent on the work. James granted this. However, trouble was brewing for Wither. The book as shown to the licenser had contained ten songs. The published work contained 41. One assumes that Wither was hoping that by appealing to James for a patent using the full text, his malefaction would be erased. However, Wither had come to the attention of the Stationers' Company who laid a serious charge against some of his hymns – which were said to be obscene. The Stationers even claimed that minors could be corrupted should they hear some of these hymns, that the text was Popish and that Wither was an ecclesiastical charlatan.[121]

The Songs of Solomon, on which the Stationers focused their complaint, certainly have a strong sexual overtone, and contain numerous passages which could offend. There are repeated references to female breasts as an object of sexual desire and beauty, for example,[122] with lines such as 'Better are those Dugs of thine, Than the most delicious wine'[123] suggesting that the breasts in question may not simply have been looked at, they may have been tasted. In addition there is at least one case where the sexual interests of a pre-pubescent, or recently pubescent girl, in an older man is presented.[124] In addition, the hymns refer to 'concubines' – hardly the subject matter of polite conversation, let alone hymns to be sung in church.[125]

Supposedly outraged by Wither's hymns, the Stationers pursued Wither with vigour. Initially they sought the revocation of the patent from James. When James refused they sought Parliamentary condemnation of the patent. This was not forthcoming. When their appeal to the King and Parliament failed, the Stationers, aided and abetted by the booksellers, provided an effective demonstration of their ability to enforce censorship: the booksellers refused to stock Wither's hymns and the Stationers refused to print them. Wither and the Stationers' Company then locked horns in a protracted battle of wills. Wither published an angry account of the affair in his 1624 book *Schollers Purgatory*. The Stationers retaliated by using the fact that *Schollers Purgatory* was unlicensed as a pretext for shutting down the press of the book's printer, George Wood. Wither appealed to the Privy Council, who confirmed his patent in 1627. However, the Stationers were not moved by this and demonstrated very effectively the ability of a printing monopoly to not merely censor, but effectively ban a work if it wished to do so. Wither appealed to the Privy Council once again in 1634. However, after over a decade, Wither decided to retreat from his battle with the Stationers and finally sold his patent in 1635. The work went back on sale and Wither received an annuity from the sale of his patent.

This case study demonstrates perfectly the multilayered nature of censorship in Jacobean England. Multiple layers of censorship and licensing merge and at times conflict. But the censorship of Wither is in some ways very difficult to understand. How did a book which was claimed to be obscene come to be approved by the King? Why was the patent of an obscene book confirmed by the Privy Council? Also, if the text was obscene, how is it that the hymns in question went on to be republished?

These questions can all be satisfied with the same answer – the objections to the so-called obscene hymns were related to economic interests and had nothing to do with obscenity.[126] Wither's true sin has its roots in his having written what would nowadays be called a 'bestseller', *Withers Motto*.[127] This work sold well, both in its official version and in pirated versions, making a tidy sum for its printers. Wither tried to use the licensing system to maximise his financial benefit from the hymns when he realised that they were popular. Wither applied for his patent shortly after the first printing of 1,200 copies of his hymns. One assumes that these sold well enough to make Wither believe that he had a book that would rival *Withers Motto* in popularity. *Withers Motto* had not been licensed and that had left the work vulnerable to piracy. With his hymns both licensed (albeit with the licence granted to only ten of the 41 hymns) and the full text granted a patent by the King himself, Wither must have expected that he would have much stronger grounds for the defence of his ownership of the hymns than he did with *Withers Motto*. In defending the hymns, he was not entirely faultless, however. The copyright of the work had gone to the printer, Augustine Matthews, when he had produced the first 1,200 copies. By going to the King, Wither was not only seeking a patent to assert his ownership of the work, he was effectively revoking Matthews' copyright. Wither wished to be the sole printer of the work, which was now to be entitled *Hymns and Songs of the Church*. It is possible that the Stationers' Company may have accepted Wither's patent if this had been all that he had sought. His patent also sought, however, that when it was published, the *Hymns and Songs of the Church* should be bound together with another religious work, *Metrical Psalms*. Wither's patent was audacious indeed – not content with the potential sales of *Hymns and Psalms*, he sought to expand his sales significantly by including the *Metrical Psalms* in the published work. The *Metrical Psalms* was an extremely popular title.[128] It is estimated that Wither would have gained an additional 87,000 sales through the inclusion of *Metrical Psalms* in his *Hymns and Songs*.[129] Crucially, these sales would be made at the expense of printers who were already making money by selling editions of the *Metrical Psalms*. While the Stationers might have accepted Wither's sharp practice in stealing Matthews' copyright, they were understandably reluctant to see

Wither actually taking away good business which they already had. They initially tried to negotiate with Wither to have the clause in the patent relating to the *Metrical Psalms* dropped. When this failed, and the King and Parliament proved unhelpful, the Stationers' Company used its might not for moral censorship, but against works which represented an economic threat to them. However, rather than admit this, the Stationers sought to discredit Wither and his work on moral grounds. The Stationers were not interested in the obscenity of Wither's work at all; if they were, they had ample opportunity to stop it being printed. If they objected to the work on moral grounds, then it is also surprising that they sought to negotiate with Wither in an attempt to leave him with *Hymns and Songs* while keeping *Metrical Psalms* for themselves. Finally, if the text was obscene, then why did they print *Hymns and Songs* when Wither eventually sold his patent? The charge of obscenity and corruption that the Stationers levelled at Wither was nothing more than a smoke screen behind which economic interests could work unseen. This is typical of cases of linguistic censorship in the period from Elizabeth I to the Restoration. Where cases of linguistic censorship appear, they are in fact cases within which economic or political considerations predominate. Without an understanding of this process, acts of linguistic censorship in the early seventeenth century can appear baffling and inconsistent. This is most apparent when one considers the censorship of bad language in plays by the Master of the Revels during the reign of Charles I.

Charles I

The role of the Church in censorship was strengthened throughout the reign of Charles I by the appointment of Laud, first as Bishop of London in 1628 and then as Archbishop of Canterbury in 1633. Before taking control of the See of Canterbury, Laud rose to effective control of the Church Court of High Commission during the last years of the tenureship of Archbishop Abbot. Laud was against Puritanism, being an Arminist, and was determined to protect both Church and State from criticism. In part Laud sought this protection through censorship which underwent a period of increased intensity from 1633, diminishing again after 1640, when the machinery of censorship began to break down as civil war approached.

While there is generally a dearth of documentary evidence related to the process of censorship in early seventeenth-century England, in the case of the Master of the Revels we not only have examples of some texts before and after censorship, we also have a fairly complete record of a desk book kept by one of the Masters of the Revels, Sir Henry Herbert, who acted in the role for both Charles I and Charles II. It is the availability of this evidence which will keep the focus of this section on dramatic texts.[130]

The role of the Master of the Revels, certainly after the 1606 Abuses of Players Act, could rather naively be taken to be that which a censor commonly has in broadcasting in twenty-first-century England – 'bleeping out' bad language in plays presented to him for licensing prior to their performance. However, such an analysis would grossly misrepresent the role of the censor – both of dramatic and non-dramatic texts – in the late sixteenth and early seventeenth centuries. As will become apparent, the Act was at best variably enforced by the Master of the Revels. Additionally, to imagine that the Master of the Revels did nothing but license plays is a mistake. He also licensed travelling shows, arranged plays at court, oversaw the rehearsal of those plays and kept the wardrobe used for court plays in good order. Nonetheless, the Master of the Revels was a key censor in this period and, through the important resource of his desk book, we have access to a number of cases where bad language is censored. Yet Herbert's censorship of bad language is inconsistent. It is only when we look beyond the claims of linguistic censorship that a situation identical to that in the Wither case emerges. A study of Herbert's censorship of *The Tamer Tamed* will serve to illustrate this well.

'I returned it to the players ye monday morninge after, purged of oaths, prophaness, and ribaldrye'[131] – a case study in early modern censorship – Sir Henry Herbert and The Tamer Tamed

The Tamer Tamed by John Fletcher was originally licensed by Sir George Buc, Master of the Revels 1610–1622. When revived for performance in 1633, Sir Henry Herbert, Master of the Revels from 1623–1673, decided to censor it. The play had been licensed by Buc, and the acting company that originally staged the play, the King's Players, planned to revive it based on the allowed manuscript, i.e. the version approved when the play was originally licensed. Herbert should never have become involved in re-editing the play unless the allowed copy had been lost, major changes to the allowed copy were proposed or if the licence had been transferred from one company of players to another. Indeed, he had already relicensed two plays previously examined by Buc on just these grounds without asking for any changes, and in at least one case without examining the text at all.[132] There is no evidence to suggest that Herbert needed to actively re-read and relicense *The Tamer Tamed*. Yet Herbert intervened to halt the performance of the play and insisted on it being relicensed. His intervention was decisive, and is another good example of the multilayered nature of censorship in this period. Herbert asked to see the copy of the text after he had the play stopped. There is evidence at this point that Edward Knight, the players' bookkeeper, censored the text afresh before the work was sent to Herbert, as Herbert thanked him for his pains in doing so, saying 'In many things you have saved mee labour; yet wher your judgment or penn fayld you, I have . . . used mine'.[133] However, Knight also received a warning from Herbert, who urged Knight in future to purge plays of 'oaths, prophaness, and publique ribaldry'[134] before Herbert received them.

What caused Herbert to act over *The Tamer Tamed*? By the time that the play was performed he had been Master of the Revels for ten years without having to change the regulations regarding the restaging of previously licensed works. Yet something about the performance of *The Tamer Tamed* provoked Herbert not merely to stop the production of the play, but to rethink whether previously licensed plays should be relicensed before being performed again, writing 'that it concerns the Master of the Revells to bee carefull of their ould playes'.[135] Herbert revised his views on licensing because of *The Tamer Tamed* and concluded that where old plays were revived they should be relicensed by him.

There is no direct evidence that the play had offended an important figure such as the King. Yet there must have been a complaint from somebody as, in Herbert's surviving notes, he refers to 'complaints of foule and offensive matters' contained in the play.[136] He also makes reference to 'oathes, prophaness and ribaldrye'.[137] One could seize on these observations as an explanation for what had happened. In the quarter century since Buc licensed the play, attitudes to bad language had changed so drastically that what to Buc was licensable had become 'foule and offensive' to Herbert. Looking at Herbert's notes, it is possible to find many examples of plays which he censored because he found the language offensive, for example, Johnson's *Magnetic Lady* was censored as it contained 'prophane speeches' which were edited out and Mountfort's *Launching of the Mary* had 'all ye Oathes left out' by Herbert before it was performed.[138] Yet it is difficult to believe that *The Tamer Tamed* contained bad language in such abundance that, when performed again, this play and this play alone exposed a fault line between the censorious views of the Jacobean and Caroline eras, leading Herbert to note 'that in former time the poetts tooke greater liberty than is allowed them by mee'.[139]

It is possible to discover what linguistic offence the play may have contained by looking at the pre-censored and post-censored version of *The Tamer Tamed*.[140] The censoring of the text is inconsistent. Oaths were indeed removed from the text by Herbert – but not all oaths, with *faith, troth, death* and *birlady* removed inconsistently. Similarly, vulgarisms are deleted inconsistently – *pisse* and *pissepot* are removed, but *pist* remains in the text. Such inconsistency is not uncommon in Herbert's censorship. Similar inconsistency is apparent in his censorship of the bad language in *The Launching of the Mary*.[141] While Herbert removed the oaths *fayth, yfaith, troth, s'life* and *by the Lord* from the play, he left in *by gisse, in god's name, a god's name* and at least 12 other examples of the use of the word *God* in such forms as *God bless* and *God shield*. Such inconsistency is typical not simply of Herbert's censorship, but of the self-censorship imposed by authors seeking licensing from Herbert. *The Inconsistent Lady* by Arthur Wilson is another example of a play where a pre- and post-censored version of the text survives, but with the censorship having been undertaken by Wilson himself.[142] While Wilson removes all oaths, he removes blasphemous expressions inconsistently. Fletcher's play *Demetrius and Enanthe* was similarly inconsistently purged of oaths in a manuscript produced by Ralph Crane.

Given that Herbert and others were inconsistent censors of language, one is encouraged to look elsewhere in the censored text to see whether some other cause of offence is consistently edited. While the language of the play is the apparent cause of offence for Herbert, we need to consider more carefully the subject matter of the play itself, and understand the views of the English ruling class, in order to understand censorship in this era.

The Tamer Tamed is something of a sequel to the *Taming of the Shrew*. In *The Tamer Tamed* a man is 'tamed' by a woman. The principal vehicle of the taming is a sex strike by the woman, in a plot device reminiscent of Aristophanes' *Lysistrata*. It is certainly plausible that the play, when played in the England of Charles rather than James, could be viewed as a political allegory, in which a woman, the Catholic Queen Henrietta, tames the weaker man, Charles I, especially as allegory became commonplace as a mechanism for making indirect political comment in an age of censorship.[143] The allegory itself had to be subtle as, especially in the case of personal attacks, plays in which it was all too obvious who was being targeted were the subject of complaint and plays were censored at the behest of the person defamed. This happened, for example, in the play *The Ball*, by Shirley, in which Herbert felt 'ther were divers personated so naturally, both of lords and others at court, that I took it ill ... Biston promised many things which I found faulte with should be left out'.[144] However, for such actions against a play to be successful, one had to have power and influence – hence Anne Ellesden's attempt[145] to force Herbert to suppress the production of the play *Keep the Widow Waking*, in which she believed she was being satirised, was unsuccessful.[146]

The allegorical nature of political criticism contained in *The Tamer Tamed* was typical. Usually, this form of political comment was tolerated, if not allowed, by the state which had an altogether patrician attitude to plays and censorship,[147] affecting a general air of unconcern when faced with minor criticisms in plays; James I was quite clear as to why ignoring criticism could be the best policy. In response to Bellarmine's *Apologia*, James chose to ignore rather than suppress the work, though it was very critical of him, 'so as not to give it importance or cause it to be sought'.[148] However, once a serious criticism was in danger of being widely known, the strategy of ignoring the criticism had to be abandoned and decisive action taken. Yet, if in taking decisive action the content of the book or play that caused offence was made yet more widely known, then this was clearly counter-productive. Finding a fault other than the true cause of offence clearly had something to recommend it as a strategy. Not only did this strategy keep the allegory coded, it also had the effect of diminishing the work – a play that is morally odious because it is obscene is much less of a threat than a keen political satire. It was censorship of this sort that Herbert was undertaking on *The Tamer Tamed*.[149]

The most troublesome censorship cases faced by Herbert can be explained in these terms very adequately. Indeed, on examination, Herbert's notes reveal that a clear and acknowledged political motivation for censorship existed at times. For example, Massinger's *Believe as You List* was censored in 1630 as 'itt did contain dangerous matter, as the deposing of Sebastian king of Portugal, by Philip the Second, and ther being a peace sworn twixte the kings of England and Spayne'.[150] Also, in 1640 an unnamed play was confiscated as 'it had a relation to the passages of the K.s journey to the Northe'.[151] Yet the two examples given are rare cases where the pretence of not noticing a political cause for offence was dropped. More often, we see exactly what happened with *The Tamer Tamed* – the censorship was focused on a matter such as language and decency rather than on the political nature of the censorship. Indeed, one is tempted to conclude that, as much today as in the seventeenth century, an offence to decency seems a less disputable ground for censorship than the suppression of valid criticism, an idea returned to in Chapter 5 of this book with reference to Mary Whitehouse. Given the choice, rather than break the coding of the text and make the criticism known, it was preferable for the censor to identify the indefensible as the cause of censorship. An interesting feature of the allegories which assisted this process is that they were often sexual in nature, as in *The Tamer Tamed* or Middleton's *A Game at Chess*. When the playwright chose to deal with politics via sexual allegory, the grounds for linguistic offence were, conveniently, often provided.

The political nature of the censorship of *The Tamer Tamed* becomes yet more apparent when the 1633 and 1647 editions are compared. The censored edition has been purged of sections that may appear anti-Catholic, with a clearly anti-Catholic exchange between two characters deleted completely.[152] Herbert censored *The Tamer Tamed* because, when restaged, the play posed a political problem for him.[153] The language of the play provided him with a covert means of censorship. Herbert chose to identify the profanity, obscenity and oaths in *The Tamer Tamed* to justify the censorship of the play. In this, he was aided by the sexual nature of the political allegories. However, since bad language was not the true target of his censorship, his removal of bad language is inconsistent. He is meticulous, however, in removing anti-Catholic scenes and sentiments from the play. That is not to say that Herbert did not, at times, simply edit out material because he found it obscene. He seemed to have had a genuine personal dislike of what he termed 'oathes, profaness and obsceanes'. Yet many of the decisions made by censors, whether they be Herbert, playwrights or book keepers of troupes of players, suggest that the role of politics in the creation and implementation of censorship laws in this period was paramount.

Civil war, Cromwell and the Commonwealth

The end of an era and the declaration of war on bad language

The social world that Herbert worked in when censoring plays for Charles I was profoundly changed by the English Civil Wars of the mid-seventeenth century. Yet the pattern of censorship survived the social change. If the Puritans were the main group apparently offended by bad language throughout the first half of the seventeenth century, it might be reasonable to conclude that, when they came to prominence at the end of the first Civil War, they would act decisively against bad language. When the Puritans went to war, profanity was one of the enemies they declared war upon.[154] In the Parliamentarian army there is some evidence that monetary penalties and even physical punishments were imposed on swearers.[155] Yet when the war ended, there was no general assault on bad language. As we will see, the bad language legislation that the government of the Saints did introduce had a goal very similar to that of Elizabeth, James and Charles – to suppress a group with opinions that were dangerous to the state, the Ranters.

The collapse of censorship, 1640

Between 1640 and 1649 the mechanisms of censorship, both linguistic and political, collapsed. That is not to say that there were no attempts to impose such censorship in this period – there were, most notably the closure of the theatres in 1642. This act neatly circumscribed the need for the licensing of plays for performance until the theatres re-opened with the Restoration.[156] A return to more systematic censorship began from 1649, with the presses, which in the period 1640–1649 had experienced a freedom long denied to them, becoming subject to attempted censorship again. Yet the presses continued to operate freely in spite of legislation designed to control them, such as the Licensing Act of 1649. Unauthorised presses were sought out and destroyed by Thomas and Elizabeth Atkin. A censor was appointed in the form of no less a person than John Milton, who acted in this role from 1649 to December 1653, when blindness brought about his resignation. However, the Licensing Act did not stop the presses in late 1649 producing large print-runs of *Eikon Basilike*, the supposed testament of Charles I. If ever there was a document which the Licensing Act could have usefully stopped, this was it. It took until 1655 for the new censorship regime to reach a peak of efficiency which surpassed the dreams of Laud.

Specifically linguistic censorship found its way on to the statute book in the form of the Blasphemy Act of 1650. The Blasphemy Act appears to be an assertion of Puritan morality over the population of England. The Act was part of a package of measures designed to re-impose censorship. Yet the aim of this censorship was not to bring about a Puritan heaven on Earth, rather its goal was to eliminate non-government opinion and radical

Protestant groups such as the Ranters.[157] More openly than in the Caroline age, the 1650 Act was a determined attempt to silence a politically problematic group. It was not an attempt to suppress bad language per se. Though the Act sought to suppress 'the detestable sin of prophane swearing and cursing' the true goal was not to suppress bad language but 'monstrous opinions and wicked and abominable practices', i.e. the Ranters. So while Cromwell himself spoke of wanting to 'make it a shame to see men to be bold in sin and profaneness'[158] there is precious little evidence that the linguistic censorship practised by the Cromwellian government was aimed at bringing this about. In order to explore this we need to consider the case of the Ranters in more detail. Following this, I will explore the limits of the public expression of bad language in the Commonwealth by looking at a newsbook of the period, *Mercurius Fumigosus*.

The Ranters – 'Oh that a man should curse, swear, whore and cry 'tis a delight to heaven's Majesty'[159]

The Ranters were a protestant sect which would be radical even by twenty-first-century standards. Far from eschewing swearing, they embraced it. The Ranters believed that the pure could not be tainted by impure actions. Hence as a demonstration of their purity they engaged in free love and embraced the use of bad language. Their beliefs scandalised the Commonwealth, and provoked the Blasphemy Act of 1650.

The introduction of the Blasphemy Act of 1650[160] is a good example both of the religious nature of Puritan objections to certain forms of language and of the essentially political nature of attempts to suppress such language in the early to mid-seventeenth century. The roots of the Blasphemy Act show its anti-Ranter nature clearly. The Parliamentary roots of the bill lie in the creation of a committee by the Rump Parliament which had a remit to examine 'obscene, licentious and impious practices'.[161] The true goal of the committee was revealed, however, when it produced its report on 'several abominable practices of a sect called Ranters'. Following from this report, the committee drafted legislation at the request of Parliament specifically designed to suppress and punish the 'abominable opinions and practices of the Ranters'. The legislation was adopted as the Blasphemy Act. All told, roughly three months passed between the creation of the committee by the Rump in June to the passage of the Act through Parliament in August.

The provisions of the Act, while in part designed to suppress certain forms of language, were much broader and clearly aimed at the Ranters. The main provisions of the Act were to make it an offence to publicly:

1   advocate drunkenness, adultery or swearing;
2   claim that heaven, hell, salvation and damnation were one and the same;
3   declare oneself to be God;

4   declare that there was no difference between moral and immoral behaviour;
5   deny the existence of God;
6   deny the existence of heaven, hell, salvation and damnation.

Anyone found guilty under the Act would be jailed for six months for a first offence. Should a person re-offend, the Act proscribed a punishment of exile from England on pain of death.

Two points should be made about this Act. First, the provisions of the Act look somewhat disparate. Indeed, unless one looks at contemporary writings on the Ranters, one would be hard-pressed to come up with an explanation for the provisions of this Act. The Act makes sense only in the context of contemporary claims about the Ranters and their practices, which pretty much match the provisions of the Act.[162] Second, this was not an attempt to produce legislation which could be used to impose a system of morality on the private sphere. The Act was quite clear in distinguishing between public and private expression, and the provisions of the Act did not apply to the private domain. In the comfort of one's home, one could in principle, for example, deny the existence of God with impunity. It was only in public that this became a crime.[163] Again, the nature of the Act is revealed here. It is not an Act which was attempting to regulate private morality – it was designed to suppress the spread of a movement of which the government disproved. The Act sought to suppress 'the most visible radical group in public'[164] during the early part of the Commonwealth. The fact that the movement was associated with bad language is the principal reason why the Act covers it. It is not covered because of the dislike of the government for bad language per se.

A case study – Abiezer Coppe

Abiezer Coppe was a preacher who lived a Ranter lifestyle. Coppe delivered sermons in the nude, freely combined religious and sexual imagery in his writings and condemned sexual monogamy. Unsurprisingly Coppe was not averse to using colourful language. His major work, the two volumes of the *Fiery Flying Roll*, abounds with choice turns of phrase and images, with 'O fool!', 'I'll laugh at thee and laugh at thy destruction', 'vile base fellows' and claims that God will make 'thine own child . . . lie with a whore before thine eyes' being but a sample. He even goes so far as to claim in the second volume that swearing is a sign of holiness saying that 'It's meat and drink to an angel . . . to swear' and 'It's a joy to . . . curse like a devil'.[165]

Appearing as they did in 1650, it is not unreasonable to imagine that the writings of preachers such as Coppe were very much in the mind of the Parliamentary committee which framed the 1650 Blasphemy Act. Certainly the provisions of the Blasphemy Act make illegal the views that Coppe espouses in the *Fiery Flying Roll*. Indeed, Parliament twice ordered the works of Coppe burned in 1650, once in May prior to the establishment of the Parliamentary committee and once on the eve of the introduction of the Blasphemy Act in August 1650. Considering Coppe's high profile it is no surprise to discover that, before 1650 was out, Coppe was charged under the Blasphemy Act. Coppe's zeal seems to have left him at this point, however, and he wrote his *Remonstrance* and later *Coppe's Return to the Ways of Truth* in 1651. Both sought to assert his innocence. The defence presented by the former work is largely that Coppe never said that which he was accused of saying. By the time of writing *Coppe's Return to the Ways of Truth*, he accepted his previous works as his own but renounced them, claiming he was intoxicated by his knowledge of the Lord when he wrote them. Coppe's second defence comes close to a plea of guilty on the grounds of diminished responsibility, and his release on the basis of *Coppe's Return to the Ways of Truth* has been interpreted by some historians as evidence that Coppe was released on compassionate grounds, as he was believed to be insane.[166]

When recanting, Coppe is expansive in his condemnation of swearing and cursing. In his *Remonstrance* he congratulates Parliament for suppressing profanity and says that a blasphemer is 'the vilest of persons'.[167] By the time of *Coppe's Return to the Ways of Truth* his condemnation has become yet more forthright, identifying swearing and cursing as sins[168] and accepting that the scriptures explicitly forbid them both.[169]

On his release from prison he abandoned his Ranter lifestyle. While he preached for a short time after his release, in December 1651 he turned from preaching to medicine and practised as Dr Higham in Surrey until his death in 1672.

Coppe's story is a perfect illustration of the goals of the Blasphemy Act. Parliament took a politically troublesome figure that had angered it before the adoption of the Act, and coerced him to recant through the expedient of imprisonment. In suppressing the Ranters and other such non-orthodox preachers, the Blasphemy Act must be counted a success; John Tickell, an Oxfordshire minister who used the Blasphemy Act to prosecute Ranters, declared that 'before the late act against the Ranters, they spoke boldly, and now they dare not'.[170] However, the Act was unsuccessful in some ways, in that, while some like Coppe and Clarkson[171] recanted, others were tried many times and did not recant, e.g. Richard Coppin. However, over time, the anti-Ranter offensive did cause the Ranters to blend into less offensive non-orthodox sects, most notably the Quakers. From the point of view of this book, however, it is crucial to note that the Blasphemy Act only ever worked at the public level. It was not an attempt to censor speech on the private level. You were only imperilled by the provisions of the 1650 Act if you tried to gain an audience of listeners or readers for your blasphemy and swearing. Even then, it was only likely that the Act would be used against you if you were politically troublesome. If you were not, you could have lewd works published under licence, as happened in the Commonwealth-era newsbook, *Mercurius Fumigosus*.

Mercurius Fumigosus

Mercurius Fumigosus was an early newsbook published by John Crouch in the period June 1654 to October 1655.[172] Crouch had previously published two other newsbooks, *Mercurius Democritus* and *The Man in The Moon*. Crouch can best be described as an early English social and political commentator who used robust language and imagery to present his views. *Mercurius Fumigosus* was the last in this series of newsbooks, and of the three it is certainly the one which is the most obscene. Yet, at first glance, *Mercurius Fumigosus* appears to abound with articles that appear to be at best whimsical, at worst crazed. Consider the following text:[173]

> The *Swarm* of *BEES* that lately lighted on the Doctor's man's *fancies* of his *Breeches*, have every day since produced such an infinite increase of *English Honey*, that it is thought the best *Butter* will be before *Michael-mas* at four Pence a Pound, if not under.

Once decoded, the text is obscene, even by modern standards. An examination of the phrase 'swarm of bees' in a corpus composed of all extant copies of the newsbook reveals the meaning of the phrase; there are nine examples of this phrase in the corpus and it always indicates male sexual arousal. *Honey* is used frequently by Crouch (13 times) and is always used to refer to sperm. Once this decoding is achieved the meaning of the text becomes apparent and obscene. This type of material is typical of Crouch – it is a coded rebuke to a figure that his readers probably knew.

Yet, as well as disguised vulgarity, Crouch also uses vulgarisms which, while Herbert would probably not have edited them consistently, would have been the subject of at least inconsistent censorship under the previous regime; for example, if we consider vulgarisms alone, Crouch frequently uses words such as (frequency of usage in parentheses) ARSE (12), BASTARD (6), DAMN (18), FART (10), PISS (19), POX (13) and SHIT (21). It is clear that even in the Commonwealth, texts which were obscene and contained bad language could be published. Crouch published *Mercurius Fumigosus* for over a year, and received official sanction to publish from the State.[174] A more powerful example of the government of the Saints not truly being concerned with bad language would be difficult to imagine.

The Restoration

In 1661, Charles II came to the throne of England in the Restoration. Sir Henry Herbert was still alive, and was appointed Master of the Revels. When the theatres were re-opened, Herbert set about his old job, applying old standards. Herbert edited out bad language from some Restoration plays. For example, he edited out oaths such as *pox* and *plague* and vulgarisms such as *fart* and *arse* from John Wilson's *The Cheats*.[175] However, *The*

Cheats shows Herbert being insensitive to the politics and morals of the Restoration. The play caused offence by implying that various professions were refuges for hypocrites. Charles II intervened and had the play censored further, with the politics rather than the language of the play being the focus of the censorship. By the time that the play was printed in 1664, the true nature of Restoration censorship was shown: the printed version virtually ignored the deletion of bad language introduced by Herbert but retained the politically motivated censorship of the text. The Restoration was not concerned with the suppression of bad language and dispensed with its use as a tool for suppressing texts. As a consequence, as is clear in *The Cheats*, politically motivated censorship became much more obvious than it had previously been.

Further evidence of the lack of interest in censoring bad language during the reign of Charles II comes from the play *The Wits*. In 1673 Sir William D'Avenant submitted his play *The Wits* to Herbert for licensing. Herbert censored the play in what he thought was the spirit of the new censorship law, the 1662 Licensing Act.[176] D'Avenant protested and took his case to Charles himself. Charles swiftly reversed all of Herbert's decisions. In doing so, Charles clearly indicated that he saw little reason to edit out bad language in plays.[177] In an age in which Puritanism had lost its power, bad language was embraced by the establishment as a means of expressing their opposition to Puritan views. Herbert, in what had been a long career as a censor, had lived through what can only be viewed as a very broad range of censorship practices. Now, in his old age, he lived to act as a censor in a period in which plays abounded with bad language. Charles attended the first performance of *The Wits* and was a regular theatre-goer. In 1663 he was present at a performance of Killigrew's play, *The Parson's Wedding*, which is littered with bad language and some interesting variations on the insult BASTARD, notably *thou son of a thousant fathers* and *Son of a batchelour*. The Restoration stage was a place where bad language found a public home for a while. Censorship existed, but as in the reign of earlier monarchs, censorship in the reign of Charles II was aimed at the suppression of groups identified as a threat to the state, notably non-conformists.[178]

Conclusion

The suppression of bad language from Elizabeth to Cromwell was only undertaken by the government in response to specific threats which, while not linguistic in nature, could best be suppressed by an accusation that they used offensive language. Ecclesiastical courts could take local action against such offences as swearing,[179] and there is some evidence that they did.[180] Yet, there is more evidence to suggest that, even at this level, prosecution was the exception rather than the norm. Social control in the sixteenth and seventeenth centuries was undertaken by local networks. Peer pressure, not the law, was the major means of correcting wrong-doing on a day-to-day basis. Indeed, the use of the courts and prosecutions can best be seen as a failure of the society – the preference was to finish disputes before they got to court using either persuasion or social pressure.[181] The laws against immorality were present not to allow the state to persecute swearers and the like, but rather to allow local courts to have a flexible response to the cases brought before them. Indeed, there is some evidence that those courts would at times accept that swearing was permissible where a woman was upbraid-ing a wayward husband in public.[182] The prosecution of individuals for single acts of swearing and the widespread application of such laws was very far from the mind of the state or the judges in the sixteenth and seventeenth centuries. On a national scale, the cases presented in this chapter match on a grander scale the day-to-day reality of prosecution at a more mundane level – the use of the law to suppress language was largely to do with the failure of persuasion and peer pressure, not a matter of state policy.

This book is not concerned with the sporadic uses of laws to prosecute swearers where no option faced a local court. Rather it is concerned with state-sponsored or widespread systematic attempts to suppress bad language. It is in this context that this chapter claims that any law appearing to promote this in the period under discussion was, in fact, a political con-venience to suppress something which was not, primarily, a linguistic cause of offence.

Yet the liberality of the Restoration stage brought about a change in atti-tudes in certain sections of society to bad language. The Restoration stage allowed the language of the streets onto the stage. Unfettered by secret codes or heavy allegories, the Restoration stage represented the English lan-guage in all of its forms, from refined to obscene. The result was bound to shock certain members of society who would rather not have bad language presented to them, irrespective of whether it was to the taste of the monarch or the many. It was in this confrontation with bad language on the stage that criticism of public use of bad language started to develop.

Hence, it is hardly surprising to discover that it was during the Restor-ation that the notion of a general assault on bad language and other forms of immorality, which was first articulated clearly late in the Interregnum, was to begin to make headway. This call for change, which aimed to bring about a reformation of manners, was to have a lasting effect on the perception of bad language in British society. Beginning with writers such as Allestree, who wrote the first edition of his *Whole Duty of Man* in 1658, a push began towards the elimination of so-called vices from polite company. There was also a clear identification of such supposedly immoral practices with the woes that had befallen England during the Civil War and Interregnum. According to Thomas Pierce in his sermons, 'swearing and drunkenness, chambering and wantonness, pride and profaneness' had brought about the Civil War and the death of Charles I. In the reformation of manners to elim-inate such sins, society would find 'the properest answer to such a blessing as the Restoration'.[183] However, the time for such attitudes to come to the fore and reshape English society was not in the reign of the merry monarch, and the group to push forward the movement to reform manners was not principally provided by the clergy. The group that was confronted and offended by this libertinage was the aspirant English middle classes and it was they who adopted the cause of the reformation of manners.

4 Modern attitudes to bad language form

The reformation of manners

Introduction

In addressing the censorship of bad language in the period from Elizabeth I to Charles II in the previous chapter, I dealt with each monarch in turn in order to demonstrate that while a change of ruler in this period may have brought a change of emphasis in the censorship of bad language, the censorship was politically or economically motivated. Morality, while useful as a smoke screen, was not the factor driving censorship. However, with the accession of James II, this general pattern changed. From the reign of James II to the accession of George III, a grassroots reform movement was active amongst the middle classes of England that was to have a lasting effect on public attitudes to bad language. Consequently, in this chapter I am shifting the focus away from monarchs to groups that, over the reigns of five monarchs, maintained a sustained campaign against bad language and other manifestations of what they saw as immorality.[184] The groups in question are the religious societies, which were rooted in the English middle classes.[185]

The rise of the English middle classes

After a century of strife, economic prosperity grew notably as the seventeenth century closed and the eighteenth century began. Up to this point the middle classes in Britain had been a negligible sector of society. However, from this period, through the massive growth in such occupations as shop-keeping, the numbers of the middle classes in Britain burgeoned. For example, a conservative estimate placed the number of families engaged in shop-keeping in England in 1688 as 50,000. By 1759 that figure had grown to 162,500.[186] In itself, this would be of no interest or importance to this book had the middle class not sought an identity for themselves predicated on asserting their social and moral superiority over the working classes. In a trend that was to become more pronounced as the eighteenth century progressed, the newly moneyed middle classes took it upon themselves to clean up society in order to:

establish a personal ascendancy above the herd as right minded, responsible and successful citizens, and at the same time to impress their worth upon their social betters, including God ... Lacking direct power at Westminster, the vocal bourgeois chose not to challenge the aristocratic political machine, but rather to consolidate their own parallel moral authority, to cower their inferiors and impress their betters.[187]

It was through the goal of distinguishing itself from the lower classes that the middle class began to seek a role of moral leadership, a role in which the pleasures of the lower orders and certain members of the middle class were problematised. In doing so, the middle-class moral reformers identified bad language as something which was morally wrong and hence not a signifier of middle-class status. So it is the contention of this chapter that the rise of a censorious view of bad language in the public sphere was linked to the rise of the middle class in late seventeenth century England. In agitating against immorality, they attacked the language of the stage. This attack set the moral framework which would later be adopted when the middle class formed religious societies to eliminate immoral practices such as bad language in everyday life. The most notable of these were the Society for the Reformation of Manners (SRM) and the Society for the Promotion of Christian Knowledge (SPCK). The bulk of this chapter is devoted to these societies, with the main focus being on the SRM.

The SRM drew their membership from the ranks of Buttonsellers, Milliners, Salesmen, Perfumers, Goldsmiths, Wig Makers and Confectioners[188] – the middle classes, not the upper classes.[189] They certainly did not draw strength from the poor, who would have found the annual subscription fee charged by such societies as the SRM prohibitive.[190]

The formation of the religious societies in England marks the beginning of the English middle classes trying to forge a distinctive identity for themselves. This identity was predicated on a moral probity higher than that of their supposed betters which also marked them as both morally and socially superior to their inferiors. As bad language was deemed to be immoral, the societies set in train the process which made swearing a mark of low class status, or at least of non-middle-classness. Similarly, through the work of the charity schools it associated bad language with a lack of education. The religious nature of the societies also associated bad language with low morals. In short, the campaign which was associated with the societies initiated a journey for the English language away from a classless attitude to bad language to a class-based one. The moral framework for the assault on public manners was formed initially during attacks on the supposed licentiousness of the Restoration stage.

'The Devil's chapel'[191]: the assault on the stage

The reopening of playhouses under Charles II was coupled with a relaxation of censorship practices concerning plays. The consequence was that plays were regularly staged in which language and topics that some members of society undoubtedly found offensive were present. The following quotation from a letter of John Evelyn's written in 1664 shows this well:

> there are more wretched and obscene plays permitted [in London] than in all the world beside ... You know, my Lord, that I ... am far from Puritanism; but I would have no reproach left for our adversaries in a thing which may be so conveniently reform'd.[192]

Such views were unpopular at the time that Evelyn wrote them, though there were calls even in the reign of Charles II for a reformation of manners which were in line with Evelyn's views. Yet, bad language, in common with the stage itself, was a token of anti-Puritanism that was bound to find popularity in the immediate wake of the Restoration, hence the limited impact of the call to reform manners in Charles II's reign is understandable. However, opposition to the supposed licentiousness of the Restoration stage did not diminish during the reign of the later Stuarts. Rather, with the fall of the Stuarts it blossomed after the Glorious Revolution, when a concerted attack on the stage began, focused in part, though not exclusively, on bad language. Chief amongst the critics of the stage was Jeremy Collier.

Collier, beginning with his 1688 work, *A Short View of the Immorality and Prophaneness of the English Stage*, which started a debate that was both to change the language used on stage and act as a precursor to the assault by the SRM on the language used by the lower classes on the streets. Collier accused the Restoration stage of using bad language that 'does in effect degrade Human Nature; links Reason into Appetite, and breaks down the Distinctions between Man and Beast. Goats and monkeys, if they could speak, would express their Brutality in such Language as this'.[193] He deplored the use of bad language on stage and claimed that some of the language used on stage clearly breached laws against the use of such language.[194] Notably, Collier also deplored the use of bad language by female characters in plays, stating that the use of modest language by women 'properly distinguishes a woman' and 'Obscenity in any Company is rustick uncreditable Talent; but among women it is particularly rude'.[195] Ladies should be protected from the use of the language of the lower class ('the Language of the Stews'[196]) being used on stage, where 'the poets make Women speak Smuttily'.[197] Further he claims that even in everyday speech 'Swearing before Women is reckon'd a breach of good Behaviour'.[198] Collier encouraged the middle and upper classes to set a good example by not using bad language. He also linked bad language to irreligiousness, stating that the lewd language of the lower classes is used in temples in pagan societies, yet has no place in a Christian church, hence linking the use of lewd language to paganism and declaring that 'Smut is insufferable' to Christianity.[199]

If one were to read Collier without reading the works he was criticising, one may develop a view that every play he saw was littered with obscenity and bad language. This is not the case. Collier had a skill for discovering offence in texts that is breath taking.[200] Collier's guide was his dictum that ''tis no matter for the sense, as long as the profaneness is clear'.[201] In short, if Collier thought a section of a play was offensive, it was indeed offensive.[202] He was particularly keen to identify blasphemy and obscenity in the language of the plays he criticised, often finding them in the most innocent of contexts.[203] For example, consider the following passage, from D'Urfey's *Don Quixote*, the language of which was thought to be 'particularly rampant and scandalous' by Collier:[204]

> Providence that formed the Fair
> In such a charming skin
> Their outside made his only care
> And never looked within

This may appear innocent enough, but for Collier this was blasphemy. If the complaints of Collier appear difficult to understand now, it should be noted that they were also difficult to understand at times in the late seventeenth century, with D'Urfey in his *Preface to The Campaigners* claiming that, in criticising *Don Quixote*, Collier was 'foaming at the mouth'.

But some took Collier's criticisms seriously and agreed with him. Collier set about his assault on the stage with a persecuting zeal, a moral certainty and a flair for publicity that easily earns him the label 'moral entrepreneur'. The controversy triggered by Collier generated over 400 books and pamphlets and started a debate that lasted well into the nineteenth century.[205] Significantly, Collier's stance drew support from periodicals aimed at the middle class, and the middle classes were active in support of Collier.[206] More importantly, it drew figures such as Anthony Horneck into the attack on the stage.[207] Anthony Horneck was a leading light in the religious societies of London. The extent to which Collier influenced the religious societies or was himself influenced by them is difficult to say. But given the similarities of the views of Collier and Horneck, and the fact that attempts were made later to induce Horneck and the SRM to support Collier,[208] it is unsurprising that the agenda of the SRM and the SPCK would bear a close similarity to that of Collier, but with the attack switched from the stage to the streets and the classroom.

The birth of the religious societies[209]

The English religious societies (RSs) may have been inspired by the religious societies of St Vincent de Paul which had been formed in France. The French societies were similar in that they drew the middle classes into religious organisations and they had a structure which the English societies mirrored, with a lay membership supervised by an ordained churchman. However, the French societies were philanthropic, while the English RSs, even in their early manifestations, were focused primarily on the spiritual salvation of their members. While this may at times have been the cause of acts of philanthropy, the goal of the members of the society was personal salvation rather than charity. While, later on, the English RSs would seek to spread salvation by imposing a moral code across society, they did not follow the French societies to become fundamentally charitable organisations. Far from it – the RSs eventually spawned the SRM, an organisation predicated on persecution.

However, it would have taken an augurer to foresee how the development of the English RSs would lead to the SRM, especially as the RSs began by capitalising on the one feature of Puritanism which remained popular after the Restoration, namely the preaching of and listening to sermons. It was via sermons given by William Beveridge, Mr Smythies and most notably by Anthony Horneck that the RSs began. Horneck in particular used his sermons to bemoan the moral ills of his age. Beginning around 1678, young men would come to such preachers to seek guidance and, slowly but surely, loose association formed. If contemporary accounts are to be believed,[210] at some point during this process of the formation of loose associations, formal RSs were established with Horneck being viewed as the *pater familias*, if not the founder, of the RS movement. The early forms of the RSs are worth reviewing as they essentially laid down the framework for what was to come in the SRM.[211] Membership was restricted to males over the age of 16 who were confirmed members of the Church of England. Members paid subscriptions to be part of the group, and weekly meetings were led by an Anglican clergyman. The main philanthropic act of the RS was an annual distribution of funds to the poor. Other than for this annual alms giving, the RSs concerned themselves solely with the spiritual instruction of the group and occasional events at which they could 'discourse each other about their spiritual concerns'.[212] Such RSs continued to grow in number throughout the reign of James II. This was in spite of state suspicion occasioned by the secretive nature of the RSs – the RSs at this period admitted members only after considerable private discussion of any candidate's suitability.[213] RS meetings were closed affairs. Considering the Anglican foundations of the early RSs, it is unsurprising that they became bases of anti-Catholicism. Their anti-Catholicism in concert with their secretiveness made them a target for the state of James II. Yet the persecution under James wrought a change to the RSs which placed them in poll position to set the moral agenda for the reign of William III. During the reign of James the RSs had widened their philanthropy to include carrying their salvation to a wider audience. From being in part a private sermon club, the RSs branched out and started to make provision for sermons to be read at a number of churches. This could take the form of the creation of an endowment for a preacher or the provision of funds to ensure an occasional lecture was read out in Church. In an attempt to sustain the church while under the scrutiny of a hostile State, the RSs had gained the capacity to take control, in part at least, of a popular form of mass media: the pulpit. This capacity to seek control through the pulpit was strengthened by a change in the nature of the RSs after the Revolution. Paradoxically, the RSs, which had remained secretive in a regime that viewed secretiveness as dangerous, moved to become more open when a regime came to power that did not have as great a problem with the RSs or their secretiveness. Under William, the RSs sought to expand their membership, with the goal that every member of the RS 'should endeavour to bring in one other at least to their society'.[214] As a result, the RSs began to grow, both in size and number. As the RSs grew they also began to spread. While initially a London-based initiative, by the 1690s societies had been formed in the provinces, such as that formed in Romney in Kent, which was vigorous and undertook such enterprises as the publication of its own hymn book.

In addition to seeking growth, the RSs also sought to shed their secretive nature by seeking official sanction for their goals and methods from the Church of England. This was given by the highest clerical authorities in the land, including the Archbishop of Canterbury who remarked that 'these societies were a Support to our Church'.[215]

With a programme of publicising its ideas through the pulpit, an expanding membership and the approval of the Church of England, the RSs in the later part of the seventeenth century were well placed to influence public opinion. Yet while the mechanism for effective militancy was established in this phase of the RSs' development, it had yet to turn into a persecuting force. The transformation of the RSs into such a force would bring it to the printing press and also bring about an increase in the different types of RSs.

The birth of the Society for the Reformation of Manners

The development that led to the evolution of a militant RS can be ascribed to two things: a moral panic which developed in the last decade of the seventeenth century regarding immorality and irreligiousness, and the existence of a set of laws which a militant RS could readily exploit to achieve their goals.

The moral panic was focused on the supposed immorality of society in this period, with claims being made by moral entrepreneurs that all forms of immorality, including swearing and cursing, were on the increase. Interestingly, each commentator viewed one sin as being more prevalent than another – Defoe saw drunkenness as the chief problem,[216] the justices of Middlesex saw such matters as the singing of obscene ballads to be a major issue,[217] while for others it was the growth of prostitution that should be combated.[218] Whatever the manifestation of vice, vice had to be combated partly on moral (which, for the reformers, meant religious) grounds, partly on social grounds. The social objection to vice was partly a class-based one – 'vices . . . undermined that system of subordination upon which the social order was based' as 'vices such as pride, envy and ambition could cause a man to try to leave his proper status and aspire to something higher for which he was not suited'.[219] The manifestations of vice were not merely a token of irreligiousness in the reformers' eyes, they were a token of the breakdown of the class divisions in society. Either irreligiousness or the threat of social disorder in themselves may have been a cause for action. Taken together, they compelled reformers to act.

Yet, is there any evidence of the moral decay which the moral entrepreneurs claimed was rampant? It is impossible to say with certainty that any behaviour which moral entrepreneurs such as Woodward deemed to be immoral was on the increase at the time. It is undoubtedly true, however, that a number of changes may have led to an apparent increase in vice. First, there are some signs that would have caused concern to the religious: church attendance was declining in this period as a consequence of the Toleration Act,[220] and religious observances, such as Sunday as a day of rest, were falling into disuse. This in itself was thought to betoken a decline in the moral fibre of the nation. Second, there was an increase in the general availability and consumption of alcohol in the late seventeenth and early eighteenth centuries[221] which, according to some observers, led to an inevitable increase in the use of bad language.[222] Third, it was claimed that entertainments, such as the masque, and sexual practices not widely discussed in England up to this point, such as sodomy, were supposedly being introduced to the land.[223] While not of direct relevance to the upsurge of activity against bad language in this period, the public discussion of such practices certainly contributed to the general moral panic of the era. The following quotation gives an impression of that moral panic:[224]

> It is very well known, That in the late times Profane Swearing, Drunkenness, Open-Lewdness, and Prophenation . . . were generally discouraged and suppressed. And it is well known, to our Shame, that those Sins have not only since revived amongst us . . . but have been committed with the greatest Impudence and without Controul . . . so that they were seen and heard at *Noon-Day* in our *Open Streets*; and as if we were resolved to out-do the Impieties of the very *Heathens*, *Prophaneness*, and even *Blasphemy* was too often the Wit and Entertainment of our Scandalous Play-Houses.

It is difficult to say whether the events outlined in the quotation above were imagined or real. What is clear, however, is that some people associated with the RSs believed this to be true and were prepared to use the mass media to establish a moral panic and to propagate their own solution to it.

However, a spark was still needed to ignite the panic, and that spark was provided at the grassroots level.

In 1690, the people of Tower Hamlets in London decided to act, in concert with the police, against what they perceived as flagrant immorality in their district, largely associated with brothels, yet including swearing and cursing.[225] One of the people behind this action then moved to the Strand and took the idea of such community action against immorality with him. This idea was fastened on by Edward Stephens, a lawyer turned preacher who had been a member of the religious societies. Seeking to emulate the activities in Tower Hamlets, Stephens and his associates began to set about the task of establishing a religious society with a difference: it would actively seek out sin and prosecute sinners, galvanising the Justices of the Peace to act against immorality. In doing so, Stephens and his associates changed the goals of the Tower Hamlets society and the RSs subtly yet crucially. The first difference was that the Strand society, unlike the Tower Hamlets society, was not a grassroots organisation. While the Tower Hamlets society had been a small parish-based affair and had counted on local support to carry out its actions, the Strand society immediately sought to use money and influence to impose moral change. The money they would provide themselves; they used it to pay informers to increase the rate of prosecutions for immorality. The influence they sought from above, by appealing to the Crown itself. Queen Mary, at the behest of Edward Stillingfleet, the Bishop of Worcester, issued a letter to magistrates to encourage them to enforce the morality laws already on the statute book. The spark caught, and by 1691 Stephens had produced a new form of RS[226] – a Society for the Reformation of Manners.[227] This SRM underlined the second major difference between the SRM and what had gone before. While the SRM was founded along the lines of the existing religious societies, it differed in that it was open to non-conformists.[228] Also, unlike the RSs the members of the SRM had the specific mission to hunt out those who broke the laws against immorality and to encourage the law enforcement agencies to apply the law.

The SRM proved popular, and, as moral entrepreneurs, they attracted support from the establishment. Beginning with the letter from Mary, the SRM drew support from the Lord Mayor and Aldermen of London, and by the time of the publication of Woodward's 1701 book, a list of illustrious names could be included at the front of the book offering support to the society. The panic about public morality had begun, and bad language, in the form of blasphemy, cursing and swearing, was a prime target for the reformers.

But what drove the SRM to believe that it could prosecute such behaviours as using bad language on moral grounds when, for the previous 100 years or so at least, nobody really seems to have tried this systematically? To understand why, one needs to understand the three assumptions on which the SRM was based. First, that God and the Devil were locked in combat, and that God needed the assistance of the good, just as sinners who used bad language aided the Devil. Second, each man had a split personality, capable of good and bad. The war they saw being fought on the divine level was also being waged in each and every human being. Just as the good could aid God, the good could aid the divine nature of each person. Conversely, just as the sinner could aid the Devil, so the sinner could promote the base nature of any individual. Finally, irrespective of the ultimately holy nature of the war against immorality, sins such as using bad language were fundamentally unhealthy – they led to mental and physical corruption as surely as they led to spiritual corruption. In these three beliefs lies the warrant for the activities of the SRM: it was waging a moral war on the side of God and, in doing so, it was on the side of moral right, intellectual well-being and physical health.[229] The SRM reinforced its need to actively pursue sinners through the courts, partly by blaming the state of moral decay they claimed existed on the failure of the judiciary to use the laws at their disposal to suppress immorality,[230] but largely by claiming that it was a duty imposed on them by God to actively interfere in the lives of others. Should they fail to act, retribution, sacred and profane, would surely fall on all of them. The great plague, the Great Fire of London, the great storms of 1703 and an earthquake in Jamaica were all cited as examples of God's wrath in the face of inaction against immorality.[231] It was also suggested that immorality could bring about a national conversion to Catholicism,[232] or cause the Stuarts to return to power in England.[233] Hence there was a need to act against the sinners if the saints were not to share in their fall. It was also incumbent on the saints to set a good example that the sinners may seek to follow.

However, while the setting of a good example did not require intervention in the lives of others, the need to act against sin did, and the SRM sought to act through the courts.

While the SRM did initially consider whether private admonitions, preaching and printed propaganda alone may achieve their goal, they settled on legal action as the most effective means of pursuing their reform programme, assuming that private admonitions would have little effect.[234] So the goal of the SRM became to work by legal means to suppress the immorality that they perceived around them, and to support their work in the courts by preaching and printing propaganda.

Stephens and his followers were aware that the laws they needed to initiate such a campaign were readily available.[235] These laws suited their purpose perfectly. While I have focused on the societies as the instrument by which concerns about swearing and cursing became a public concern in England, there had been unsuccessful attempts to turn it into a public issue in the past. A number of statutes had been passed in the reign of earlier monarchs against blasphemy, cursing and profanity. There had even been a forlorn attempt to pass laws against profaneness in the reign of Charles II, though this had never been formally adopted into law. The statutes that survived into the 1690s[236] did so largely because they had been so rarely used that they were, to all intents and purposes, dead letters. The laws were invoked from time to time and could be a cause of consternation, such as when the Earl of Pembroke was committed to the Tower on a charge of blasphemy in 1678. But, by and large, the laws against public bad language were so rarely used and the issue so rarely discussed that by 1687 the Mayor and Aldermen of London felt compelled to issue a proclamation against profaneness and immorality, imploring constables to enforce the laws in this area. However, the laws were ineffective while there was no public support for them and the constables were unwilling to enforce them. The moral panic which the societies fuelled and exploited from the 1690s was exactly what was needed to revivify the laws in the statute book. When revivified, the laws proved to be potent for two reasons. First, they required only one witness – the word of one person was sufficient evidence to convict another. Second, on conviction, the accuser could be given a financial reward for making the accusation, i.e. paid informers could be used to bring charges. If the moral panic of the societies was not enough of an inducement to the public and constables to enforce these laws, the added bonus of a financial reward from the SRM was. However, before turning to the methods that the SRM used, one needs to examine a sister organisation of the SRM and then explore the growth and spread of the RSs.

The societies multiply – the Society for the Reformation of Manners and the Society for the Promotion of Christian Knowledge

Not all RSs decided to pursue the tactics of the SRM. In 1698 the Society for the Promotion of Christian Knowledge (SPCK) was launched. The SPCK adopted different tactics from the SRM, though it shared the concerns of the SRM and sprang from the same crucible of the religious societies and the moral panic regarding immorality. The SPCK decided to focus on the sin and not the sinner, and worked to root out the cause of, rather than the manifestations of, vice. For the SPCK, 'it was the catechism learned young, rather than the informer, that was to make England secure against atheism and vice'.[237] With that said, the SPCK and the SRM were very closely linked.[238] While the tactics of the SPCK differed from those of the SRM, and while it survived much longer (indeed it survives to this day), the SRM and the SPCK were very much joined at birth. Leading lights in the establishment of the SPCK were also leading lights in the SRM. For example, John Evelyn was 'a principal founder and supporter of the Societies for the Reformation of Manners and Promoting Christian Knowledge'[239] and the first Secretary of the SPCK, John Chamberlayne, was also later Secretary of the SRM.[240] In 1700 the SPCK agreed to inform its stewards to 'co-operate with the Societies for the Reformation of Manners by giving information'. The SPCK also distributed large numbers of texts such as the SRM's *Help to a National Reformation* and handbooks arguing against cursing.[241] The link between the two was not simply in terms of the object of their complaint and the personnel staffing the societies, it was also constitutional. Indeed, so close were the links between the two societies that in the public mind they were often viewed as being one and the same.[242] However, the SPCK, over time, became increasingly interested in asserting a separate identity from the SRM, even resorting to a newspaper advert in 1719 to achieve this aim.[243] While the SPCK's members may have supported the SRM, they were pursuing a separate policy – change through education.

The SPCK decided to work through educating and informing, rather than preaching and prosecuting[244] as the SRM did. It was also an expressly Anglican organisation, unlike the SRM.[245] While the SPCK did not have the initial dramatic impact of the SRM, it certainly ensured the long-term survival of the agenda of moral reform.

The diversification of the approaches of the religious societies to the problems they perceived in late seventeenth century England led to a moral panic that was enduring. For while the SRM was riding the wave of the moral panic, the SPCK was busy setting up an educational framework that would perpetuate the basic message of the moral panic across three centuries and throughout British society. Yet, neither society would have had much of an impact if their appeal had been limited and their moral panic had failed to take off. Quite the reverse happened.

The original Strand Society developed rapidly, with branches spreading across London and moving into the provinces. By 1697 there were 20 societies in London.[246] Beyond London, the SRMs grew until most of the major cities of England had a society, as Table 4.1 shows.[247] The SRM also spread beyond England, with branches in Scotland,[248] Wales and the North American Colonies.[249]

Table 4.1 Local and regional Societies for the Reformation of Manners in England in the early eighteenth century

Region of England	Places having SRMs
Northern	Alnwick, Carlisle, Chester, Derby, Hull, Kendal, Leeds, Liverpool, Morpeth, Nantwich, Newcastle-upon-Tyne, Nottingham, Penrith, Warrington, Wigan, York.
The Midlands	Bedfordshire, Coventry, Lapworth, Leicester, Newbury, Northampton, Norwich, Reading, Shrewsbury, Tamworth, Wendover.
South and South West	Bristol, Isle of Wight, Kent, Kingston, Longbridge Deveril, Lyme Regis, Portsmouth, Shepton Mallet.
West of England	Gloucester, Kidderminster, Newcastle-under-Lyme.

The methods of the societies

The SRM sought to prosecute as a means of affecting the salvation of both the individuals prosecuted and the society in which they lived. This was especially true for those the SRM deemed to be 'too unintelligent, ill-educated or obstinate to understand reasoned argument'.[250]

Prevention

For some crimes the SRM sought to prevent the cause of the crime by seeking work for the potential sinner. Prostitution was a good example of a sin thought to be caused by want. If the person who might be tempted to enter a life of prostitution could be given honest work, the sin would be prevented. However, as far as bad language goes, two forms of prevention were pursued by the religious societies – education (the domain of the SPCK) and the suppression of temptation (largely the domain of the SRM).

Education

It was the SPCK and the charity school movement, rather than the SRM proper, which was to carry forward the project of educating the children of the poor to be morally upright.[251] Assessing the impact of the SPCK charity schools is somewhat problematic. The SPCK charity schools swelled an existing charity school movement. Education was provided free initially, but by 1723 the wealthy benefactors that the movement attracted in its early days dwindled in number and children were often required to undertake some labour on the school's behalf. Where a child could not be freed from work to attend the charity school, Sunday schools were used to allow working children to receive instruction from the SPCK.

But what was the purpose of this education? The SPCK brought about a new type of schooling – schooling in which enforcing class distinctions and moral codes were the primary goals, with the aim of education being to establish a social hierarchy.[252] The following quotation, establishing the order for a new charity school in Nottingham, sums up the aim of the schools quite well:

> That the [master] be a member of the Church of England ... [be] of sober life and conversation of sufficient ability to teach children at least to read well and to instruct them in the Church Catechism ... and from time to time ... to reform what he finds amiss in them by admonition and reproofs and sometimes by several Corrections where the faults require – such as those of Lying, Swearing, Stealing etc.[253]

The charity school sought to teach the children of the working class 'the duties of humiliation and submission to superiors';[254] the charity school classroom was one in which the children of the poor were educated to accept their position within the social hierarchy of the day. Consequently, even the education of the children of the poor with those of their betters was unthinkable, so much so that schoolmasters who attempted this were accused of perpetrating 'mischiefs' by an SPCK inspector, Mr Skate.[255] At best, the education prepared the children of the poor for their working life. Yet, most importantly, the SPCK asserted the moral superiority of the middle class by imposing the moral agenda of the middle-class reformation of manners movement on the children of the poor. The assertion of the social authority of the middle classes reinforced their right to dictate a moral code to the children, while simultaneously the supposed superiority of their moral code justified their higher position in society. As such, Bible study and prayer book reading took precedence over writing and arithmetic in the charity school classroom.

As stated, the morality of the charity school classroom matched that of the SRM. The stage was abominated, so much so that an enterprising schoolmaster who organised a school play, Mr Honeycott, had his teaching licence revoked for his pains.[256] Bad language was also a focus of the moral agenda of the classroom. There is evidence that children were taught to recite, by heart, relevant sections of Acts of Parliament relating to acts such as blasphemy.[257] Also, bad language was punished in the classroom. While the SPCK, by the standards of the time, did not mete out punishment freely in the classroom, cursing was one of only eight misdemeanours which merited punishment according to a faults book published by the SPCK in 1707.[258] In the classroom materials used by the SPCK, bad language is identified as a sin to be avoided. One notable text used by the SPCK charity schools was *The Whole Duty of Man*. This book, by Richard Allestree, was a teaching text in some SPCK schools. The book sought to provide moral, rather than secular, education, and had two main objectives, both of which matched the goals of the SPCK classroom. First, the book sought to provide moral guidance as to what was morally acceptable and unacceptable behaviour. Second, it sought to educate children to fill their predestined position in society, and to establish in the minds of the children that this was as morally acceptable as acts such as swearing were morally unacceptable. Given the importance of this book to the SPCK charity school movement, it is worth exploring it a little further.

The book seeks to set out, in plain and bold language, what it sees as acceptable and unacceptable behaviour. Swearing is identified as quite unacceptable. Allestree devotes a 12-page section of the book to this topic. Swearing is identified as an offence to God, as with regard to offences to be avoided:[259]

> The first is, All Blasphemies, or speaking any evil thing of God, the highest degree wherof is cursing him. . . . A second way of dishonouring God's name is by Swearing.

Allestree goes further, claiming that swearing is 'the basest affront and dis-honour that can possibly be done to God'.[260] Swearing, according to Allestree, was a work of the Devil that was becoming ever more common, claiming, 'This is a sin that is (by I know not what charm of Satan's) grown into a fashion amongst us; and now its being so, draws daily more men into it'.[261] He even claims that children are swearing at their parents more fre-quently:[262]

> What shall we then say to those children, that instead of calling to heaven for blessings on their parents, ransack Hell for curses ... and pour out the blackest excrations against them? This is a thing so horrid, that one would think they needed no persuasion against it ... alas! Our daily experience tells us, 'tis not only possible, but common, even this of uttering curses.

The consequences of swearing were secular as well as spiritual. For example, Allestree believes swearing is a sign of untrustworthiness.[263] Allestree seeks to dissuade his readers from swearing by claiming that, in the case of a child who swears, 'For this heinous offender ... Let it be considered, that God hath ... The power of punishing'.[264] More generally, one imperils one's immortal soul by swearing, as the act of swearing is likened to a black magic mass which brings about damnation:[265]

> How common it is to hear men use the horridest Execrations and Curs-ings upon ... the slightest cause of displeasure? Nay, perhaps without cause at all ... This is a kind of saying our prayers backward indeed, which is said to be part of the ceremony the Devil uses at the making of a witch: And we have in this case also reason to look at it, as a means of bringing us into acquiantance and league with that accursed spirit here, and to a perpetual abiding with him hereafter. 'Tis the language of Hell, which can never fit us to be citizens of the new Jerusalem, but marks us out for inhabitants of that land of darkness.

The advice that Allestree offers to his readers is to 'Pray earnestly, that God will enable thee to overcome this wicked custom; say that the Psalmist, Set a watch, O Lord, over my mouth, and keep the door of my lips.'[266]

In books such as Allestree's, bad language was set out as a certain pathway to hell. One must conclude that tracts such as this being used as textbooks by the middle-class teachers of poor children must have had some impact on attitudes to bad language, if not on the practice of using bad lan-guage itself. This is made all the more likely by such books simultaneously telling children to accept without question the views of their social superiors lest they offend God: 'All inferiors are to behave themselves to their super-iors with modesty and respect, and not by rude boldness confound that order which it hath pleased God to set in the world.'[267] Gaining clear evidence of such an effect is, however, problematic, if not impossible. We can say that the charity schools provided a foundation for British classroom education that remains influential to this day. In terms of their immediate impact, the charity school movement was active throughout the eighteenth century, and books such as *The Whole Duty of Man* remained in print for over 100 years as a consequence.[268] It is difficult to calculate the number of children that were influenced by the SPCK over this period, but it was undoubtedly huge, as the movement saw hundreds of charity schools and Sunday schools in operation for a century or more. One estimate calculates that, at the height of its popularity, the SPCK charity schools were educating 100,000 children annually in Great Britain.[269] As such, if attitudes to bad language were changed in an enduring way by the religious societies, it is likely that a century of the SPCK educating hundreds of thousands of children to believe in the immorality of bad language had a more enduring effect on the attitudes of speakers of English to bad language than did 40 years of the SRM arresting swearers in the street. Yet the activities of the SRM had a lasting effect on British political attitudes to bad language, as we will see shortly, so we must now return to the activities of the SRM.

Suppression of temptation

While education was the province of the SPCK, much more work was done by members of the SRM in rooting out what they viewed to be major sources of temptation. Principal amongst these were the theatre, alehouses, fairs and Sunday sports. Of these, it is doubtless the theatre which, just as it had in the early seventeeth century, proved to be a focus for linguistic censorship.

Propaganda

The SRM also used print and the pulpit to propagate their message. The SRM was a prolific publishing body. In part, it is through the distribution of printed materials that the actions of the SRM can best be traced. The SRM published an annual report, detailing the convictions that they had secured that year, amongst other things. Early in the history of the SRM this annual list, then known as the Black Roll, included the names of those accused and those convicted – an early form of the 'name and shame' approach to moral reform which abides in England to this day.[270] The annual reports also detailed the number of published works the SRM had distributed. While a complete set of the annual reports of the society no longer exists, there is a near-complete run of the reports available for the period 1715–1738.[271] The first year in which distribution figures are given, however, is 1721. The number of publications that the 1721 report states had been distributed by the society from its start up to 1721 was 400,000. Over the next three years that figure did not grow, hence Table 4.2[272] shows the growth of the distributed works of the society from 1725.

Table 4.2 The expansion of the distribution of propaganda by the SRM, 1725–1738

Year	Total books	Increase from previous known year
1725	410,000	10,000
1726	412,000	2,000
1727	415,000	3,000
1728	417,000	2,000
1729	418,000	1,000
1730	420,000	2,000
1731	–	–
1732	423,000	3,000
1733	440,000	7,000
1734	442,000	2,000
1735	443,400	1,400
1736	–	–
1737	444,750	1,350
1738	–	–

While Table 4.2 shows what appears to be an ever-expanding market for the promotional materials of the society, one must be cautious when interpreting these distribution figures. First, the figure of 400,000, while impressive, actually distracts attention from the fact that the main promotional activities of the society had been in an earlier era. From 1721–1724, the society did not distribute a single book to add to the total of 400,000 it had managed between 1691 and 1721. In its first 30 years the distribution activities of the society must indeed have been impressive. There is evidence that books promoting the cause of reformation and books offering assistance to the judiciary in prosecuting offenders were distributed for free in very large numbers.[273] However, with the movement of publication activities from the society to the SPCK from 1698, the society gradually gave up any serious work in the area of the distribution of promotional material. Table 4.2 shows this clearly. Considering that, on average, the society distributed over 9,400 printed works per year in the period 1691–1738, its involvement with printed materials from 1721 onwards was negligible and publication to that date must have been prodigious (running at 20,000 printed works a year). The 1691–1738 average brings us, however, to the second note of caution one should sound: it was in the best interests of the society to give the false impression that its message was becoming ever more widely accepted and sought. Unless one had a copy of every annual report, one could easily have gained the impression from looking at any one of the society's reports from 1730 that it was a vigorous distributor of promotional literature. By 1730 this would certainly have been a false impression. A final point that one should make is best achieved by drawing an analogy with the modern religious groups who stalk shoppers on Saturday afternoons. For example, while it is doubtlessly the case that followers of the Hare Krishna cult press thousands of free copies of the writings of Bhaktivedanta Swami Prabhupada into the hands of British shoppers each week, the count of copies distributed would not allow one to easily estimate the impact of the Hare Krishna cult on twenty-first-century British society. The analogy is both useful and misleading, however. It is useful in showing that these were materials which, in part, were not purchased or even particularly sought out. For example, the SRM had admonitions printed covering a range of topics. These were:

> printed in half a sheet of paper that it may be made up in the form of a letter and directed to any persons when they are informed against, or are brought to punishment ... by the magistrate at which times the giving or sending of it to them may be most likely to promote their reformation.[274]

Such publications were undoubtedly common, but had a readership that one would imagine was at best resentful. However, the analogy with modern cultists in shopping centres is misleading in that, unlike shoppers who can simply discard such a work at the nearest litter bin or donate it to a jumble sale, the recipients of much of the promotional material of the society were churchgoers and children. The society distributed sermons which could readily be used by vicars. They also provided materials that could be used in schools. While some of the recipients of the message of both the SRM and the SPCK may have been no more willing than modern shoppers badgered by cultists, at least some of those receiving the message of the SRM and the SPCK were in a less empowered position and were forced to read or hear the message of the societies. It must also be accepted, however, that some of the material produced by the SRM found a willing audience. While we will never know how much of the material published by the SRM was read willingly, that which was caused widespread alarm:

> the societies in London have been so industrious in spreading their books, and the success they have had ... in this way has made such a noise everywhere that the whole nation has taken the alarm.[275]

Prosecution – 'A sort of popular sport'[276]

While the SRM was indeed engaged in preventative measures to suppress vice, it was through prosecution that the SRM sought most vigorously to wage its moral war against the Devil. In doing this, they exploited existing laws, encouraged their enforcement by the judiciary, used warrants of arrest to bring prosecutions against sinners and encouraged informers to report transgressions of the law.

Exploiting existing laws

As noted already, the people who started the SRM were well aware of the provisions and workings of the English legal system. They were also clearly aware that a battery of laws to combat immorality did actually exist in English law, but were rarely applied. The SRM sought to apply these laws to effect a change in society by prosecuting those who acted in a manner which they deemed immoral. With reference to bad language, the SRM had a wide range of laws to choose from with which to begin their campaign. James I had passed laws against swearing and cursing (21 Jac. I, c. 20). Charles I had also passed laws in this vein (Act 3, Car. I, c. 4). Both provided for conviction on the say so of one witness, without the defendant even having to appear before a magistrate. The fine for these offences was two shillings. William III passed a further Act against swearing and cursing (6 & 7 Gul. III, c. 11).

Throughout the early eighteenth century a number of changes were effected to the laws against cursing and swearing. Under George II the Acts of James, Charles and William were repealed and replaced (19 Geo. II, c. 21). George II's reform was important, as it removed the possibility of a defendant being charged *in absentia* and also effectively removed the possibility of people being convicted on the basis of evidence provided by a single, anonymous, person. George IV finally repealed Charles I's Act (9 Geo. IV, c. 61, §35).

With regard to blasphemy, the blasphemy Act of James I (3 Jac. I, c. 21) and the later laws of William III (9 and 10 Gul. III, c. 32) were also available. Both of these Acts proved more durable than the laws against cursing and swearing, with the Act of James being repealed by Victoria (6 & 7 Vict., c. 68, §1) and William's being repealed by George III (53 Geo. III, c. 160, §2).

In short, throughout the last decade of the seventeenth century and the first half of the eighteenth century the SRM had adequate laws with which to pursue their moral agenda. The only thing they had to do was ensure that the laws were enforced.

Encouraging the enforcement of laws

As noted earlier, there was little point in trying to exercise the law if the agents of the law were not interested in pursuing prosecutions. Simply passing laws against bad language had no effect, with Defoe going as far as to say that the passing of such laws 'never had, as far as I could perceive, any influence . . . nor are any of our magistrates fond or forward in putting them in execution'.[277] It is little surprise then that from an early stage the SRM sought official support to encourage constables and Justices of the Peace (JPs) to enforce the morality laws, even arguing that the pursuit of those who committed such sins as using bad language should take precedence over the pursuit of thieves and murderers.[278] The SRM sought very actively to promote their work by the 'Influencing of Magistrates'[279] to both carry out the law and to chivvy the constables beneath them to enforce the morality laws. For example, the London Court of Aldermen ordered citizens to report constables who failed to carry out their duty in the face of vice.[280] The attempt by the SRM to encourage the enforcement of the morality laws was fundamental to their enterprise, which would be helped:

> by Furthering in as many Places as you can the Choice of good Officers in Corporations, who will have the sense of the Obligations that their office lay them under, to endeavour to be serviceable in this Matter; and by letting Constables know how great a Power they have for the Suppressing of all publick Disorders.[281]

In addition to this, the SRM was active in providing help and guidance to lawyers and JPs regarding the enactment of the morality laws. For example, the lawyer Sir Francis Pemberton was asked to provide opinions on questions such as whether or not a constable could perform an arrest without a warrant.[282] Also, books were produced to assist the lawyer and the layman alike that summarised the relevant laws and contained sample warrants, most notably *A Help to a National Reformation*, published in 1700.

At times, however, the advice and help that the SRM proffered was ignored, as members of the legislature proved unwilling to enact the law. In such circumstances, the SRM was at times powerful enough to bring about the exclusion of that person from their office. For example, in 1691 a constable who refused to execute a warrant against Sunday trading lost his office.[283] This pressure on the constabulary was exerted by the SRM keeping a register of warrants it had caused to be issued, and checking that against the actions taken by the constables. Those warrants which were not executed were pursued by the SRM. This could lead to the enactment of the warrant or, as noted, to the removal of the constable in question.

While it is difficult to gauge exactly how successful the SRM was in encouraging the enforcement of these laws, there is some evidence to show that in counties where the SRM was active, the levels of prosecutions for immorality exceeded those in counties where the SRM was not active.[284] Given that the SRM gained many thousands of prosecutions, it must have been successful, to some degree at least, in making the judiciary enforce the morality laws.[285]

The use of warrants

The SRM became, to all intents and purposes, a police force in itself. It could become such a force because English law allowed it to do so. While the constabulary of the time could arrest on the basis of a warrant or by virtue of having caught a criminal red-handed, it was also possible for members of the public to issue warrants provided by JPs or magistrates, which were then executed by members of the constabulary. In short, as long as one could furnish sufficient evidence to a JP or magistrate, one could issue a warrant which would in effect oblige a constable to execute it. The SRM took full advantage of this provision of English law. Indeed, they took to printing and publishing pro-forma warrants which members could use in order to speed the prosecution of a malefactor:[286]

> I have likewise, Sir, sent you some Blank Warrants for particular Offences, which those that give Informations are to keep by them, and to fill up when they have any Informations to give against any prophane and viscious Persons, with the Offenders Names, Offences, Places of Abode &c. and to carry them thus filled up to the Magistrates.

As noted above, these warrants were typically held by agents of the SRM. When an informer or SRM member wished to issue a warrant, they went to the agent, outlined the nature of the offence and were issued with a warrant. Armed with this warrant, the person would then go to the magistrate and present their evidence. Assuming that the evidence was satisfactory, the magistrate would sign the warrant. The warrant was then returned to the agent. Warrants were lodged at the agent's office and would be collected by the SRM periodically. Each warrant was forwarded to an appropriate constable of the constablewick in which the malefactor resided. In choosing the constable to be involved in the case, the society was careful, where possible, to select those which were sympathetic to both their cause and their methods, choosing to send their warrants to 'the best disposed Constables to be executed'.[287] The constable then executed the warrant. As noted, the SRM ensured warrants were executed by keeping records of the warrants it had issued and the results of the warrant. It was able to discover what the effects of each warrant had been by sending its agents to the Quarterly Sessions at which constables had to report on the warrants they had received and their execution. The agents of the society ensured that the process of bringing a prosecution was as straightforward as possible and that the prosecution itself was executed.

It is clearly reasonable to say that the SRM did indeed view itself as a moral police force of sorts, and would ensure that, within the areas it had a care for, it policed widely and effectively wherever possible, as is clear in the following quotation:

> we agree at each meeting how we shall divide ourselves in our walkes to the most advantage And so as to take in all parts of the City and that we change our walks as oft as may be convenient.[288]

Nonetheless, members of the society could not be everywhere at once. In order to increase the effectiveness of their campaign, they used another device which English law afforded them: informers.

Informers

The SRM encouraged both its members and members of the general public to keep a watch on their fellows, and to report those people who had broken a law.[289] Informers became the engine which drove the prosecutions of the SRM along, for informers were 'so highly instrumental in this undertaking that they may be reckoned as the very cornerstone of it'.[290] The SRM encouraged informers by paying them. One must not, however, form the mistaken impression that the SRM invented the informer as a legal instrument. Paid informers had been a part of the English legal system for some time before the creation of the religious societies, and had garnered a poor reputation from the Restoration onwards. What the SRM did once again was to take a provision already existing in law and harness it to their 'puritanic and militant'[291] zeal in pursuit of their goal. In doing so, however, they knew that the use of informers was unpopular and pleaded with the accused to realise that:

> The Persons that bring them to Punishment do therein as becomes good Christians, and Members of the Community, for religious ends and with Charitable Intentions towards them; [do] not therefore add to ... Sin and Folly, by entertaining any unchristian Resentments for their thus acting.[292]

Such pleas fell on deaf ears. Consequently, as well as financial encouragement, the SRM and courts sometimes encouraged informers by granting them anonymity. Those who informed on another person had their identity kept secret by the society wherever possible. The warrants issued to an informer by a magistrate were returned to and forwarded by the SRM, not the informer himself. It may have been that the informer need never see the inside of a court room in order to bring about a prosecution, as swearing his evidence before a magistrate was sufficient under the laws used by the SRM. In the case of some London justices, they actually went as far as to guarantee the anonymity of informers, with the specific purpose of encouraging an increase in informing.[293]

It is also the case that, inspired by the work of the SRM, individuals did step forward to inform and received no payment, nor anonymity. An example of this is the case of three soldiers from Buckinghamshire who accused Thomas Bromley of 20 charges of swearing, and Thomas Bigg, a servant who accused his master of swearing.[294]

In short, the SRM encouraged espionage, either through payment or by example. The SRM was more than willing to take the fruits of this espionage to the courts to gain convictions against people who may have never even known their accusers. It is hardly surprising in such a situation that cadres of informers became attached to the societies. With the SRM prepared to pursue prosecutions against those informed against and with anonymity and a financial reward for the informer, it was certainly possible for an informer to fashion something of a livelihood from the act of informing.[295]

However, where members of the SRM themselves were involved in the arrest of a person who was subsequently convicted, they were supposed to forego the financial reward that this would bring. Whether they did so or not remains a moot point. What is indisputable is that the informers themselves were unpopular, in spite of attempts by both the Crown[296] and the Church[297] to make informing against immorality an acceptable act. Members of the society were killed while going about seeking prosecutions.[298] Others received death threats, such as that received by an informer who reported a soldier for swearing. The soldier sent him a note saying, 'Thou immortal informing dog, thy days are numbered; I'll surely be the death of thee.'[299] In spite of such threats, the informers kept up their work, some doubtlessly for temporal rewards, others for spiritual.

An early setback – the case of Ralph Hartley

While the methods outlined would become the mainstay of the operations of the SRM, these tactics were used before the SRM began, and were found to be less than satisfactory. The first Justice of the Peace to use these methods to the full was Ralph Hartley of Middlesex. Hartley was a very early and vigorous exponent of the use of warrants to suppress vice and, in the summer of 1691, under the direction of Sir Richard Bulkeley, Hartley began to issue warrants against it. Unfortunately, the zeal with which the warrants were issued was greater than that used to investigate the cases brought by Hartley. Not only did Hartley have people tried *in absentia*, he even managed to convict people who had been dead for two years. Hartley's actions were brought before the Middlesex justices and his warrants were investigated and mostly repealed. The Middlesex justices expressed a view that the methods used had been 'illegal, arbitrary and oppressive'.[300] This finding could have spelt the end of any attempt by the societies to use the law in this way to suppress vice. However, in areas where the justices were more favourably inclined to the use of the law to suppress vice, convictions continued, as in Buckinghamshire. These convictions sometimes extended as high as the bench itself, as was the case in 1704 when a Buckinghamshire justice was found guilty of profane swearing.[301]

When the SRM came into being, it sought to defend the actions of Hartley, largely to legitimate its use of similar tactics. Stephens, in his *The Beginning and Progress of a Needful and Hopeful Reformation in England*, both outlines the need for a reformation of manners and stoutly defends Hartley. The defence is partly undertaken by an attack on the probity of the Middlesex justices, and in particular on their unwillingness to accept the evidence of informers.[302] Stephens' defence must be accounted a success. His rebarbative style invited a counter-attack. The failure of the counter-attack to materialise, the better investigation of cases brought to court and the passing of further bills to aid the work of the SRM by William III meant that the SRM could proceed with its legal persecutions in spite of the failure of Ralph Hartley.

Education, information and persecution

The strategy of the SRM and the SPCK balanced opportunity with terror, the carrot with the stick.

The SRM provided the stick – seeking to weed out bad language and other sins through punishment. In achieving this goal, they forced the judiciary to implement long-neglected laws against bad language while simultaneously providing a steady stream of cases for trial by their own policing activities and those of informers actively encouraged by them.

The SPCK and the charity school movement, on the other hand, focused on the carrot, offering secular and spiritual education. They provided education, which was beyond the means of the poor of the time,[303] so that the children of the poor could be inculcated with the morality of the new middle class. Throughout, both used the mass media, notably the press and the pulpit, to get their message to an ever-wider audience, though the use of the press largely passed into the hands of the SPCK in the early part of the eighteenth century.

The double attack on bad language was successful in forming a public and private agenda on the issue of bad language: to use it was immoral, betokened low social class and low education. These themes will be returned to at the end of this chapter. For the moment, let us consider how successful the SRM was in prosecuting those it viewed as malefactors.

'A just Terror to Offenders'[304] – a legal reign of terror

Armed with a well-informed and zealous membership, and laws which allowed people to be convicted on the say-so of professional informers, sometimes guaranteed anonymity and paid for the information they furnished to the court, the SRM was in a strong position to begin a wave of morally motivated prosecutions. Where they motivated the judiciary to enforce the laws, the SRM could truly set about imposing their moral agenda on an area.

Once again, the published annual reports of the society are a good source of evidence one may use to estimate the impact of their activities. Table 4.3[305] shows the numbers of prosecutions brought about by the society for cursing and swearing, as shown in the available annual accounts in the period 1708–1724.[306]

These figures represent only a fraction of the prosecutions brought by the society. Up to 1724, the society had brought a grand total of 89,393 prosecutions for a range of crimes, including Sabbath breaking,[307] lewd and

Table 4.3 Prosecutions for swearing and cursing brought by the SRM

Year	Total prosecutions for cursing and swearing	Total of all prosecutions brought that year	Swearing and cursing prosecutions as % of the total number of prosecutions	Running total
1708	626	3,299	19.98	626
1709	575	2,976	19.32	1,201
1715	263	2,571	10.23	1,464
1716	102	1,820	5.60	1,566
1717	400	2,909	13.75	1,966
1718	205	2,006	10.22	2,171
1719	–	–	–	2,171
1720	114	1,959	5.82	2,285
1721	161	2,199	7.32	2,446
1722	201	7,251	2.77	2,647
1723	96	2,224	4.34	2,743
1724	108	2,449	4.41	2,851

disorderly practices,[308] drunkenness and the keeping of gambling houses. By the time of the 1738 annual report, the SRM had brought a grand total of 101,683 prosecutions to the courts. Of these, 59,689 occurred in the periods 1691–1707 and 1710–1714 combined. What proportion of these might one reasonably assume were for cursing and swearing? Table 4.3 shows, fairly clearly, that prosecutions for swearing and cursing generally declined in the period 1708–1724. Given that we might assume that, in the period 1691–1707, the proportion of swearing and cursing offences might be higher than those recorded in 1708–1709, and that from 1710–1714 they would be, on average, lower, it would seem reasonable to suggest that around 19 per cent of the 59,689 remaining prosecutions were for swearing and cursing. If this figure is defensible, this would give a grand total of 14,192 prosecutions brought by the SRM for cursing and swearing in the period 1691–1724, an average of around 430 prosecutions a year over the period. Such a figure, however, must remain speculative.

There is little doubt that this level of litigation had an impact on English society. Indeed, contemporary writers sympathetic to the goals of the SRM concluded that 'the blasphemies of licentious tongues are manifestly abated on our streets',[309] because of the prosecutions brought by the SRM. There was much encouragement given to the public to become informers, and where encouragement did not work, threats may, with one writer warning that 'he who is privy to swearing and cursing and will not inform against the person so offending, has the same guilt before God'.[310]

While threats and promises may have swelled the army of informers and consequently increased prosecution, this increase was achieved by means which, to a modern reader, probably seem more immoral than the sins being prosecuted. Trial without representation, accusers profiting from the conviction of the accused and entrapment were the mainstay of the societies. Yet such tactics were undoubtedly successful in allowing the society to achieve its aims. A document which shows how effective these tactics could be is the report of SPCK agents,[311] John Skeat and Thomas Morrison, who visited Kent in 1701. This document is revealing as it shows how the SPCK agents could also act as SRM agents. It also gives a flavour of what a visitation by members of the SRM to an area was like. Skeat and Morrison had the apparent goal of visiting Kent to encourage the establishment of societies, distribute promotional literature and make contact with societies already in existence in the area. Along the way, they also carried out the work of agents of the SRM, rooting out malefaction by the placement of warrants, attempting to entrap the unwary and chivvying the local constabulary into doing their duty. For example, they visited a public house on a Sabbath day in Canterbury and 'found twelve with company in them, whereof one was a constable'. Justice was swift as the malefactors were 'next day convicted before the mayor'. Skeat and Morrison did not stop there – they ensured that justice was done:

> Several of the offenders paid the same day, we having warrants levying the money which amounted to [Blank] ourselves, and went with them to the execution of them. We gave to Mr Alderman Gibbs and Dr Taylor an account of those warrants which were not with the Constables' names, to whom they were delivered, who promised faithfully to put them into execution.

The effect of the prosecutions was immediate as they report that 'The whole city was alarmed at our proceedings'. It certainly led to a reform of linguistic behaviour:

> As to swearing . . . 'tis almost suppressed, we not hearing an oath all the while we were there.

Considering the fright that Skeat and Morrison had caused, it is hardly a wonder that nobody dared to swear within earshot of them. Undaunted, the pair proceeded to try a little entrapment; they asked a barber to come and shave them on the Sabbath. If the barber had accepted the pair would have issued a warrant on him. However, the barber proved to be wise and said that he 'durst not do it'.[312]

The report of Skeat and Morrison, while only recording the events of a single day in a single town, gives a strong flavour of what it must have been like to live in an area in which members of the societies were active. Any opportunity to prosecute was taken, even where that amounted to entrapment. The agents and books of the SRM inspired others to persecution. A good example here is Thomas Powell, mayor of Deal. Inspired by the SRM, he began a campaign against immorality in Deal when sworn into office in 1703. His first victim was a sailor who was prosecuted for profane swearing, his second was a prostitute who he had whipped. At church, when a particular sin was mentioned in the sermon, he took to standing up and pointing at members of the congregation who he felt were guilty of the sin. Powell was delighted with his work, and reported that in the wake of his prosecution of the sailor and the prostitute 'twenty and five such like characters left the town, taking the road to Canterbury and Chatham, uttering the most fearful oaths'.[313]

It is difficult to avoid the conclusion that to have lived under the watchful eyes of men like Morrison, Powell and Skeat was to have lived in an oppressive atmosphere. However, it is also hard to conclude that the societies did not effect a change in attitudes to bad language, whether that simply be through the suppression of such language in certain contexts, or the self-imposed exile of inveterate swearers from towns where they were not welcome. Yet, the oppression that brought about the change in attitudes that the societies sought also slowly undermined them.

Objections to the societies

From the beginning, the SRM had opponents. Some simply recoiled from the pious persecution that the SRM brought in its wake. This can be well illustrated by returning to the case of Thomas Powell. Powell's reforming activities in Deal did not make him popular, and in time he became isolated, marginalised and ridiculed.[314] Even Skeat and Morrison on their journey through Kent found people who were openly resentful of their actions. Travelling by Canterbury, they stopped at the Red Lyon Inn and heard a man swear. They offered him SRM papers by way of admonishment; the man refused them as 'he said a justice made him pay for swearing: who at the same time offered him the same [papers] which he refused'. The man was clearly resentful of Skeat and Morrison's actions, and considered them to be 'fanatics'.[315]

Some objected to the SRM on principled grounds. Notable amongst these were Daniel Defoe and Bernard Mandeville. Neither writer necessarily agreed with immorality per se – indeed Defoe at least was very much in favour of a moral reformation. Defoe objected to the SRM, as it persecuted the lower classes while allowing members of the upper classes to carry on in their immoral ways free from persecution. Defoe likened the application of the laws against immorality to a cobweb which let through the big flies, but caught all of the little ones. Defoe's criticism is telling, and was never addressed by the SRM – the SRM remained a class-based organization, persecuting the lower class to assert the moral superiority of the middle class, while simultaneously prosecuting members of the middle class to ensure that they complied with the developing moral code of the middle class.[316] Defoe's criticisms of the SRM were accurate, but are best understood in terms of the class-based aims of the SRM, and, for that matter, the SPCK; the creation and continuous reinforcement of a morality which created and delimited the lower, middle and higher social orders. Within this view of the world, the failure of the SRM to prosecute their social betters becomes obvious – morality, education and prosecution was applied laterally, or in a downward fashion in the social hierarchy, not upwards.[317] In criticising the SRM, Defoe not only highlighted an essential unfairness in their operation, he also characterised the essence of the prosecutions undertaken by the society.

The criticism of writers like Bernard Mandeville is best likened to modern libertarianism – Mandeville wanted to apply the principles of free-market economics to the moral economy of England. In doing so, he argued that the vices targeted by the SRM were in fact good for the nation, as they stimulated the economy, and that the very social striving that the SRM sought to suppress was in fact exactly what the economy of England needed, as being 'Content [is] the bane of industry'.[318] Mandeville's ideas were certainly the most novel that appeared in opposition to the SRM, and some of his proposals, such as the establishment of legalised brothels, are proposals that even twenty-first-century England finds difficult to accept. In reality, however, Mandeville's voice was not as decisive as that of critics such as Dr Henry Sacheverell, who will be dealt with later in this chapter, perhaps simply because Mandeville's arguments were so radical. For the moment, it is fair to say that the existence of dissenting views from those of the SRM up to the campaigns of Dr Sacheverell are mainly of interest in demonstrating the plurality of views held at the time, but also, in the case of Defoe, of demonstrating the class-based nature of the SRM and the moral reform movement.

The decline of the societies: from triumph to disillusion – 'I have laboured in vain; I have spent my strength for nought and in vain'[319]

The SRM began with high hopes. Early reports from the societies indicated that vice was being rolled back everywhere and that bad language and other sins were on the decline. Only a year after the creation of an SRM in Carmarthen, the society claimed to have been so successful that 'drunkenness, swearing, profanation of the Lord's day &c are generally suppressed'.[320] The apparent success of the reformation of manners filled preachers such as Samuel Wesley and John Ryther with the conviction that the army of reform was unstoppable and its triumph inevitable.[321] Ryther went so far as to see close at hand a 'joyful day when profaneness, irreligion, and immorality will be banished from this land'.[322] Yet the joyful day never came. The rhetoric of the SRM did not change – in spite of the prosecutions they still claimed that immorality was rife. After nearly 40 years of prosecutions, Arthur Bedford complained in 1734 that on the streets of Bristol 'horrid oaths and curses ... are heard every minute of the day'.[323] The targets of the SRM proved to be more durable than they had anticipated and the easy victory over sin that had been expected was slowly abandoned, as they found that 'corrupt nature and long custom in sin are not so easily conquered'.[324] While prosecution may curb public swearing within earshot of an informer, swearing in private or in groups which did not disapprove of the act continued.[325] Indeed, the aim of the SRM eventually changed to accept that reality, when they restated their aim to be the achievement of an appearance of salvation – not salvation as such. In the words of William Bissett, talking about those who offended the members of the societies:

> They may be as secretly wicked, lewd, and worldly as they please; we won't force them (they need not fear it) to an heavenly mind, much less to Heaven against their liking. But we would oblige them (if possible) to be civil upon Earth and let their neighbours live by them a quiet and peaceful life in all godliness and honesty.[326]

As disillusionment set in amongst the members of the SRM, they changed their tactics from Heaven for all to peace on Earth for those who did not want to hear bad language or observe lewdness. The later SRM sought to eliminate bad language from polite company rather than to prosecute it wherever it was spoken. Bissett's speech, while initially attacked by the SRM itself,[327] encapsulated nicely the state of affairs with regard to bad language in English society throughout the next 300 years. However, this state of affairs represents a defeat for the original SRM, which hoped to eliminate immorality rather than chase it from the view of the saved. The defeat for the SRM became final in 1738, when the last accounts and sermons were published.

In some ways, the defeat the SRM experienced was yet more profound. One of the fears that had driven the SRM forward was that England was becoming a less godly place. Indeed it was, at least in terms of church attendance. In spite of the moral crusade of the SRM, church attendance declined steadily throughout its existence.[328] If the SRM and its zeal had not occasioned this decline, it certainly seems to have done nothing to arrest it.

The indifference and hostility of the establishment – 'Lay hands suddenly on no man'[329]

As noted, the SRM, unlike the SPCK, admitted non-conformists. Over time, it became clear that this decision meant that the SRM would only ever receive fitful support from the Anglican establishment in England.[330] While individual ministers, bishops and even archbishops may have shown enthusiasm for the SRM, the Anglican Church as a whole tended to be wary of it. With the creation of the SPCK, a wholly Anglican alternative to the SRM slowly developed that received much more obvious and sustained support from the Anglican Church than the SRM had ever done. Worse still, rather than fitful support or passing indifference, the SRM at times encountered outright hostility from the Church of England, with views such as this being common:

> Should they long continue ... they'd eat out the bowels of the Established Church, their mother. But what did I say, the Church their mother? That I recant. They are only seedlings of the good old cause and sprouts of the Rebellion of '41.[331]

For some within the Anglican Church, the SRM represented a modern form of Puritanism that was every bit as dangerous to the Anglican Church as the Puritanism which had finally brought the country to civil war. Indeed, in 1698, Archbishop Sharp registered his fears that the aim of the SRM was 'to undermine the Church' under 'the pretense of a reformation of manners'.[332] Church opposition to the SRM finally found flower in the writings of the Reverend Dr Henry Sacheverell, who opposed a society that was 'always declaiming against the vice of the age and the insufficiency of our laws to restrain it [which in order to] more securely to cloak it ... screens [itself] under a pretend society to reform it'.[333] Sacheverell's opposition alienated the high church further from the SRM and was taken up as a Tory cause, thus shearing a substantial body of the political establishment off from the SRM's supporters. By 1702, the identification of the Whigs with the SRM was well in train, and the consequent opposition of the Tories thus guaranteed.

It is more surprising to discover that the Crown was also suspicious of the goals of the SRM. While the public proclamations of monarchs against immorality may appear to be endorsements of the SRM, the SRM was nonetheless viewed with suspicion, because of their acceptance of nonconformists. It was also felt that their claims that society was in decay reflected badly on the State, and may thus be an attempt to undermine it. This led William III, though he appeared to support the SRM through public proclamations, to use James Vernon to have some of the meetings of the SRM spied on and the methods of the societies secretly investigated.[334] These investigations revealed, amongst other things, that the illegal prosecutions undertaken by Ralph Hartley were still being undertaken, with the use of anonymous informers against swearing being a common event, even though the procedure breached 'the received rules of law that provides no man shall be condemned unheard and that the party may expect to have his accuser face to face'.[335] Vernon concluded that the SRM were paving a road to hypocrisy, in a judgement that preceded Sacheverell's claim by three years. He also thought that their extra-legal methods, while they may be approved of by God, would not be tolerated for long in England, as 'such an inquisition will not be borne in this kingdom, let the pretense be what it will'.[336] The State tolerated the societies after this enquiry, but perhaps only because the inquiry found no evidence that the SRM was likely to undermine the State and, crucially, because Vernon concluded that their methods and goals were such that they were bound to fail. The State need only wait, not act, to be rid of the societies.

The SRM itself was mindful of the disapproval of the established Church and the concerns of the State. A London SRM amended its constitution to state that 'in our said meeting we will never meddle with affairs of Church or State'.[337] Numerous SRM sermons sought in vain to allay the fears of the established Church. Yet in spite of these efforts, the SRM, unlike the SPCK, was never welcomed in the Anglican Church establishment. Worse still, the SRM itself became a political issue, with their goals being associated with the Whigs.[338] Support for the reformation of manners became an issue in the 1702 election, with at least one prospective Parliamentary candidate, Sir John Pakington, accusing Bishop Lloyd of Worcester of slandering him by claiming, amongst other things, that Pakington did not support the reformation of manners.[339] It was in response to this case that Sacheverell began his crusade against the SRM. As both a high churchman and Tory pamphleteer, Sacheverell was important in mobilising both the State and the populace against the SRM. By 1709, Sacheverell's words were falling on receptive ears, though his outright condemnation of the Whig government of the time brought him to trial.[340] As the Government charged him in part with opposing the reformation of manners, the case in effect put the SRM on trial. Even though Sacheverell was convicted, the SRM was not vindicated. Rather, the conviction of Sacheverell simply confirmed him as a popular hero and proved to be the prelude to the defeat of the Whigs in the election of 1710. While it was to take a further 27 years for the SRM to expire, 1710 undoubtedly represents a turning point for the SRM and its estrangement from the establishment.

The judiciary

While the SRM, especially in its early days, did encourage the enforcement of the laws against immorality, obstacles to this encouragement slowly re-emerged over time. The problems that had beset Ralph Hartley never went away, and manifested themselves once more, slowly but surely, over time. Three major factors represented impediments to the actions of the SRM waxing. First, constables were liable to be held personally responsible if an SRM-inspired prosecution went awry. A good case in point here is Walter Chapman, who was an SRM member and constable. He brought a case against a malefactor and was subsequently embroiled in a legal dispute with the accused that cost him 14 pounds, five shillings and eight pence.[341] Cases like Chapman's show that bringing prosecutions was not entirely hazard free, and, as the executing officer, the constables in particular were in a vulnerable position. As this vulnerability became apparent, so the willing-ness of the constables to do the bidding of the SRM must have declined.

Second, as with modern police forces, the constabulary in the early eight-eenth century had to prioritise. While bad language may have been an important issue for the SRM, it probably ranked lower on the constables' list of priorities. As the initial zeal of the SRM faded, so too did the willingness of constables to adopt the priorities of the SRM in pursuing prosecutions.[342]

Finally, the attempt of the SRM and a number of monarchs to bully the judiciary into applying the anti-immorality laws were at best fitfully successful. Sometimes the justices would appear to comply, issuing demands that constables and citizens take the laws seriously, only to fail to convict people brought before the bench on the basis of those laws. A good case in point is the London Aldermen, who, as noted, encouraged citizens to act as informers. It was the London Aldermen, amongst others, however, who were later accused by the SRM of making the work of informers difficult by refusing to accept their evidence.[343] On other occasions, there is evidence of a solitary justice, who wished to aid the SRM, being frustrated by the other members of the bench who did not, as appeared to have happened in Derbyshire.[344] In general, the SRM never had the wholehearted backing of the judiciary nationally and strived against 'discouragements . . . from the magistrates'.[345] Where the SRM was backed by the judiciary, they did achieve prosecutions. However, without their backing, it was difficult for the SRM to proceed. What backing they had received melted away as the eighteenth century proceeded, leading to a major decline in the number of prosecutions for swearing, causing the SRM in its annual report of 1730 to complain that the small number of convictions for swearing recorded was a result of:

> the late proscribed method in the granting of summons and warrants against prophane swearers etc. which the justices of the peace thought themselves obliged to follow, had rendered the prosecution of these offenders more dilatory, which with some other difficulties occurring the past year, are the cause of why so few persons have been punished for prophane swearing.[346]

Without a judiciary willing to accept the extra-judicial activities of the SRM, the ability of the SRM to bring prosecutions against bad language in particular was curtailed.

The Victorian era began early

While the SRM slowly faded during the 1730s, their moral agenda was continued by the SPCK, and their views were picked up and championed by the so-called Country elements in Parliament. While the SRM would never be revived, in spite of attempts to do so, there was in fact little need for it. While the SRM had not succeeded in stamping out bad language, it had helped to establish a moral agenda which was to persist through to the Victorian age and beyond, in which education, private/public virtuousness and work were enduring blessings, whereas immorality, vice and bad language were viewed as curses. Though the SRM and its methods eventually came to be discredited, it set the moral agenda for a number of other approaches to addressing bad language and other forms of immorality that were enduring and effective, most notably in the classroom and on the stage. In the class-room it led to centuries of teaching that problematised bad language. On the stage, the arguments of reformers such as Collier started a process which was to lead to a reform of the stage, with bad language being eschewed, partly in the face of encroaching censorship,[347] but also because the audi-ences for plays changed – the middle classes took to the theatre and, in doing so, took their attitudes to bad language with them. The success of the reform movement in reforming the theatre 'was another triumph for the middle class in its struggle for recognition'.[348] With legal and audience pres-sure placed on the stage, it evolved rapidly, moving away from the norms of the Restoration towards a view of language espoused by Collier and the SRM.[349]

As the eighteenth century progressed, the refinement of manners and taste led to the rejection of bad language, and to an ever more refined definition of what bad language constituted. PISS as a swear word gained potency through-out the eighteenth century.[350] The mainstay of swearing, DAMN, slowly fell out of use, and over the century its potency was lost, with words such as FUCK developing to replace it. Some started to become aware that certain words with innocent meanings were homophonous with swear words and thus should be avoided. For example, terms such as *mother mastiff* were coined to avoid the use of the word *bitch*. The developing sensibilities of the age led to words which were simply viewed as vulgar being avoided or replaced in polite company; words such as *stink* and *sick* became unacceptable in polite company, while in conversation terms such as *shift*, *belly* and *big with child* became replaced by supposedly less vulgar equivalents such as *chemise*,[351] *stomach* and *pregnant*. The process by which bad language was to become a marker of distinction, whereby class could be defined, was well underway.

Similarly, the view that women should not swear and that they were somehow the guardians of the nation's morality intensified throughout this period. As with many facets of the reformation of manners, Allestree was an early writer who provided a view that was to be very influential in the reformation of manners, in this case the view that women should be pro-tected from bad language, and that they were too delicate to deal with such immorality. Allestree, in his book, *The Ladies Calling*,[352] portrays the perfect woman as being modest and passive.[353] This view contrasts very sharply with earlier depictions of females. For example, in the press of the 1640s, 1650s and 1660s, women are often portrayed as very dangerous indeed – unruly, sexually predatory and even violent.[354] Women were condemned 'for their active part in spreading evil'.[355] Yet with the passivisation and angelicisation of women that began in the Restoration and was intensified during the reformation of manners, the views of society towards a stereotypical woman changed. Women were assumed to be naturally inclined towards 'submissive and docile femininity',[356] and immodest behaviour such as using bad language became the negation of womanhood.[357] This distinction of male from female became rooted in language to the extent that it was thought that those women who used male language, such as bad language, may experience a 'Metamorphosis . . . being affectedly masculine',[358] for while 'an Oath sounds gratingly out of whatever mouth . . . out of a woman it hath an uncouth harshness, that there is no noise on this side of Hell can be more amazingly odious'.[359] From being dangerous creatures, women had been reduced to passive angels by the end of the seventeenth century, with femininity in part being defined by a purity of discourse.[360]

Such was the reaction against bad language, that by the end of the eighteenth century it was viewed as more of a sin to swear in some quarters than to engage in 'free association with carnal company', and bad language was viewed as being but a few steps away from death and damnation and only marginally less reprehensible than infidelity, according to *The Evangelical Magazine* in 1800.[361]

The wave of reform sparked by Collier, the SRM and the SPCK led to a lasting change in what was viewed as publicly acceptable language. Though the form and zeal with which moral reform was pursued in the eighteenth century varied, and English society retreated from attempts to legislate against the use of bad language by individuals after the experience with the SRM, the current attitudes of the English to bad language were formed in the late seventeenth and early eighteenth centuries. The use of such language was frowned on by a censorious middle class, and the public expression of such language via the mass media became an area of concern for the state. The greatest triumph of the SRM was not necessarily in its prosecutions, but in the impetus it gave to others who were spurred on to seek reform through other means. The tide of reform initiated by the SRM and like-minded reformers was to have a profound effect on how we view bad language in English. It characterised bad language as irreligious. It associated bad language with a lack of education by making the lack of bad language a token of having received and absorbed an education founded on the principles of the SPCK, which sought to suppress bad language through the classroom. It also associated bad language with social class – the absence of bad language in one's speech was a token of being middle class. 'Delicacy' in conversation became a signifier of membership of this class. Finally, it came to be firmly believed that not using bad language was somehow a particularly feminine trait. In establishing these associations with bad language, groups such as the SRM established a set of attitudes to bad language that would endure and strengthen throughout the following 300 years. Indeed, it is possible to see exactly those attitudes in the writings of those who campaigned against language once more, nearly 300 years later. Then a new form of mass communication, television, provided a means by which the bad language could be presented in a way that the moral middle classes felt it must control. This is a theme returned to in the next chapter.

Conclusion

By the end of the reformation of manners, modern attitudes to bad language had formed. The end of the reform movement may well have led to the erosion of those attitudes – but it did not. Rather the reform movement established a discourse related to bad language that survives to this day. While it is undoubtedly the case that periods of relative liberality and illiberality with regard to attitudes to bad language followed the end of the reformation of manners movement, the discourse that they had established to discuss bad language dominated, and in counter-reactions to liberal attitudes to bad language, the discourse of Allestree and Woodward was dominant. While this point will be made with reference to the twentieth century in the following chapter, let this chapter close with a few quotations from the English press of the early nineteenth century,[362] in which the manners of the young middle class were criticised. Writing in the newspaper *The Oracle* in 1800, a writer complained of the sight of 'seeing our young gentlemen cutting a swell, as the fashionable phrase is, and adopting the manners and the language of the brothel'. In *The Universal Magazine* in 1810, a writer complains that males had dropped their manners with respect to women from 'a formal, precise and ceremonious demeanour, constituting good breeding' and replaced it with an 'indifference to the convenience and accommodation of the softer sex'. Yet the paper also criticised changes in female linguistic behaviour, decrying the immodest use of 'double entendres' by females. These criticisms are clearly made within the context of a discourse established by the reformation of manners. While the group itself had long expired, its influence on society lived on, and the discourse it had established regarding the use of bad language as an element of distinction between groups – middle and lower class, male and female, young and old – remained dominant. So dominant was the discourse that the process of the refinement of language continued throughout the nineteenth century, with more and more words and phrases being identified as problematic and replaced. By 1818, *breeding* and *with child* had become unacceptable as terms to describe pregnancy and had been replaced by terms such as *lying-in*. Reference to processes of the intestines, or reference to particular parts of the bowels other than the stomach, had also become problematised.[363] As is the case today, language could become bad language in the nineteenth century with bewildering speed:

> So rapid are the changes that take place in people's notions of what is decorous that not only has the word 'smock' been displaced by the word 'shift', but even that harmless expression has been set aside for the French word 'chemise', and at length not even this word, it seems, is to be mentioned, nor the garment itself alluded to, by any decent writer.[364]

The search for offence and purity established by Collier was active throughout the nineteenth century and lives on into the twenty-first.

5 Late-twentieth-century bad language

The moral majority and four-letter assaults on authority

Introduction

The attitudes to bad language developed in the late seventeenth and early eighteenth centuries entrenched themselves ever deeper in English society to the extent that, by the Victorian era, the public representation of bad language was very rare indeed. Such was the potency of bad language, that, on occasion, it was banned from the courtroom, especially in blasphemy cases, where defendants would find themselves at times unable to even mention what they were being tried for lest they were summarily fined for using such language in court.[365] Such was the suppression of the language of the courtroom that from the nineteenth century it was not possible to publish the proceedings of a trial verbatim where 'a correct account of proceedings . . . contain[ed] matter of a seditious, blasphemous, or indecent nature'.[366] Public scandal could be caused by certain words in print or the enunciation of a word on stage.

When bad language finally returned to the stage, most notably in Shaw's *Pygmalion*, the resultant scandal left nobody in any doubt as to the success of the agenda set in motion by Collier, the SRM and the SPCK. Bad language was not for public consumption. The twentieth century brought with it new mass media – the radio and television. The response of the government to the new mass media was initially to monopolise, as it had been in the sixteenth century. In the establishment of the British Broadcasting Corporation (BBC) the government developed an institution which was largely self-censoring, as the printers had been initially some 400 years earlier. Laws to specifically censor or prohibit what may be broadcast were unnecessary where the BBC itself exercised a restraint that would not lead to a reaction from its listeners or the Government. This restraint lasted until well into the late twentieth century, and was in place throughout the early years of television. This chapter, in part, is about the journey of British television towards a clash with those who sought the censorship of its representation of bad language. The attempt to impose censorship on broadcast and printed bad language, from the early 1960s onwards, parallels in many ways the attack on bad language ushered in by the Glorious Revolution, though this time a group entitled the National Viewers' and Listeners' Association (VALA) was the vehicle of the moral panic.

The VALA was an organisation established to 'clean up TV' in the early 1960s. Its founder, Mary Whitehouse, is the UK's single most notable moral entrepreneur of the past 50 years. This chapter is concerned with the VALA for two principal reasons. First, the agenda, aims and methods of the VALA are a powerful argument in favour of the hypothesis put forward in this book that modern English attitudes to bad language were formed in the later seventeenth century. While some of the aims of the VALA are different from those of Collier and his fellows, these changes reflect both the aftermath of the activities of the SRM and the changes in the world since the time of Collier. The core values and methods of the VALA and the moral reformers of the Glorious Revolution are, however, remarkably similar. Second, the imposition of those values on films, radio and TV in Britain are, if not exclusively, then largely, due to the work of Whitehouse and the VALA. However, before exploring these two claims further, the role of bad language in the mass media of the twentieth century and reactions against it must be explored.

Twentieth-century firsts and the retreat of censorship

Bad language fitfully re-entered public life in the early to late twentieth century. Shaw's *Pygmalion* famously included the use of the word *bloody* when performed on stage in 1914.[367] After the outcry over *Pygmalion*, the word *bloody* slowly began to be used more widely on the English stage, with the Lord Chancellor having a notional quota of how many times the word may be used in a stage play.[368] If the stage door opened early to the slow return of bad language, radio was tardy in allowing its use. When it did, however, the results were thrilling and shocking to listeners.

'Bill Blaster (the Crimson Cockney) Takes the Air. And he swears!'[369]

The first public broadcast of bad language over the radio occurred during the Second World War. A German propaganda programme, *Worker's Challenge*, was broadcast from Germany to Britain. The show debuted on 7 July 1940, and ran daily broadcasts until 26 January 1945. The show purported to be broadcast from within the UK, and had the express aim of trying to incite British workers to 'revolt' against the British establishment. The show featured a number of announcers, notably two British Guardsmen, William Humphrey Griffiths and Sergeant McDonald,[370] who had decided to work for the Germans. They discussed matters such as the character of current British politicians and the conduct of the war by the British. The presenters, who were working class, used what may be characterised as the language of the barrack room. It was on *Worker's Challenge* that bad language was first regularly broadcast over the airwaves. The BBC acknowledged the use by the programme of 'foul language here and there, foul words particularly when speaking of personalities'. With reference to the type of words typically used, the BBC noted that 'The word "bugger" was one of the most frequent, with "bastard" and "sod" and things like that' also being used on the programme.[371] In a small corpus of transcripts from the *Worker's Challenge* programme, amounting to 16,787 words, the following swear words appear (frequencies in parentheses): *bastard* (2), *bastards* (3), *blasted* (4), *bleedin'* (3), *bleeding* (9), *bloody* (54), *buggered* (9), *bugger* (1), *buggers* (9), *damn* (10), *damned* (3) and *hell* (14).[372] Following is an extract from a 'playlet' broadcast on *Worker's Challenge*[373] in which supposedly late warnings of air raids are being discussed by two British workers:

Worker A: Mistakes be buggered. Do you call it a slip up when my pal had his house blown to bits and his wife and kiddies killed whilst he was at work? Now where the hell does the mistake come there thick-head? The bosses have been hollering and whingeing about workers trooping down to the shelters when there's a raid. So the khaki buggers have the alarm delayed.

Worker B: Strike me bloody pink! Things must be in a queer state when they start blocking the workers like that.

Worker A: Why you bleeding twerp it's as simple as ABC! A delayed alarm means more production from the workers, and more profit for the bosses, and besides they don't care about Jerry dropping a few bombs on the factory, as long as they're out of the danger zone. I suppose they'll say 'what's a few workers' lives to us, when our democratic country is at stake'.

Worker B: Well, I'll be buggered.

As is apparent from this example, the language used on *Worker's Challenge* was unlike anything that had been heard before on British radio broadcasts. Nor would such language be broadcast for a long time after 1940. It is hardly surprising that the use of such language caused the programme to attract an audience – people were tuning in to be scandalised by the novelty of bad language being broadcast over the radio[374] and the programme had 'a heavy following ... The novelty was on [sic] the language'.[375] Listeners confessed to finding the bad language and working-class accents 'very amusing after the proper BBC accent'.[376] The station also attracted comment from the British press who were scandalised by the station's use of bad language.[377]

The use of bad language in the broadcast media was not to happen again for over two decades after this, but the *Worker's Challenge* case is a powerful example of the shock and novelty value of hearing a form of language, normally banned from public life, being broadcast and used in public. It was also an early example of bad language being used as a challenge to authority

– a theme returned to later in this chapter. Yet *Worker's Challenge* was an isolated case of the use of bad language in the media for this purpose in the mid-twentieth century. The true watershed occurred after the popularisation of television in the 1960s.

Bad language from 1960

Bad language was certainly not a feature of early television programmes. Indeed, throughout the era in which television ownership initially boomed in Britain, the 1950s, the BBC moved markedly away from trying to cater for working-class listeners and viewers, and took a determinedly middle-class approach to broadcasting, as the 'BBC confirmed its role as an instrument of middle class hegemony'.[378] The BBC showed a marked 'preference for middle-class accents' and was 'a monument of safe middle class respectability'.[379] Presenters with non-RP accents were marginalised.[380] Bad language, construed as a token of working-class status, was barely allowed on the BBC in this era. However, by the mid-1960s, working-class life and bad language were being represented on television, notably in a more realistic attempt to portray working-class speech, on the comedy programme, *Till Death Us Do Part*, with its multiple uses of *bloody* in each episode, of which more later.[381] Kenneth Tynan, the theatre director, notched up what is probably the most notable first for the use of bad language on television, however, when he used the word *fuck* in a discussion on BBC television in 1965 when he commented that, 'I doubt if there are very many rational people in this room to whom the word *fuck* is particularly diabolical or revolting.' The response to Tynan's use of the word was explosive, yet Tynan remained steadfastly and, ultimately, triumphantly unrepentant. Unapologetically, Tynan uttered a word the like of which had not been heard on the British airwaves since the early 1940s, yet was to be heard on the airwaves many times after his use of the word.

Tynan was not the only pioneer in bringing bad language back into public discourse. Other firsts were also scored, for example, by Marianne Faithfull, who gained some fame as a singer and actress in the 1960s. Faithfull was the first woman to utter the word *fuck* in a mainstream film in the now little remembered *I'll Never Forget What's'name* in 1968.[382] Faithfull scored another first when she became the first woman to use the word *cunt* in the mass media, when, in 1979, she recorded the song *Why'd Ya Do It?*, which uses direct, uncompromising language to express a woman's rage at her cheating lover, including the line, 'Every time I see your dick I imagine her cunt in my bed.' Faithfull recalls that during recording the musicians she worked with were 'all absolutely appalled and horrified because they . . . had this odd perception that a . . . lady . . . couldn't sing words like *fuck* and *cunt*'.[383] While Faithfull could indeed sing the words, radio stations found them difficult to broadcast and resorted to bleeping them out.[384]

However, the debate about the use of bad language in the media predates

Tynan's *fuck* and Faithfull's *fuck/cunt*. Whitehouse began her crusade in earnest on 5 May 1964. To understand the genesis of her campaigning, one must first understand the changing nature of British society in the 1960s.

The move from absolute morality to humanist liberalism

The early 1960s in Britain was a period in which technological and social changes came to the fore that fundamentally changed the nature of British society. The major change which was apparent was the rapid increase in television ownership. Between 1947 and 1964, the number of households owning television sets in the UK boomed from 0.2 per cent to 90.8 per cent.[385] This increase in television ownership in itself was not necessarily a challenge to long-held middle-class values. Indeed, a high rate of radio ownership had long been sustained in Britain without a threat to middle-class values being perceived. Mass communication itself was not the cause of the change in British society. What happened was that broadcast television in the early 1960s began to change, wanting to reflect a broader view of society than previously represented in the mass media. It was this change which occasioned the clean-up-TV campaign. The prevalence of television sets simply exacerbated the threat felt by this change in direction by broadcasters, most notably the BBC.

However, to truly understand the change occasioned in British television in the early 1960s, one needs to consider the broader changes which were underway in British society. The moral and political landscape of Britain was changing. Church attendance was declining up to this period, a decline that has continued from then into the twenty-first century.[386] The move away from organised religion went hand-in-hand with a shift from an intrinsically moral society towards a new, humanist, orthodoxy. Emblematic of this shift were a series of laws passed from 1959 to 1969, which rejected previously held Christian moral absolutist positions in English law. The *Obscene Publications Act* (1959), *Abortion Act* (1967), *Sexual Offences Act* (1967), *Theatres Act* (1968) and *Divorce Act* (1969) all rejected a moral absolutist position. For example, homosexuality was partially decriminalised by the *Sexual Offences Act* and censorship of the theatres by the Lord Chancellor was ended by the *Theatres Act*. Rather than legislation reflecting a right/wrong morality rooted in the orthodoxy of conservative Christian theology, the law moved to a progressively more humanist position within which moral relativism, rather than moral absolutism, was the norm.

These changes were driven along by changes in society, some grand in scale, some smaller. At the grand level, a change of emphasis from a production-based economy to a consumption-based one has been assumed to have affected a change in attitudes, with continence being rejected in favour of indulgence.[387] The switch to a culture of consumption also generated an affluence which, it is assumed, militated in favour of more permissive attitudes in society.[388] On a smaller scale, there were key individuals in the period who became committed to forcing through legislation in the teeth of opposition from pressure groups opposed to liberalisation. MPs in the Labour administrations of 1964–1970, such as Roy Jenkins, were key figures in this process. This is not to say that there was no linkage between the micro and macro forces. With the exception of the end of capital punishment, the MPs pushing through the liberalising reforms were actually reflecting the wishes of their constituents, if opinion polls of the time are to be believed.[389]

It was not simply in Parliament that individuals committed to the propagation of the new humanist orthodoxy made their mark. The Church hierarchy itself was influenced by the new humanism and, crucially for this chapter, the BBC was led robustly in the direction of the new humanism by Hugh Greene.

Greene became Director General of the BBC in 1960. When he took up his post, Greene was faced with a major crisis at the BBC. It was losing a ratings war with its rival, the commercially funded ITV network, with BBC audience share falling as low as 28 per cent compared to ITV's 72 per cent.[390] In response to this, Greene changed the direction of the BBC away from portraying a safe, cosy middle-class vision of England towards a more realistic representation of British society that would see good and bad, working class and middle class, Christians and humanists all represented on television. Greene caused a change at the BBC which showed that 'the working man was a fit subject for drama, and not just a comic foil in a play in middle class manners'.[391] It was in this change in society, a humanist reform of the law by the Labour government and a more inclusive BBC, that a centuries-old vision of the moral supremacy of the middle class in British society was challenged. It was Mary Whitehouse who would rise from the ranks of the middle classes to answer that challenge and defend their supremacy. However, before examining Whitehouse's response to this challenge, it is worth investigating in some detail the relationship between the BBC and bad language in the 1960s.

The BBC and bad language

A crucial component of the BBC's shift of emphasis to a more inclusive approach to broadcasting in the early 1960s was to try to produce high-quality drama which reflected the interests and concerns of contemporary society. In doing so it was following on from a trend in the theatre which, with the advent of kitchen sink dramas and the works of the 'Angry young men' of the 1950s, had moved decisively in this direction already. This change was a major one for the BBC. Up to that point, output was completely sanitised as a matter of policy. The following quotation, from a booklet produced to provide guidance to programme makers at the BBC during the 1940s and 1950s, shows very well the prevailing attitudes at the BBC up to the 1960s:

Programmes must at all cost be kept free of crudities. It must be cut. . . . When in doubt, take it out.[392]

This changed with the advent of Hugh Greene. The shift towards realism at the BBC led it to produce drama series such as *Play for Today* and the *Wednesday Play*, the authors of which read like a who's-who of modern British drama, including the likes of Ken Loach and Harold Pinter. This drama, along with other BBC output, most notably the comedy series *Till Death Us Do Part*, was based on an approach to social realism which included an attempt to represent language as it was actually spoken, rather than how any one group in society thought it should be spoken. Importantly, this included the use of bad language in the form of blasphemy, homophobic language, racist language, sexist language and swearing. The introduction of bad language to the television by the BBC was no accident, and as a policy it certainly pre-dated Tynan's use of *fuck*. However, the reaction of the BBC to Tynan's use of *fuck* clearly shows that the BBC did not completely deregulate language use in television broadcasting in the 1960s. The BBC operated a form of self-censorship, respecting a 9 o'clock watershed before which bad language was not permitted, a policy revealed in a letter to a VALA member from the BBC:

with . . . plays . . . or with adult comedy shows which may contain traditional vulgarities we transmit such programmes after 9.00 p.m., a time of the evening when children may be expected to have gone to bed.[393]

The BBC also tried to gauge what it felt the public would and would not accept when it came to the use of bad language in television shows. Sometimes, as in the case of *Till Death Us Do Part*, the BBC believed it was operating at 'the very edge of what is acceptable'.[394] In spite of the restraint that the BBC demonstrated, however, its policy of allowing bad language to be used on television meant that bad language was repeatedly identified as the major cause of offence to the viewing public in the period up to the *Annan Report* on the future of British broadcasting in 1977. Nonetheless, the BBC was robust in defending its decision to allow bad language on television. The following extract from a letter from Lord Hill, Chairman of the BBC, to Whitehouse, in response to a complaint from her regarding the use of bad language in two plays and an edition of the documentary series *Man Alive*, is a clear statement of the liberal humanist position introduced by Greene. As a statement of moral relativism it represented wormwood to the moral absolutist Whitehouse:

You ask whether I believe language used in two recent plays and edition of 'Man Alive' would be acceptable in my household. By 'language' I assume that you mean 'bad language'. If I am right in my assumption, I should be grateful if you would explain rather more fully what you have in mind, given the nature of the two plays and of 'Man Alive' and of the placing of the programme. Is it your view that we should place an absolute veto on the use of certain words or simply a veto on some words at some times? In either case, it would be helpful if you would develop this point. Whatever one may say about the suitability of the language included in broadcast programmes, the question of whether I should wish my own family circle to use such language is different from being prepared to have them hear such language used by others in a public representation.[395]

Given such a fundamental difference of opinion, it is hardly surprising that, by the time that the Annan Committee sat to consider broadcasting standards,[396] bad language, violence and sex had taken centre stage as the three major causes of complaint about television output.[397]

Whitehouse and bad language

The impact of the use of bad language by the BBC on the campaigns of Mary Whitehouse was significant, yet, as will be shown, not in proportion to its salience as an issue in complaints to the BBC.

There is no doubt that Whitehouse found bad language offensive and in her campaign against 'moral pollution'[398] on television she identified bad language as a major cause of such so-called pollution. Whitehouse developed four major objections to the use of bad language. First, it was offensive. Second, it was a vehicle of political subversion. Third, it was a childish form of language. Finally, its use debased culture. The offence which the use of bad language caused Whitehouse was predictable – indeed the expression of distaste for the use of bad language from the predominantly middle-class VALA was simply to be expected after the intervening centuries in which it had been loaded with a number of negative associations.

Yet Whitehouse's identification of bad language as a vehicle for subversion deserves closer examination. Whitehouse showed a clear understanding of the role that language had to play in establishing moral, social and sexual orthodoxy from the late seventeenth century onwards. Given this awareness, it is hardly surprising that she saw in the move away from standards of acceptable speech the possibility of an associated move away from the values and social hierarchy that had established those norms of acceptable speech. Hence, for Whitehouse, 'language carries within it the accumulated values of society, and can therefore be readily used to carry other values, which may supplant and replace existing ones'.[399] Whitehouse was encouraged in her belief by those who argued that bad language did have a political, indeed revolutionary, role to play in society, with the phrase 'the weapons of revolution are obscenity, blasphemy and drugs'[400] being one which Whitehouse often referred to.[401] Just as a reform of language had been the vehicle for a moral revolution in the 1690s, Whitehouse feared that it had the potential to be a vehicle for a revolution that she disapproved of in the late twentieth century.

Another of Whitehouse's complaints about bad language also deserves further discussion – the claim that bad language is childish. Whitehouse makes reference to bad language as a childish form of behaviour on a number of occasions. For her, the discourse of childishness had three goals: (i) to identify those adults who use bad language to be childish and bad examples to children; (ii) to portray the use of bad language by children as a transient phase; and (iii) to emphasise the role of moral guidance in moving children from this immature form of language to responsible adult language use. In attacking adults who use bad language as being in some way immature and poor examples for children to follow, Whitehouse was echoing earlier critics who made much the same point. In the 1811 edition of the *Whole Duty of Man*, Charles Atmore asserts that: 'Filthy conversation is most unbecoming in those who are advanced in years; because it argues a mind extremely depraved, and gives too great countenance to youthful follies.'[402] These sentiments are echoed over 150 years later when Whitehouse complains that:

> To set standards of speech and expression was felt, in days gone by, to be the responsibility of the older generation in the arts, the classroom and in the home.
>
> Now, it would seem, this is no longer so. Rather are the young encouraged to believe that within adolescence and immaturity are ultimate values to be found; they see the spectacle of an older generation so bemused by the blandishments of the 'new libertarians' that they no longer have faith in their past, their future, their culture, their faith – or themselves. 'Let's all be kids together,' cry the adults as if only the fantasies of child's play help them to come to terms with what they have made of the world. And in so doing, they deny the young the basic security without which they cannot grow to a mature and responsible exercise of freedom.[403]

Adults who use bad language, according to Whitehouse, are not simply betraying their linguistic and cultural heritage, they are robbing children of the opportunity to inherit the linguistic and cultural certainties that had been established for a long, though unspecified, time. In doing so they are condemning these children to immaturity, irresponsibility and insecurity. This condemnation of adult users of bad language is an amplification of the views of the SRM and Charles Atmore.

The cultural values supposedly corrupted by the use of bad language were, according to Whitehouse, the finer aspects of art and culture:

> Anyone with teaching experience will know that the four-letter syndrome on lavatory walls was a manifestation of the burgeoning sexuality

of the adolescent, to be corrected without too much pomposity because one had confidence that with growing maturity such language would be left behind as more elegant, more civilized ways of expressing sexual feelings would be discovered as the young mind was fed on poetry and great literature.[404]

Yet the use of bad language was not merely the choice to avoid supposedly superior forms of communication, it was also the denigration of finer forms of communication, as Whitehouse asserted that TV was leading to 'the degradation of the English language and culture through coarse and too often obscene and blasphemous language'.[405]

While the VALA clearly saw bad language as a major problem on television, and bad language on television was regularly identified as a cause of complaint by the public, two conundrums remain. First, considering the salience of bad language as a complaint, why was bad language not the principal focus of the VALA? Even contemporary commentators, such as the one-time BBC Director General, Alasdair Milne, were surprised that campaigners focused on 'sex and violence' at the expense of campaigning against bad language:

> It is . . . absurd to talk about 'sex 'n' violence' on television as . . . this silly and easy formula seems to ignore something that research shows offends the viewer much more than the odd sexual encounter or moment of violence: bad language on the screen.[406]

Yet bad language on TV was never the main focus of the VALA. This leads me to my second point. Given that the VALA did from time to time campaign against bad language, why was it that some programmes which contained bad language, such as *Steptoe and Son*, were rarely, if ever, complained about, while others, such as *Till Death Us Do Part* excited concerted opposition from the VALA because of its use of bad language? Both questions have a single answer, but in order to understand the answer it is necessary to consider the role of language in the political landscape as viewed by both Whitehouse and political theorists of the 1960s and 1970s.

Four-letter threats to authority[407]

As noted in the previous section, the VALA objected to bad language as offensive, childish, subversive and degrading to high culture. However, these objections cannot be taken singly – they form a complex within which the act of objecting to bad language, or the failure to object to the use of bad language, can be understood. While Whitehouse may not have approved of the use of bad language by children, she certainly did not object to it vehemently, seeing it rather as a passing phase worthy of correction without 'too much pomposity'. Similarly, while she herself would not approve of bad language, she shows some acceptance of the use of bad language in everyday contexts. In the following anecdote, told by Whitehouse, it is clear that she does not always object to bad language and can even see it as a source of amusement:

> A television crew once spent two or three days in the Whitehouse home . . . she remembers their kindness, good humour and informality . . . but nonetheless they were so conditioned by their preconceptions that they found their normal subject and style of conversation, well-larded with lewd and vulgar language, so inhibited that they apparently never so much as employed a swear-word; the result was they were no sooner clear of Triangle Farm than they opened wide the windows of their car and hurled obscenity after obscenity into the air, to relieve their pent-up feelings.[408]

There are other examples of Whitehouse, if not being amused by bad language, at least not being unduly perturbed by it. Whitehouse, for example, discusses workmen who use 'unprintable remarks'[409] without expressing particularly censorious views about them, or even labelling them as childish.

These two examples serve to show that the individual elements of Whitehouse's objection to bad language were not sufficient in themselves to provoke a response from her. It was when the elements acted in concert that Whitehouse was most likely to object, as it was when they were present in conjunction that they were likely to be subversive. As noted, in objecting to this attempt at subversion, Whitehouse was responding directly to a deliberate attempt to overturn the linguistic and moral orthodoxy established in the late seventeenth century. By bad language having been established as emblematic of exclusion from the establishment, the possibility was created to use bad language as a token of rebellion against that establishment. Language, when used as the bedrock of a political system, could be used to undermine that political system. The model in Figure 5.1 summarises this point well.[410]

According to the model in Figure 5.1, the ultimate basis of any political mandate is linguistic. A discourse of power is established whereby laws can be conveyed. Access to that discourse becomes a token of membership, or at least acceptance, of a ruling group. To subvert that linguistic mandate is akin to undermining the foundations of a building. It was this process of subversion that was identified in attempts in the 1960s and 1970s to generate 'models for disobedience'[411] with which to confront the establishment. If the arguments of Chapter 4 of this book are accepted, the system of language underpinning authority was formed, at least in part, by groups in the late seventeenth century who associated the use of bad language with immaturity, immorality, irreligiousness, low educational attainment and licentiousness. In short, they identified the use of bad language as being indicative of the unsuitability of a person to be a source of secular or

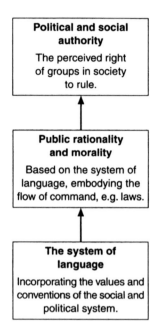

Figure 5.1 The linguistic mandate of power.

spiritual authority. It was this orthodoxy, amplified throughout the following three centuries, that Whitehouse was defending and which, she believed, those intent on challenging the restrictions on the use of bad language were determined to destroy. In this context, it is the use of bad language with the express intention of political subversion that entails the repudiation of social/cultural norms. The reaction to the user of the language must be that which was established some three centuries before – their views are not valid because their use of language is childish and offensive. There is certainly evidence to support this analysis in the writings of Whitehouse. One of the persistent features of her writing is that, where faced with opposition, she notes the use of bad language by those who disagree with her, with the clear intention of characterising her detractors as people who have put themselves beyond the pale and hence are not valid interlocutors, in much the same way as the early Modern English censors discussed in Chapter 3 used an objection to the use of bad language to cloak censorship. The following, where Whitehouse is discussing a speech she gave at Leicester University, is typical of her identification of the use of bad language as grounds for claiming that those who disagree with her are beyond the pale:

> Unreason took over and obscenities flew hard and fast the whole night
> . . . It was quite clear that they wanted to make me go away.[412]

The use of bad language is a token of unreason. This, then, is the basis of a claim that the students, who had invited her to debate, did not actually wish to debate with her, but simply wanted her to go away. Bad language, for Whitehouse, was the negation of acceptable discourse. For her detractors, it could be the basis of rejecting her discourse and hence the view of society that that discourse supported. However, not all of those who objected to Whitehouse and the values she stood for rejected the discourse which she used to support those values. In the case of such objectors, Whitehouse identified some other factor which invalidated their views – Whitehouse was unstinting in her praise of 'experts' who agreed with her, yet damning of those who disagreed with her. She refuted the value of formal research by wishing that 'we could somehow get back to the business of commonsense instead of trying to computerise and interpret',[413] saying that, in order to study the effect of TV on children, 'you should go directly to the people who are likely to be able to tell you; for instance, headmistresses of Junior and Infant schools'.[414] Whitehouse was keen to exclude academic debate of her views, calling for 'evidence directly from people like teachers, doctors and the rest ... for pity's sake don't let's have ... sociologists who will start interpreting it [data] so that it doesn't prove anything'. Such a view seems clear-cut: those who support the views of Whitehouse should have their opinions listened to, those who may wish to take an objective view of the data should be excluded from the debate.[415] However, Whitehouse was prepared to blur this distinction; where an expert agreed with her views, she was a proud champion of their research, such as that of Dr John Court, a consultant psychologist whose research supported Whitehouse's views. His research was praised by her as being of international standing, and of approaching its subject 'objectively and in depth'. Throughout her writing and speeches, Whitehouse was unswerving in one aim, the defence of the values, linguistic, moral and political, which preserved society in the image in which she found it acceptable. Where those who debated with her used the discourse associated with those values, they were dismissed as lacking commonsense. Where they shifted the discourse to use bad language in a direct attempt to subvert values based on a discourse which excluded bad language, they were beyond reason and not worthy people with whom to debate.

Returning to the question of the role of bad language in subverting the values that Whitehouse supported, if the model presented has any validity in explaining the objection of the VALA to bad language, then where there is an attempt at political subversion and a repudiation of established linguistic norms, one should expect to see the VALA object to the use of bad language, labelling it as childish, offensive, etc. Where bad language is not being used to subvert, then one would expect an altogether more lenient attitude to bad language to be taken, though individuals using it may well still be branded offensive, childish or both. However, the vehemence of the objection should be much reduced and may not even occur. Should this

hypothesis hold, we simultaneously have an explanation for why some programmes which used bad language were not objected to and, hence, why
bad language, although the major concern of viewers, was not the major
concern of the VALA. The VALA only objected to the politically subversive
use of bad language. The following case study, looking at two TV programmes, *Steptoe and Son* and *Till Death Us Do Part*, will provide evidence to
support this hypothesis.

Case study 1: bad language in comedy – the subversive and the servile

Till Death Us Do Part was a BBC comedy which ran from 1965–1975.[416]
The central character, Alf Garnett, was an opinionated bigot who, while
revering the Establishment and God, was lavish in his use of bad language
both in defending that which he cherished and condemning that which he
despised (see Figure 5.2[417] for an example of this). His use of bad language
covers blasphemy (e.g. *God* as an exclamation), homophobia (e.g. *poof*),
racism (e.g. *coon*, *nignog*) and swearing (e.g. *bitch*, *bloody*, *cow*). He was a con-
summate hypocrite, by turns condemning others and acting in a way that he
himself would condemn. His creator, Johnny Speight, wanted to enshrine in
the character of Garnett an assault on 'the man in the street or in the Big
House or the pretentious middle class box who are responsible for some of

---

(Alf and his son-in-law Mike are discussing whether or not God is a
capitalist. Elsie, Alf's wife, and Rita, who is both Alf's daughter and
Mike's wife, are listening.)

Alf: You ... blasphemous Liverpudlian Socialist ponce! He'll see
you burn, don't worry. He'll have you. Jesus might have been
a bit soft, dying for us ... and letting them Jews knock nails
in His hands ... but His Father ain't! He's no bloody fool.
He'll have you. He'll see you get a bloody fork up your back-
side ... a bloody hot one.
Mike: God? He can't do nothing.
Alf: He'll have you mate.
Mike: All right ... all right. I'll challenge Him. If there's a God up
there, let Him strike me dead in ten seconds from now.
Alf: Don't worry he will.
Mike: Right, start counting now. (Looks at watch) One!
Alf: (*panics*) Not in this house, I ain't insured against acts of God.

Figure 5.2 An excerpt from *Till Death Us Do Part*, transmitted 11 October 1972
('Dock Pilferring').

the most stupid utterances of our time on race, religion, philosophy and politics'.[418] The aim was to make Garnett a living embodiment of all that Speight believed was wrong with British society as it stood, and, hence, produce an opportunity for change. Speight caused Garnett to act 'as a distorting mirror in which we could watch our meanest attributes reflected large and ugly'.[419] Viewers were 'expected to laugh contemptuously at this wild old reprobate and buffoon'.[420] Through Garnett, Speight 'attacked unthinking acceptance of many of ... society's standards and establishments'.[421] It is hardly surprising then that contemporary commentators noted that 'Such a programme, with its vigorous realism of language, was certain to arouse the anger of those who ... want to impose their own morality on viewers'.[422] Speight's comedy was an attack on two levels on those who, like Whitehouse, wished to impose their morality on society. It was an explicit attack on them, in that their views and attitudes were ruthlessly lampooned on the show week after week. Yet, on another level, the use of bad language in arguments setting out, often ludicrous, defences of the establishment was a negation of the discourse that would normally be associated with the defence of those values. In using bad language in this way, Speight both undermined this discourse of power and suggested hypocrisy on the behalf of the moral campaigners, a charge at least as old as the early eighteenth century, when it had been part of Sacheverell's attack on the SRM.

It is hardly surprising that Whitehouse singled out *Till Death Us Do Part* for signal criticism. What is slightly more surprising, though this is evidence in favour of the model presented in the previous section, is that Whitehouse's objections to *Till Death Us Do Part* were focused almost exclusively on bad language in the programme, though she did wonder about Speight's political motives and credentials as a writer.[423] Whitehouse, and other VALA members, kept up a concerted stream of complaints about bad language in the programme and claimed that 'the bad language and the blasphemy mounted week by week'.[424] Blasphemy, racist language and swearing were the staples of the complaints levelled at *Till Death Us Do Part* by the VALA. Interestingly, while the programme also used homophobic terms of abuse, the VALA, disapproving as it was of homosexuality, never complained about them. The programme was credited with a number of unlikely effects on the English language, such as a rapid rise in the use of Alf's favourite swear word, *bloody*.[425] Yet the VALA did not object to the politics of the programme. Whitehouse pointedly refused to accept that the bad language in the show was used in a sophisticated manner and was not intended to insult per se. This had two notable effects. First, it allowed Whitehouse to dismiss the programme as smut, much as political protesters who used bad language were dismissed as unreasonable. In her view, the programme was simply awash with bad language used unwisely by Speight which meant that '"bloodies" could be picked by the bunch every Monday smack in the middle of Family Viewing Time, with a good chance of a "bitch", a "dirty devil", a "git" and a "coon" being thrown in for good measure'.[426] An example of her avoidance of the political goals of Speight's use of language is her claim that, as he was 'convinced that there was nothing offensive about the word "coon" he could not accept that coloured people in this country could look upon it as an insult'.[427] The fact that the language was not in itself intended to be offensive, but was used, rather, to demonstrate the offensive nature of bigotry, was never accepted by Whitehouse. Second, in a manner wholly reminiscent of monarchs in the early seventeenth century, by failing to acknowledge the true meaning of the use of bad language, the propagation of this decoding of the programme within society was hindered. This hindrance was exacerbated by Whitehouse condemning the programme very publicly on the basis of a literal interpretation of the bad language used in the show. As her views were widely reported, it is not simply the case that she failed to spread the intended interpretation of the show; she actively propagated a view of the meaning of the show that ran counter to the intentions of the author. But it served her political and rhetorical purposes well. Given Whitehouse's depiction of the show, it is little surprise that *Till Death Us Do Part* was widely misunderstood in just the way that Whitehouse intended, with even Speight forced to admit that only 'a few people sensed what we were up to. The majority just enjoyed the show and missed the point.'[428] Contemporary commentators agreed, with some, such as Malcolm Muggeridge, a noted journalist and VALA supporter, writing that:

> Far from being the clown-villain of the series, Alf is the hero. His crazy outpourings ring the bell for millions of viewers; he's their hero, they dote on him and hang on his words.[429]

Other commentators sounded a more mournful note, conceding that 'Alf Garnett was compulsive watching for millions, even for those unfortunate ones who relished the confirmation of their own intolerance unable to see the parody behind the prejudice'.[430]

This treatment of bad language in *Till Death Us Do Part* by Whitehouse was a deliberate defence of the discourse of the establishment, as she herself acknowledged:

> 'Old Alf' was the man we were supposed to hate. He was foul-mouthed and bigoted – he was also a Tory, and a patriot, who believed in God and was devoted to the Queen. If we could be made to hate his offensiveness and prejudice, then we would perhaps also turn against his loyalties.[431]

The bad language in *Till Death Us Do Part* was attacked consistently by the VALA because it had a political motive – Garnett was foul-mouthed and, hence, according to the usual VALA formula, a cultural degenerate, childish and a poor example to his juniors. Yet Garnett was a four-letter threat to authority as he used a discourse littered with bad language to support an establishment predicated on a bad-language-free discourse. It was in this tension between the anti-establishment discourse of Garnett and his vehement defence of that establishment that Speight thrust at the values defended by the VALA. It was this attack which ensured that bad language was to the fore in the enduring campaign of Whitehouse against the show. This campaign reached a peak in 1972, when Whitehouse accused a particular episode of the show, *The Bird Fancier*,[432] of blasphemy as it had mocked the supposed virgin birth of Christ and suggested that further offspring of Mary and God had been prevented by Mary taking contraceptive pills. Whitehouse criticised the episode as containing 'talk that was not only obscenely blasphemous, but a calculated offence to a great many viewers'.[433] In doing so, Whitehouse is lining herself up with Garnett – in the programme Garnett takes a high moral tone in this discussion, condemning the blasphemies of his Liverpudlian son-in-law, Mike, while gazing up to heaven, talking in a tremulous voice and wagging his finger at heaven. The four-letter threat to authority that Garnett finishes with – calling Mike 'a blasphemeous [*sic*] Scouse git' – is a perfect example of what Whitehouse truly found objectionable. The discourse of the righteous subverted by the use of bad language.

The BBC defended the programme, arguing that 'the programme is so well known that it is difficult to suppose that many, if any, will turn it on without a clear idea of the kind of language ... they will hear'.[434] Yet Whitehouse was not satisfied, and actively attempted to invoke the blasphemy laws to prosecute the BBC. Whitehouse wrote to the Director of Public Prosecutions, arguing that a case for blasphemy should be brought. The DPP, with the support of the Attorney General, declined. Yet this incident demonstrates that she was alert to the possibility of using the blasphemy law, one of the few pieces of anti-bad-language legislation that remained on the statute books at the time, to legally enforce her views on society. As will be seen later in this chapter (pages 138–142), Whitehouse was to return to the possibility of the blasphemy laws and to use them successfully a few years later.[435] But *Till Death Us Do Part* escaped the law, if not the ire of Whitehouse, in its ten-year run due to the legal situation regarding public broadcasts at the time.

From its inception, the VALA was interested in imposing a system of moral censorship on public broadcasting, especially the BBC. Throughout the 1960s and 1970s the VALA was frustrated in its attempts to regulate the language of television by two simple facts. First, the BBC was not overseen by any regulatory body other than Parliament through the Royal Charter renewal process. More importantly, it was legally difficult or impossible to prosecute the BBC under the few laws that could have been used to prosecute bad language. For example, the *Obscene Publications Act*, 1959, section 1 (3)(b) specifically excluded broadcasting from the provisions of the Act.[436] With reference to blasphemy, the *Law of Libel Amendment Act*,

1888, meant that a case against the BBC for blasphemous libel could not be brought as a private prosecution without the permission of a judge. In short, there was little likelihood that any legal case focused on bad language could be brought against the BBC at all. Garnett was safe.

A possible objection to the model used to explain the attack on *Till Death Us Do Part* by Whitehouse is that, while it appears to explain the vehemence of the attack on the programme, it may not explain the failure to attack programmes that were not employing bad language as a means of political subversion. A good example of a contemporary comedy which helps to counter this objection is the programme *Steptoe and Son*.

Steptoe and Son was the creation of Ray Galton and Alan Simpson. The show focused on the lives of a father and son who ran a so-called rag and bone firm, living a hand-to-mouth existence collecting, recycling and reselling discarded household goods. The father Albert was an offensive elderly man, and the son Harold, pathetically dependent on the father, was a dreamer, forever striving above his social station, but forever being pulled back down to the reality of his life in a scrapyard by his clinging father. *Steptoe and Son* bore many superficial similarities to *Till Death Us Do Part*. Both featured working-class characters as protagonists, both started life as BBC one-off specials in the *Comedy Playhouse* series and went on to a lengthy run (from 1962–1974 in the case of *Steptoe and Son*), both were immensely popular programmes and both took a realistic approach to the dialogue of their characters, with both the father and son in *Steptoe and Son* using bad language, including blasphemy, homophobic language, racist language, sexual innuendo and swearing. The most significant difference between the two programmes is that, while the VALA regularly denounced the language of *Till Death Us Do Part*, *Steptoe and Son* escaped all criticism by Whitehouse,[437] in spite of using language that was every bit as offensive as *Till Death Us Do Part*. This led some commentators to wonder why *Steptoe and Son* evaded criticism when 'there is just as much bad language, both distasteful and sexual, in *Steptoe and Son* as in *Till Death Us Do Part*'.[438] See Figure 5.3 for an example of some dialogue from *Steptoe and Son*.

Sympathetic commentators put the failure of Whitehouse to complain about the language in some programmes while vigorously attacking it in others down to her being simply 'unselective'.[439] Yet Whitehouse was, on the contrary, highly selective, and her failure to criticise *Steptoe and Son* was as much a product of the model of discourse and power as was her decision to criticise *Till Death Us Do Part*. *Steptoe and Son* presented a fundamentally different and more acceptable view of the working class, and the use of bad language, than *Till Death*. I will illustrate this with a discussion of the use of bad language in the *Steptoe and Son* episode *Men of Letters* broadcast on 21 February 1972.

Men of Letters starts with the father and son playing a game of Scrabble. The use of bad language is frequent, and the comedy is largely centred around the use of bad language by the father as part of the game. The true

(Albert and Harold are in hospital after a fire at their house discussing who is to blame for the fire. Before the fire, they had split the house in two, taking half each and allowing passage to shared areas via a turnstile. They had done this as Harold wanted to get away from Albert, but would not leave home.)

Albert: Oh Gawd, I'm dying. It's your fault. If you hadn't put them bloody silly partitions up, this wouldn't have happened. The bleeding firemen had to put pennies in the turnstiles to get at us.

Harold: That was because they came in the wrong door. If they'd come in your door they wouldn't have had any trouble at all.

Albert: Oh, they know that, don't they? They're always going to houses with turnstiles in the passageway. They're used to it. Just because you wanted to be on your own. Because you wanted to get away from me. Well, look where it's got us.

Harold: (*bitterly*) Yeah, and in the same ward.

Albert: Yeah, well, you'll have to put up with it. Here, give us some of your orange juice. They ain't given me any. Come on, hurry up, I'm thirsty.

Figure 5.3 An excerpt from *Steptoe and Son*, broadcast 27 March 1972 ('Divided We Stand').

difference between the two programmes only becomes apparent when, at the end of the Scrabble game, the local vicar calls. From the moment that the vicar appears Harold is grovelling and apologetic, seeking the social acceptance of the vicar. Harold is mortified by his various social *faux-pas*, all of which centre on the use of bad language. The vicar, blissfully unaware of cockney rhyming slang, can, without any spite, recall odd expressions used by Harold which are obscene, noting that he does not 'pretend to understand all the colloquialisms' that the Steptoes use. A good example comes when Harold begins a theological debate with the vicar. Summoning much pomposity, Harold recalls a past debate where he explained that he ranks himself alongside Bertrand Russell and René Descartes as a humanist. The vicar recalls the conversation, and notes with some hesitancy and a clear lack of understanding, that he recalls Harold called Russell and Descartes 'berks'. Harold is mortified, and instantly says that he 'should not have used language like that'. Even the father, usually forthright in his speech, is notably cowed by the presence of the vicar, and the worst bad language that he utters in his presence is 'Oh God'. The Steptoes are humble in the presence of their social and spiritual superior, and instantly change their discourse from one using bad language to one excluding it. Additionally, both Steptoes are deferential in the extreme towards the vicar. The use of bad language in the show is very much a private affair between the Steptoes – before their superiors they make a sustained effort to avoid such language and are apologetic for its use. The vicar was a recurring figure in the Steptoe programme,[440] and when he did appear the result was the same: a modification of language use and a suitable display of deference.

Bad language provides the punch line of the show. Both Harold and his father produce materials for the hundredth-anniversary issue of the vicar's parish magazine. Harold produces a local history piece. The father produces an obscene crossword, with, one assumes, words appearing in the magazine which are every bit as obscene as those he has used in the Scrabble game at the start of the programme. The result is that the magazine is impounded by the police on the grounds that the crossword constituted 'obscenity, filth and hard-core pornography'. This punch line shows two further clear differences between *Till Death* and *Steptoe*. The use of bad language in *Steptoe* has clearly negative consequences, in *Till Death* it does not. Also, in *Steptoe*, the language used is evaluated and condemned; Harold claims that his father uses swear words because he is 'dirty and crude and horrible' and his father, when Harold swears at him, admonishes Harold saying, 'I will not be spoken to like that, I'm your father.'

In short, the bad language of *Steptoe and Son* is not subversive. On the contrary, it reinforces many attitudes to bad language: the users of bad language in the programme are untrustworthy, working class, ill-educated and male. They accept that their language use is unacceptable in polite company, and both are servile in the presence of their supposed superiors. They accept the social hierarchy and hegemony, with this being reflected in their speech. Harold, who is supposed to be the leftwing foil to his father's rightwing opinions is no leftwing firebrand – rather, he aspires to middle-class status, forever trying to better himself, always failing and finding himself firmly put back in his caste, in his ramshackle junk yard. *Steptoe and Son* is a comedy in which, when middle-class characters appear, Greene's vision fails and the working class are not 'a fit subject for drama' and are 'just a comic foil in a play in middle-class manners'.[441]

Returning to the model and the argument presented, *Men of Letters* could certainly be objected to on a majority of the grounds that Whitehouse disapproved of bad language on television. By Whitehouse's standards, Steptoe is an appalling example to his son – his use of bad language is more frequent than Harold's, and he is the first to utter a specific piece of bad language in the episode more often than not.[442] The father also debases culture – the game of Scrabble, a game for the erudite, is used by the father to display his grasp of bad language. Finally, the language is represented as offensive. The acknowledgement of the offensive nature of bad language in the programme comes through clearly in Harold's description of the aftermath of the publication of the crossword containing bad language. First, the police are said to have declared the crossword 'obscene material likely to corrupt public morals' (i.e. it fits the legal definition of obscenity in force at the time). Second, Harold says that two old ladies fainted when they discovered the nature of the crossword. Finally, Harold reports that the few issues of the magazine which escaped the 'police dragnet' were changing hands at twice the price of the *Schoolkids* edition of *Oz* magazine.[443] The language used by the father is clearly represented as being unacceptable and offensive. The one thing that the bad language in the programme is not is politically subversive. On the contrary, as noted above, the programme is accepting both of the social hierarchy and the discourse that supports that hierarchy. In this respect the programme contrasts markedly with *Till Death Us Do Part*. The trigger to Whitehouse's complaints about *Till Death* was its intended political subversion, not its use of bad language as such. This becomes more apparent if we contrast the language of *Men of Letters* with the controversial *The Bird Fancier* episode of *Till Death Us Do Part*, broadcast on 20 September 1972. Both were screened in 1972, and both used bad language. Indeed, *Steptoe* used a wider range of bad language and, arguably, more offensive terms than *Till Death Us Do Part* (see Table 5.1). *Till Death* has a greater volume of bad language, but most of that is made up of one word used very frequently – *bloody*. Yet, the bad language of *Steptoe and Son* confirms prejudices and reinforces the discourse of power. *Till Death Us Do Part* actively seeks to undermine that discourse.

The failure of *Steptoe and Son* to use bad language to subvert the discourse of the establishment is the reason why, I would contend, the programme did not attract the wrath of Mrs Whitehouse. This explains both why Whitehouse did not complain about all uses of bad language, and why her concern with bad language was not as great as that of the general public. Her principal complaint related to four-letter challenges to authority, not the four-letter words themselves. For viewers, the reverse was true. Hence Whitehouse fell out of step with viewers on this matter. It was the viewers' number one concern. Yet it was, at best, the third most important focus of complaint for Whitehouse, behind sex and violence. The one occasion when it came to true prominence, Whitehouse's complaint brought to light a

Table 5.1 The uses of bad language in *Steptoe and Son* ('Men of Letters') and *Till Death Us Do Part* ('The Bird Fancier')

Show	BLWs used (frequency of usage in parentheses)
Steptoe and Son	*bloody/bleeding* (2), *brahms & liszt* (1), *bristols* (1), *bum* (10), *bums* (1), *berk/berks* (1), *cock* (1), *crucify* (1), *crumpet* (1), *knickers* (1), *oh god* (2), *pox* (1), *sod* (2), *spunk* (1), *tit* (1)
Till Death Us Do Part	*blimey* (5), *bloody/bleeding* (31), *berk/berks* (1), *coons* (6), *cow* (1), *git* (2), *jocks* (3), *micks* (3), *moo* (2), *pillock* (1), *sod* (1), *taffy* (3)

much neglected anti-bad-language law, the common law offence of blasphemy, as reviewed in the next section.

Case study 2: prosecuting twentieth-century blasphemy – 'I felt moved and humbled that such a privilege should have been given us by the Lord'[444]

As noted already, as early as 1972 Whitehouse had considered invoking the Blasphemy Act in response to an episode of *Till Death Us Do Part*. On that occasion the Director of Public Prosecutions (DPP) had refused to proceed with the prosecution that Whitehouse called for. Whitehouse did not forget the Blasphemy Act, however, and in 1976 the possibility of using the Blasphemy Act arose again over an article in the newspaper *Gay News*, an early example of a newspaper for Britain's gay community. *Gay News* appeared once a fortnight. In *Gay News* number 96, a poem appeared written by the poet Ronald Kirkup. The poem, *The Love That Dared to Speak Its Name*, concerned the homosexual attraction a Roman centurion feels for Christ. In the poem, Christ has just been crucified. The language of the piece is direct[445] – there is mention of Jesus' *great cock* and his *ejaculation*. Both Jesus and the centurion *come* (with the word used in the sense of orgasm) many times as the centurion explains that he 'came and came and came'. The phrase *kingdom come*, part of the Lord's Prayer, becomes part of a sexual image, as Jesus (miraculously revived) penetrates the centurion and drives him into *kingdom come*. After the act, the lovers lie in a *horny paradise*. The piece as a whole is adorned with a large, Aubrey Beardsley inspired, illustration of a nubile centurion carrying the body of an equally nubile, yet dead, Christ, whose *great cock* is on display for all to see.

The poem is certainly provocative, both in its use of language and its subject matter. The poem fits the model of four-letter assaults on authority introduced in this chapter. Bad language here is, once more, subversive. Jesus, a figure who is usually represented as being quite sexless, is not merely represented as engaging in homosexual activity with the centurion, the poet assures us that Jesus 'loved all men, body, soul and spirit'. In addition to this, the actions and body of Christ are discussed in terms normally reserved for somewhat more pornographic descriptions of sex. Yet, not only is the discourse surrounding Christ's body a subversion of the normal discourse surrounding Christ, the poem takes well-worn religious phrases and imbues them with this quasi-pornographic spirit. Hence *kingdom come* becomes, in effect, the state one is in while orgasming. Resurrection is sought on *a green hill far away*, but the quaint phrase, borrowed from the hymn *There is a Green Hill Far Away*,[446] does not focus on the 'redeeming blood' of the hymn, rather it refers to the hope that an erection will eventually return after the joy of an orgasm. The poem does not merely subvert by the use of bad language, it subverts further by turning familiar religious phrases into bad language by imbuing them with a sexual meaning. Hence, when one considers both the subversion of discourse that the poem represents and the presentation of Jesus as homosexual, a claim bound to attract the wrath of the homophobic Whitehouse, the *Gay News* poem looks very much like a piece that Whitehouse should have opposed vigorously. She did, though she was not the first to complain about the poem.

In the very next issue of *Gay News*, readers of the newspaper registered their disquiet. One letter writer[447] identified the poem as 'insulting and blasphemous' while accepting that the intention to cause outrage may have a political end as 'Deliberately offending our opponents may be a political move'. Another writer[448] complained that the poem was 'thoroughly distasteful' and represented 'blasphemy'. The criticism intensified in issue 98, with five further letters published criticising the piece, with the poem being condemned for 'vulgarity and bad taste'[449] and for using 'sensual and obscene terms'. The editor, Denis Lemon, was prompted to reply, and while not apologising for publishing the piece, he defended Kirkup on artistic grounds and claimed that the piece was not, in fact, printed simply to cause offence. Nonetheless, the debate rumbled on. Issue 99 included three letters supporting Kirkup, and condemning those who had written in to complain, with at least one person writing, in rebarbative terms, that he found it 'curious to see such strong reactions against the idea of screwing the dead Christ from people who sit around on Sunday mornings eating bits of him before breakfast'.[450] With this salvo of letters, the immediate debate of the Kirkup poem ceased in *Gay News*.

Issue 96 of *Gay News* clearly provoked many, and one person at least sent the newspaper to Whitehouse. She immediately developed a view that with regard to blasphemy 'a successful action can be brought in this case'.[451] Whitehouse was so swift in coming to this conclusion not simply because of her attempt to use the blasphemy law against *Till Death Us Do Part*, but because she had sought legal opinion in May 1976 from a lawyer, Robert Ward, as to how, and under what circumstances, a prosecution for blasphemy could be brought. She was encouraged to consider using the blasphemy laws against a proposed film entitled *The Many Faces of Christ* by Jens Jorgen Thorsen, which she objected to, as its subject was the sex life of Christ. The British Home Secretary at the time, Merlyn Rees, had suggested that Whitehouse look at the law of blasphemy as a means of deflecting her from assailing him with requests to act against the film:

> The Home Secretary was being harassed, so to get himself out of this difficulty he mentioned the common law of blasphemy ... he didn't mean it seriously – it was just a way of dodging out of trouble.[452]

It would appear that Rees had not seriously thought Whitehouse would ever use the law. Rather he thought that while she was busy in a futile exploration of the blasphemy laws she would be out of his way. But because of her past explorations of the blasphemy law, when the *Gay News* case arose

Whitehouse was able to move relatively swiftly, as she was in possession of legal opinion regarding the law of blasphemy. Whitehouse had to seek an opinion in large part because the law she wished to invoke had not been used since 1922. It was unlikely that any lawyers serving in the mid-1970s had personal, direct experience of a blasphemy prosecution.[453] Hence there was a need to carefully review the provisions of the law before reviving it. By the time that Whitehouse received the copy of *Gay News*, she was well versed in the law of blasphemy, and understood the circumstances under which a successful prosecution might be brought. For Whitehouse, the stage was set for a legal battle which, if successful, was to be the first of many, with the law of blasphemy being used to prosecute *Gay News* and 'a great deal more'.[454]

The intention of Whitehouse to bring the case was announced on 29 November 1976, when she issued a statement claiming that the poem was 'obscenely blasphemous' and announcing that consequently she intended to bring a prosecution for blasphemy. In retrospect, the *Gay News* case was both a triumph and a disaster for Whitehouse. The triumph was legal. Whitehouse was granted the right to bring the case on 9 November. On 20 December a so-called voluntary bill of indictment was granted to Whitehouse, which meant that pre-trial hearings in lower courts were dispensed with and the case went straight to criminal trial at the Old Bailey in London. The case was heard between 4 and 12 July 1977. Whitehouse won, with the jury declaring by a majority of 10–2 that 'the words and drawing are blasphemous'.[455]

Yet, in an important sense, Whitehouse also lost. If she imagined that the case would pave the way for a new reformation of manners, she was mistaken. The political, Church and media establishment were clearly against the action brought. MPs campaigned on behalf of *Gay News*. The news media in the UK, and worldwide, covered the case, and comment seemed to be decisively against Whitehouse. But most frustratingly of all for Whitehouse, the Church establishment distanced itself from her actions. Senior Church figures declined Whitehouse's offer of the opportunity to give evidence at the trial, with the Archbishop of Canterbury, Donald Coggan, and the Catholic Cardinal, Basil Hulme, both refusing to appear. Coggan responded to Whitehouse when she wrote to admonish him for refusing to appear saying that he was:

> puzzled by your letter. Cardinal Basil Hulme and I refused to come forward as witnesses in the *Gay News* trial only after most careful thought, and Mr Ross-Cornes[456] assured my Registrar . . . that he fully understood our reasons.

Whitehouse was clearly bothered by the failure of the Church hierarchy to support her, and stated that she 'couldn't believe that there was no member of the hierarchy of the church willing to speak up'[457] in her favour in public or in court. Her response was the only one which she knew – she hit out at the Church, claiming that 'the church is powerless to stand up in a situation like this because it is compromised' by its acceptance of homosexuality. In spite of this, Whitehouse acknowledged that:

> Some Christians have gone into print to say that Christ needs no defence, so why should I bother? I've even had a lot of people accusing me of being thoroughly un-Christian in what I did.[458]

As well as finding that the establishment did not support her, the legal case with *Gay News* became protracted. The case began in 1976, but by the time that the case had been heard, the first appeal at the Court of Criminal Appeal and the final appeal at the House of Lords had taken place, nearly three years had passed. The case then dragged on further as it went to the European Court in Strasbourg where it was finally dismissed in 1982. The use of the *Blasphemy Act* was no rapid and easy means of prosecution. This, in combination with the lack of support Whitehouse received, ensured that she did not invoke the law again.

The appeals in the *Gay News* case were mainly of interest as they established the importance of the language used in the poem; there is the possibility, of course, that it was the propositional content of the poem that was blasphemous rather than the language of the poem itself. The House of Lords appeal in particular seems to indicate that it was the 'violent and scurrilous'[459] language of the poem rather than the message of the poem that was the grounds for the poem being judged blasphemous as outlined, for example, by Lord Diplock:[460]

> To publish opinions denying the truth and doctrines of the established Church or even of Christianity itself [is] no longer held to amount to the offence of blasphemous libel so long as such opinions [are] expressed in temperate language and not in terms of offence, insult or ridicule.

Lord Scarman went further by saying that:[461]

> Had the argument for acceptance and welcome of homosexuals within the loving fold of the Christian faith been advanced 'in a sober and temperate . . . style' (Reg. v. Hetherington, at p. 590), there could have been no criminal offence committed.

It was the language – the four-letter assault on authority – of Kirkup's poem that constituted the blasphemy, not the proposition that Christ may have been a homosexual. The legal response was not against the content of the poem – it was expressly a response to the four-letter assault on authority itself. The Lords' view in this matter reinforced the view, earlier expressed by the Court of Appeal, that 'A treatise attacking Christian doctrine . . . may well, as a matter of ordinary language be described as an attack on Christianity. Yet such publications have long been within the law because they neither insult nor offend nor vilify.'[462] The act of blasphemy is closely associated with the tenor of the text in which it is expressed and part of that expression of blasphemy is in the choice of words which, in context, become blasphemous because they are 'indecent, offensive, insulting' and tend towards 'ridicule', 'vilification', 'irreverence'.[463] In such circumstances, Lord Scarman notes 'Everyone who speaks blasphemous words is guilty of . . . blasphemy'.[464]

The prosecution of *Gay News* ended in a short-term triumph for Whitehouse, yet it led to a defeat for her long-term project – the extensive use of the blasphemy laws. While the blasphemy laws had been dusted off, and their applicability reaffirmed, Whitehouse never used the blasphemy laws again, though films like Monty Python's *Life of Brian* certainly, on the face of it, may have fallen under the provisions of the blasphemy law.

Case study 3: the *Little Red Schoolbook*

As noted in Chapter 5, with reference to *The Whole Duty of Man*, the control of discourses presented to children in the classroom, and the legitimisation or illegitimisation of discourses in teaching materials, is a way of ensuring the continuity of the views regarding certain discourses or, crucially, a way of affecting a change in those attitudes over a number of generations. The *Little Red Schoolbook* is a good example of both of these processes: an attempt by one group to introduce a new discourse to the classroom, and an attempt by an opposing group to exclude that discourse, so as to defend the discourse that was viewed as acceptable in the classroom. The book itself, and Whitehouse's reaction to it, can certainly be accounted for by the four-letter assault on authority model. However, before these issues can be explored in more detail, the background of the *Little Red Schoolbook* case must be presented.

The *Little Red Schoolbook* was published in Britain by Richard Handyside.[465] The book drew inspiration for its title from Chairman Mao's famous *Little Red Book*, but was aimed, amongst other things, at providing an effective framework for protest to children. Children were encouraged to question the authority of adults, and practical advice was presented to them regarding how to revolt against adult authority. The infiltration of ruling bodies, the generation of unrest, rebellion against established rules, the production of propaganda, the use of intimidation and attacking those in authority are all recommended as courses of action to the unsatisfied child. Children are also encouraged to contact various leftwing organisations for assistance in their cause. The book, as well as attacking the established roles of child and adult in society, also rejected the established discourse of education, and elected instead to use what were viewed as swear words in discussing sex in the book. Instead of the standard terms accepted by the classroom discourse of sex education, such as *vagina* and *penis*, the *Little Red Schoolbook* elected to use words such as *cunt* and *cock*:

> The usual word for a boy's sexual organ is cock or prick. The usual word for a girl's sexual organ is pussy or cunt. Many grown ups don't like these words because they say they are rude. They prefer words like penis and vagina.[466]

The description of coitus itself is couched in similar terms:

> When a boy puts his stiff prick into a girl's vagina and moves it around it is called having intercourse or making love or sleeping together (even if they don't sleep at all). The usual word for intercourse is fucking.[467]

The book provides a very frank and liberal view of sex and sexuality to its readers. Given the goals of the VALA, it is unsurprising that the book became a target of legal action from Whitehouse. On 29 March 1971, she wrote to the Director of Public Prosecutions asking him to take action to prosecute the book as obscene. He replied on 1 April 1971 to say that he had done so. The trial was swift and on 1 July 1971 the book was found to be obscene and Handyside was fined £50 and additionally required to pay £100 costs. An appeal against the ruling failed.

The language and supposed obscene content of the book was clearly a deliberate assault on authority on Handyside's behalf. The intention of the book was a general assault on authority, part of which was a four-letter assault. Handyside was engaged in an attempt to influence and persuade the school child every bit as much as those SPCK teachers who, nearly 300 years before, had used Allestree and others to reform the morals of the nation. Handyside's aims were clearly the same, though the shape of the society that he wished to forge was clearly different from that of the moral reformers of the seventeenth century. Whitehouse, on the other hand, was defending the heritage of the moral reformers – she was principally rebutting the Marxism of the *Little Red Schoolbook* which she saw as 'a revolutionary primer'.[468] Whitehouse herself makes it quite clear that it was the politics of the *Little Red Schoolbook* with which she was principally preoccupied:

> It followed very closely the format and philosophy of Quotations from Chairman Mao – indeed the two books were side by side on the counter of 'Stage One' before legal action stopped the distribution of the first edition. Open rebellion against the 'system', be it school, parents or authority generally, was openly advocated, while children were constantly exhorted to collect evidence against teachers of alleged injustices or anything which was likely to enhance revolution.[469]

Whitehouse was strong in her condemnation of the Marxism of the book, and made much of the fact that Handyside has also published works by Che Guevara and Fidel Castro. However, the espousal of revolutionary Marxism to children was no more illegal in 1971 than the profession of homosexuality or the right of a rightwing figure like Alf Garnett to be a ranting bigot. Whitehouse focused on the obscenity of the *Little Red Schoolbook* because it was the obscenity of the book which could bring about its prosecution and suppression under law. Much as the censors of the early seventeenth century, who, under the guise of deploring the language of a book, sought its censorship on grounds which were not linguistic, Whitehouse was able to bring about the suppression of the book as a whole by focusing on its supposed obscenity. By doing so she was able to censor the revolutionary Marxism of the book as surely as if that revolutionary Marxism was itself illegal. Whitehouse admits as much when she writes that, prior to the publication of the book in Britain, she was 'already aware, through our contacts in Denmark, of the revolutionary nature of this manual and instantly drew it to the attention of the Director of Public Prosecutions'. Yet she did not bring the revolutionary nature of the book to his attention. While it is the revolutionary nature of the book that was clearly the impetus for action, it was the supposed obscenity of the book, of which the language formed no small part, which provided the grounds for prosecution and Whitehouse's letter to the Director of Public Prosecutions:

> I would like to draw your attention to the chapter on sex. This book is now being sold freely to children of all ages and it is intended, by the publishers, to be read by children of eight and upwards. In my view this book would corrupt and deprave young children and I draw it to your attention in the sincere hope that you will find it possible to take action against the publishers.[470]

Indeed, such was Whitehouse's dislike of the revolutionary nature of the book that when it was reprinted, with the offending sections and language removed, she was reduced to impotent declarations of dismay, and speculated that:

> in the light of the fact that over 70,000 copies were distributed among schoolchildren in its revised form, it cannot have been without influence in creating a value-free society amongst the generation reaching maturity today.[471]

However, Whitehouse's discussion of the *Little Red Schoolbook* is misleading. In her 1977 book, *Whatever Happened to Sex*, Whitehouse discusses the book at length. By this time, the prosecution of the book had been confirmed by the European Court of Human Rights, and the censored edition had been accepted as within the bounds of the law by the Director of Public Prosecutions. Without looking at the censored version of the book, if one were to read the description of the book presented by Whitehouse, one may well gather that dysphemism was a central focus of the case against it. After discussing the prosecution of the book, Whitehouse proceeds to quote from it, to demonstrate how inappropriate it is for 'children of eleven and over'.[472] Whitehouse gives three examples to support this claim, the first of which is rich in dysphemisms, including words like *come, fuck, fucking* and *prick* (2).[473] The other two quotations contain no dysphemisms or other forms of bad language, but deal with the topics of contraception[474] and pornography.[475] When the censored version of the schoolbook is examined, however, the dysphemism-rich passage has indeed been edited – but not to remove the dysphemisms. To understand how censorship alters the section Whitehouse quotes, I need to reproduce that particular quote in full:

> When a boy puts his stiff prick into a girl's vagina and moves it around it is called having intercourse or making love or sleeping together (even if they don't sleep at all). The usual word for intercourse is fucking.
>
> A boy and a girl can 'make love' and give each other pleasure without necessarily fucking. If you don't want to fuck, perhaps because you're afraid of having children, you can find lots of other ways of giving and having pleasure – for instance by kissing and cuddling, petting or masturbating each other.
>
> A boy and a girl can give one another more pleasure by touching it and caressing each other in the right places and in the right way. Each person enjoys being touched in different places. They should talk about it and tell each other what they really enjoy. It's easier for boys to come than for girls. A boy only needs to have his prick stroked by the girl.

The first two paragraphs that Whitehouse quotes, which contain all but two of the examples of dysphemism, are not edited at all in the revised edition of the book. As they are not essential to the understanding of the third paragraph, which is the subject of censorship, one can only assume that her intention in quoting the first two paragraphs is to provide the impression that these passages, containing bad language as they do, were in fact censored.[476] They were not. The revised third paragraph is given below:[477]

> Each person enjoys being touched in different places and ways. The neck, ears, breasts, thighs and of course the sex organs and the area around them can be caressed. Don't be shy about telling each other what you really enjoy.
>
> It is easier for boys to come than for girls. A boy only needs to have his prick stroked by the girl.

The changes seem difficult to understand and largely focus on innocuous matters, with sentences such as 'A boy and a girl can give one another more pleasure by touching or caressing each other in the right places and in the right way' being deleted. After the deletion, the dysphemism is very much in place.

The passages relating to contraception and pornography were more heavily edited, with the section on contraception having been changed almost beyond recognition. Whitehouse's choice of opening quote on the schoolbook is misleading, as it implies that dysphemism at least in part must have been the cause of legal offence, a view certainly picked up by others who have followed the case.[478] Yet this is clearly not so, and by the time of the publication of Whitehouse's book this was clearly known to her. Additionally, the focus on the politics of the book, and its encouragement to school children to question authority is highlighted in her discussion of the *Little Red Schoolbook* case – yet, once again, this was not a cause of concern for the courts. Indeed, the publishers of the book complained that the magistrate who condemned the book refused to consider anything other than the section on sex education in the book.[479] This was also known to Whitehouse. However, both facts were likely to be unknown to readers of her book. The proceedings of magistrate's courts, or other courts for that matter, are not easy either to access or to interpret. In quoting passages containing legally permissible dysphemisms, what effect was Whitehouse achieving? In a context where she has constructed bad language as something which signals a non-serious or childish discussion and inappropriate language use by adults, as noted earlier in this chapter, the net effect of the quotation of such language is clear – to demonstrate that the authors of the book were irresponsible and certainly not to be viewed as intellectually serious.

In the confusion of bad language, political objection and legal censure in her discussion of the *Little Red Schoolbook*, Whitehouse certainly gives the impression that she has vanquished a dangerous and obscene revolutionary work. Her discussion of the book in the past tense, when she claims that the *Little Red Schoolbook* 'was a revolutionary primer', implies that it is no longer even available, or at least no longer available in a form in which it could be viewed as a revolutionary primer. This was clearly untrue. The book changed little as a consequence of re-editing, and went on to achieve wide circulation – indeed, in its original form it was never even banned in some parts of the UK.[480] The presentation of the *Little Red Schoolbook* trial as a defence of obscene language, sexual promiscuity and revolutionary thought by Whitehouse was clearly, at best, an exaggeration of the truth. However, the facts which could help to change that view of the trial were difficult to access, and as such Whitehouse's claims went unchallenged, making it a *de facto* triumph of the sort she mendaciously claimed it was.

This case is a good example of both the intentions of the four-letter assault on authority and its principal failing. Its intent was to subvert – to replace one discourse with another and, in doing so, to undermine the authority which rested on the usurped discourse. But the discourse with which they attempted to subvert took the revolutionaries perilously close to illegality. While *Till Death Us Do Part* escaped prosecution by virtue of the provisions of the Law of Libel Amendment and Obscene Publications Acts, no such Act protected the *Little Red Schoolbook*. Consequently, it was prosecuted successfully, and the four-letter assault on authority was deflected and failed.

The purity of the discourse of power[481]

What do the case studies presented say about the role of the VALA in censoring language in the media? On one level, their role appears somewhat similar to that of the SRM – a 'grassroots', largely middle-class, group seeking to impose linguistic and moral absolutism on society using a moral panic, this time apparently focused on bad language, sex and violence in the media.[482] However, the differences between the two groups are also striking. The legal triumphs of the VALA are petty by comparison to the SRM. The SRM undertook thousands of prosecutions – the VALA undertook nowhere near as many, and faced much more hostility from the State and the judiciary than the SRM did in its early years. If the VALA faced no Sacheverell, it was largely because there was no need for a Sacheverell – the relative impact of the VALA in legal terms was much less than the SRM, and consequently the backlash against it was not as marked. However, the VALA was also working in a very different context to the SRM – the VALA was working within the society that the SRM and other such societies had created – the nature and scale of the task presented to such groups as the VALA was fundamentally different from that which faced the SRM. The VALA was fighting to retain the society that the SRM had helped to forge – the SRM was actively defining a new approach to morality in society as part of establishing the role of the moral middle class in English society. The VALA was conservative while the SRM was revolutionary. It is in this difference, conservatism versus revolution, that a further difference between the VALA and the SRM can be seen. The VALA was fighting to retain a status quo. With regards to language, this meant defending it from an oppositional discourse of power, the four-letter assault on authority. The SRM were defining a new discourse of power, and at least in the works of Collier, we can see that the moral reformers of the seventeenth century were themselves espousing an oppositional discourse – a discourse of moral purity – to replace what they saw as an immoral and licentious discourse inherited from the Restoration. The success of the moral reform movement was the establishment of their discourse of purity as the discourse of power. The success of the VALA was in their maintenance of the purity of the discourse of power. In the case of the SRM, the establishment of that discourse was a step towards the expression of power through that discourse. For the VALA, the maintenance of that discourse was a key element in ensuring that the relationship of various groups to power within society remained unaltered.[483]

In supporting that discourse, the VALA, in turn, adopted a discourse of moral panic. That discourse will be explored in detail in Chapter 7. In the next chapter, the discourse of the revolutionary SRM will be explored. In part, this is to look at the discourse of the SRM in its own right. However, the study of the discourse of the SRM will also facilitate a comparison of the discourse of the SRM and the VALA in Chapter 7.

Part 3
Discourses of panic

6 Sea change

The Society for the Reformation of Manners and moral panics about bad language

Introduction

In this chapter I will explore the two moral panics relating to bad language discussed in this book, one which began in the 1690s and another which began in the 1960s. In doing so, I want to achieve two things. First, I want to demonstrate how a corpus of writings representing a moral panic can be used to rapidly and effectively populate a model of the discourse of moral panics. Second, I wish to characterise, compare and contrast the two moral panics in question, in part to see how bad language is represented in them.

Comparing the SRMC and Lampeter

In this section, I will compare the SRMC and the Lampeter corpus as a means of identifying the core discourse in the SRMC associated with moral panics. However, before focusing on the discourse of the moral panic, I need to explore the keyword lists yielded by the corpora in more detail.

Lampeter and the SRMC

An initial comparison of the SRMC and Lampeter identified 99 positive and 20 negative keywords in the SRMC corpus.[484] These words are given, in descending order of keyness, in Table 6.1.[485]

A striking feature of the positive keywords of the SRMC is that they include numerous religious references (e.g. *christ*, *christians*, *soul*) and archaic pronouns (*ye*, *thy*). This in itself is an indication of the religious nature of the writings of the SRM. This should come as no surprise considering the history of the SRM, as outlined in Chapter 4. What the keyword list does suggest, however, is that while a comparison to general English may identify both the content and the register of the SRMC, a comparison of the SRMC to religious texts of the period may allow one to filter out keywords which are register-based and to focus exclusively on those keywords which differentiate the SRMC from general religious texts of the time. Fortunately, it is possible to explore this hypothesis with the Lampeter corpus, as the

Table 6.1 Positive and negative keywords in the SRMC when compared to the Lampeter corpus

Positive keywords	Negative keywords
god, and, sin, vice, drunkenness, magistrates, public, profaneness, reformation, men, etc., swearing, evil, ourselves, offences, judgement, thou, our, we, sins, guilt, virtue, ye, thy, religion, excess, debauchery, swear, penalties, us, profane, judgements, christian, holy, unto, laws, soul, world, day, examples, heaven, fear, reproof, man, lord, christ, societies, intemperance, sabbath, offenders, christians, wickedness, manners, vain, wicked, vices, worldly, saviour, souls, punishment, worship, vicious, endeavours, persons, neglect, chastity, suppressing, lust, good, shame, heart, divine, execution, love, duty, dishonour, honour, virtuous, informations, sinful, shall, zeal, hearts, oaths, lusts, conversation, drinking, offender, guilty, thee, magistrate, contempt, ruin, mind, reprover, publicly	*lord, said, french, lords, at, she, could, were, parliament, small, my, sir, england, the, trade, her, had, was*

corpus contains religious texts as one of its genres. Consequently I carried out the keyword analysis of the SRMC with the Lampeter corpus, but focused exclusively on texts in the Lampeter corpus occurring in the religious writing category in the period 1690–1750 (this data amounted to 92,210 words and will henceforth be referred to as Lampeter B). The results are shown in Table 6.2.

The dramatic reduction in the number of keywords between Tables 6.1 and 6.2 is strong evidence that the SRMC texts are written in a religious register, in that the language itself is less distinct from Lampeter B than from the Lampeter corpus as a whole. This conclusion becomes more pronounced when one compares the keyword lists generated by a comparison of the SRMC with Lampeter B, and a comparison of the Lampeter B with the

Table 6.2 A comparison of the SRMC and Lampeter B, yielding keywords for the SRMC texts

Positive keywords	Negative keywords
and, public, sin, drunkenness, magistrates, vice, profaneness, men, offences, judgement, etc., guilt, oath, virtue, ourselves, offenders, will, penalties, swear, swearing	*you, clergy, he, i, was, that, bishops, bishop, church*

other texts in the Lampeter corpus in the same period as that covered by Lampeter B (amounting to 452,684 words, henceforth called Lampeter A). In Table 6.3 the keywords for Lampeter B are shown. Those words underlined are also keywords when the SRMC is compared to the Lampeter corpus as a whole.

Looking at the keywords of Lampeter B has two functions. First, it underlines the distinctiveness of Lampeter B from Lampeter A. Second, it asserts the similarity of Lampeter B to the SRMC. Many positive keywords are shared by Lampeter B and the SRMC. Nearly all of the negative keywords for Lampeter B are also negative keywords for the SRMC. Focusing on the positive keywords first, those not shared by the SRMC are easily explained in terms of the differences in purpose and nature of Lampeter B. Unlike the SRMC, there is frequent close discussion of the scriptures in Lampeter B (yielding positive keywords such as *page, scripture, canons, treatise, apostles, communion* and *psalm*) and a discussion of the structures, practices and institutions of the Church (yielding positive keywords such as *baptism, bishop, bishops, church, godfathers, godmothers* and *schism*). Where the SRMC and the religious texts overlap, however, is with reference to the discussion of faith (*religion, christian, christians*), the discussion of the principal components of Christianity (*god, christ, saviour, world, heaven*), the identification of problems (*profane*) and the use of register-specific words (*unto, ye*). The negative keywords are interesting, because of the great similarity between the Lampeter B data and the SRMC. Yet, even here there are telling dissimilarities – *money* and the coordinator *or* are not negative keywords for the SRMC, yet they are negative keywords for Lampeter B. The former can be explained easily – there is much discussion of the use of monetary fines in the SRMC as a

Table 6.3 A comparison of Lampeter A and B, yielding keywords for the religious texts

Positive keywords	Negative keywords
god, church, bishop, religion, bishops, text, christian, christians, page, scripture, canons, treatise, apostles, schism, clergy, children, communion, christ, temporal, holy, adversaries, deliverance, psalm, providence, religious, sureties, divine, stage, schismaticks, sermon, baptism, saviour, our, paul, godfathers, world, that, civil, special, authority, prophets, david, fathers, are, godmothers, his, blessed, heaven, jews, presbyter, mackbeth, learning, ye, deprivation, gallio, unto, caesar, praise, salvation, profane, sadducees, persecution, emperor, primitive, powers, state	*money, at, england, small, her, parliament, or, trade*

means of punishing miscreants. This is absent from the Lampeter religious data. The presence of *or* as a negative keyword in Lampeter B but not the SRMC will be discussed later in this chapter – for the moment it is important to notice that another coordinator, *and*, is a positive keyword for the SRMC data, whether it is compared to general English or the religious texts alone. *He* as a negative keyword in the SRMC is also interesting. Given that, as we will see later, males are a focus of discussion in the SRMC (see pages 165–168), it is somewhat surprising that *he* is a negative keyword. One possible explanation is that references to males in the singular in particular are rare, and hence the pronoun *he* is rare. However, there is no evidence for this in the keyword list – while *he* is a negative keyword, *man* and *gentleman*, for example, are not. The truth about *he* is revealed when the occurrences of the word in the SRMC are examined. *He* is used in the SRMC, almost exclusively, to refer to God. *He* has become a pronoun with a fixed referent in the SRMC, and, as such, its frequency is reduced to such a degree that it has become a negative keyword.

Given that the consideration of Table 6.3 has shown that the SRMC is written in the religious register and that it shares some elements of its discourse with religious texts, where does the SRMC text differ from Lampeter B? We can now refer to Table 6.2. I will deal with the negative keywords first, as these link most clearly to the positive keywords in Table 6.3. Note that a major discourse of the Lampeter religious texts, what I have termed the structures, practices and institutions of the Church, is not merely absent from the positive keyword list – it appears in the negative keyword list of the SRMC/Lampeter B comparison. Mention of the *clergy*, *bishop*, *bishops* and *church* is avoided in the SRMC. In order to discover whether the frequency of the use of these words in the SRMC is only low when compared to the Lampeter religious texts, where it is high, I compared the SRMC data to Lampeter A. Table 6.4 shows the result of this comparison, with keywords shared with Lampeter B underlined.

Three things are notable about the positive keywords in Table 6.4. First, as one would expect, when compared to Lampeter A, the number of register-specific keywords in the SRMC surges, with archaic forms such as *thou*, *shalt*, *thee* and *hath* being positive keywords when Lampeter A and the SRMC are compared, but not when Lampeter B and the SRMC are compared. Second, when the SRMC is compared to Lampeter A, a great many words with an evaluative content are keywords, e.g. *vicious*, *sinful*, *zeal*, *piety*, *chastity* and *lusts*. This shows that these words, while used by the SRMC with a higher frequency than in general English, are not used with a higher frequency than in religious texts in general, i.e. they are key when the SRMC is compared to Lampeter A, but not Lampeter B. Finally, the keywords which the SRMC shares with the Lampeter B corpus, when they are compared to Lampeter A, are pretty much unchanged from when we considered the SRMC compared to the whole of the Lampeter data. The main area where the keywords of the Lampeter B data and the SRMC converge are around the discussion of faith

Table 6.4 A comparison of the SRMC with Lampeter A, yielding keywords for the
SRMC

Positive keywords	Negative keywords
god, and, sin, vice, magistrates, profaneness, reformation, drunkenness, religion, public, thou, men, christian, our, ye, sins, evil, swearing, we, ourselves, etc., thy, holy, christians, offences, judgement, christ, virtue, guilt, unto, us, heaven, world, excess, soul, profane, saviour, debauchery, swear, penalties, wicked, examples, judgements, divine, vices, worship, souls, laws, fear, societies, man, lord, day, manners, vain, wickedness, worldly, religious, reproof, apostle, intemperance, contempt, wrath, sabbath, s-day, magistrate, vicious, thee, persons, lust, offenders, shall, shame, honour, righteous, duty, zeal, love, sinful, shalt, though, virtuous, hearts, punishment, piety, execution, dishonour, neglect, heart, endeavours, let, suppressing, example, lusts, chastity, good, spiritual, are, conversation, hath, repentance, behold, almighty, jesus, salvation, mind, is, their, glory	*france, two, english, money, said, french, lords, could, were, she, at, my, parliament, small, sir, i, the, england, trade, her, had, was*

(*religion, christian, christians*) the discussion of the principal components of
Christianity (*god, saviour, world, heaven*), the identification of problems
(*profane*) and the use of register-specific words (*unto, ye*). With regard to
negative keywords, while the SRMC/Lampeter A comparison yields more
negative keywords than the Lampeter A/B comparison, there is only one
word from the negative keywords in Table 6.3 which is not a negative
keyword in Table 6.4 – the coordinating disjunction *or*. It would appear
that, of all of the Lampeter B negative keywords, this keyword alone is a
word which is not a negative keyword for the SRMC, i.e. the SRMC shuns
the same words as Lampeter B, except for the word *or*; as promised, this will
be investigated later. In short, the SRMC and Lampeter B corpus are not
simply similar when compared to one another; when we compare them sep-
arately with the same reference corpus, in this case Lampeter A, they are
shown to be similar again.

Returning to the point of departure for this discussion, what of the negative keywords shown in Table 6.2? Are the negative keywords associated with
the Church negative solely because they appear very frequently in Lampeter
B? Do they still occur frequently enough in the SRMC that, by contrast with
Lampeter A, the Church-related lexis in the SRMC constitutes a set of keywords? Looking at Table 6.4, the answer to these hypotheses is clearly no.
While the words *clergy, bishops, bishop* and *church* are not positive keywords

when Lampeter A and the SRMC are compared, they are not negative key-words either. So we can confidently say that the SRMC differs from Lampeter B in that it discusses the Church and its structures far less frequently than would be normal for a religious text, and discusses them no more frequently than would be typical in general English of the time. The reason for this, I hypothesise, lies in the relationship between the SRM and the established Church. The SRM was at pains not to offend the established Church, but it was also relatively non-denominational.[486] As such, it did not discuss the workings of the Church – as it was not part of it – and shied away from a discussion of the Church and its hierarchy for fear of the consequences of doing so. While this can only remain informed speculation, in the context of the history of the SRM it is an explanation which makes sense.

I wish now to consider the positive keywords yielded by a comparison of Lampeter B and the SRMC. If the hypothesis put forward in this chapter, i.e. that frequency can be a guide to the lexis and nature of a moral panic, and if the SRMC/Lampeter B comparison is the most relevant for this purpose, then it follows that the positive keyword list should be analysable in terms of the major elements of a moral panic as introduced in Chapter 1. How do the positive keywords in Table 6.2 match these categories? Table 6.5 categorises the words.

Note that the words *magistrates*, *men* and *oath* are entered in this list twice. *Magistrates* and *men* function as both a corrective action and as a scapegoat. *Oath* appears both as a corrective action and as an object of offence. This will be explained for *magistrates* and *oath* in the section dealing with corrective action keywords. The discussion of the double entry of *men* will be deferred until the 'scapegoat' section.

In the following short sections I will present the keywords with their overall frequency, the collocates for the word in the SRMC (if any, up to a maximum of ten)[487] and the collocates of this word in Lampeter B and A.[488] Collocates are listed from strongest to weakest.[489] I will typically not comment on the patterns of collocation in Lampeter A and B as my expectation is that they will usually be different from the SRMC, as they are not representing the

Table 6.5 The positive keywords of the SRMC/Lampeter B comparison categorised according to the major themes of a moral panic discourse

Category	Positive keywords in that category
Consequence	*guilt, public*
Corrective action	*judgement, magistrates, oath, penalties, men*
Desired outcome	*virtue*
Moral entrepreneur	*ourselves*
Object of offence	*drunkenness, offences, profaneness, sin, swear, swearing , vice, oath*
Scapegoat	*men, offenders, magistrates*
Moral panic rhetoric	*and, etc., will*

moral panic of the SRMC, i.e. the different pattern of collocation between the SRMC and the Lampeter corpora is evidence of the distinctiveness of the SRMC discourse. However, on occasions where similarities do arise, I will discuss them. If any collocate is also a keyword, it is underlined. Following each table I will present a brief justification, where necessary, for the inclusion of the keywords in question within the category presented.

Consequence

The words in Table 6.6 represent the consequences of the problems identified by the SRM and show, first, that the consequences will not merely be private, they will be *public*. Additionally, the nature of the consequence is made clear by the keyword *guilt* – guilt is the lot of those who commit the sins identified by the SRM. But as these guilty parties bring shame on those around them and the nation, that guilt will be national also, and consequently the *judgement* brought to bear on the nation will be national. Guilt is commodified to the extent that it becomes the moral equivalent of the national debt.[490] To give some support for this view, both *national* and *public* collocate with *guilt*. In the concordance of *guilt*, there are numerous examples of personal guilt brought about through some misdemeanour translating to guilt for a larger social group. For example, consider the SRMC extracts in Figure 6.1 (keyword underlined).[491]

In the first and second examples, the guilt of an individual has consequences for others, with the second example seeing it as injurious to the

Table 6.6 Consequence keywords

Word	Frequency	Collocates in SRMC	Collocates in Lampeter B	Collocates in Lampeter A
public	98	*exercising, disorders, trade, promotion, worship, tipling, immoralities, scandalous, taken, offender*	*frequented, worship, service, spirit, churches, stage, name, already, private, manner*	*contribution, prefer, attention, debts, contracts, payment, breaking, impose, taxes, parliamentary*
guilt	83	*contract, load, transgressions, heap, lays, involved, remove, double, deeply, perjury*	*lest, without*	*involve, jane, treason, innocent, blood*
judgement	62	*submit, stability, righteousness, actions, behold, death*	*heat, enter, till, according, give*	*arrest, reverse, decree, entered, sentence, verdict, pass, severe, obtain*

1   The Laws of God forbid it, the Laws of Men are against it, our Souls are Involved in the <u>Guilt</u>, others are injured by it, we cannot Practice it but at our own Perils...

2   And I wish they would seriously lay this Truth to Heart, and consider how much <u>Guilt</u> they thus contract to themselves, derive upon their Children, and convey into the World, and learn from hence to keep...

3   Every time we Swear rashly and falsely, we are adding to the heap of National <u>Guilt</u>, and Treasuring up Wrath against the Day of Wrath.

4   Farther yet, This dishonouring the Name of God by common Swearing has this other aggravating Circumstance of <u>Guilt</u>, that it leads to destroy all solemn Worship of God and Obedience to his Laws.

Figure 6.1 Four examples of the consequences of guilt.

young and the world in general. The second example is particularly noteworthy as it presents guilt as an almost virus-like entity, which, once contracted, spreads worldwide.[492] The third example presents guilt as a national problem – the guilt of the individuals in society, contracted in this case by swearing, weighs on the nation and invites the wrath of God (a common theme for the SRM).[493] Finally, in the fourth example, we can see the ultimate consequences of guilt for a society, once again occasioned by swearing: the complete breakdown of Christian society. The public consequences of these acts are made clear in examples such as those in Figure 6.2.

The examples in Figure 6.2 illustrate nicely the role of *public* as a *consequence* keyword. In the first example, the consequence of a large number of

1   the great Mischief that is done the <u>Public</u>, by suffering an unnecessary Number of Public-Houses.

2   unrestrained Vice and Profaneness are as fatal to <u>Public</u> Societies as they are destructive to Private Persons.

3   Where we may observe, that for the suppressing of Sin, and the preventing of <u>public</u> Guilt, even Parents were commanded to bring their own Children to be punished with Death.

4   Then indeed Severity to punish is truly Mercy, Mercy to the Offender, and Mercy to the <u>Public</u>.

Figure 6.2 Four examples of the consequences of wrongdoing for the public.

public houses is bad for the public. In the second example, sins cause the damage to both public institutions and individuals, a theme echoed in the *guilt* keyword. In the third example, the suppression of sin, in this case in a rather dramatic form, is the best way of avoiding the burden of guilt falling on the public.[494] Finally, the separation of the public from the offender implied throughout these examples is clearly spelt out – to be harsh to the offender is to be kind to the offender. This harshness is also a kindness to the public. I will return later to the question of the separation and identification of the offenders from the public. For the moment, it is sufficient to note that guilt, with its supposedly infectious nature, is the key consequence of the moral panic outlined by the SRM, and that that guilt has one notable victim: the public.

The supposed ultimate consequence of this national burden of guilt will be that the nation will be judged by God and found to be wanting. The consequences of this divine judgement will be profound indeed, as the examples given in Figure 6.3 show.

As in the case of the *guilt* keyword, what begins as a cause for the judgement of an individual (first and second examples) translates to the judgement of the nation as a whole (examples three and four). The actions of sinners threatens the exclusion of the entire nation from the Kingdom of God, as well as the assured expulsion of the sinner from that kingdom.

Corrective action

The keywords focused on corrective action (see Table 6.7) relate to legal processes (*judgement, magistrates, penalties*) or to actions individuals should

---

1   Hear, O ye Swearers, the Judgement that GOD has denounced against you! Every one that sweareth shall be cut off, from GOD.

2   But the pronounced Sentence after they are brought to Judgement, will be most fatal, reaching to an utter Exclusion from the Kingdom of Heaven.

3   [the actions of sinners] endangers our Cure, and makes our Condition desperate, if not irrecoverable. O England, my native Country, come to Judgement! Bring thy Deeds to the true Light; see whether they are wrought in GOD or no.

4   [sinners] make this Nation as guilty as most under Heaven, if not to be ripe for Judgement, than the Discountenance and Unsuccessfulness of pious and regular Endeavours for the Reformation of Manners.

Figure 6.3 Four examples of the nature of the judgement which will be brought on those guilty of sin.

Table 6.7 Corrective action keywords

Word	Frequency	Collocates in SRMC	Collocates in Lampeter B	Collocates in Lampeter A
magistrates	113	subordinate, unfaithful, brief, unfaithfulness, negligence, governors, worthy, ministers, reign, obligation	No collocates of magistrates with an MI greater than 3	ministers, whom
men	406	wisest, lower, election, ranks, promotion, distinguish, bargains	plots, virtuous, united, understanding, skill, mere, flood, useful, orders, write	sett, landed, elect, council, quarentine, natures
oath	54	solemn, church-warden, appeal, credit, commission, taking, taken, sacred, run, lawful	No collocates of oath with an MI greater than 3	tendred, perjury, examined, grand, promise, tender, solemn, witnesses, takes, jury
penalties	58	rogues, forfeit, sureties, shillings, pounds, pence, levied, witnesses, imprisonment, month	No collocates of penalties with an MI greater than 3	inflict, inflicting, pains, law

take to avoid sin (*oath*). To deal with the first set of keywords, *magistrates* and *penalties* are clearly enough associated with corrective action, with the emphasis, as Chapter 4 would lead us to expect, being on those magistrates who enforce the laws against immorality. The SRM urges respect for 'those Magistrates that conscientiously apply themselves to the Suppressing of Vice and Prophaneness' and commends 'Worthy magistrates' and 'Religious Magistrates'. Magistrates, however, as well as being presented as the means of suppressing vice, are also identified simultaneously as scapegoats – certain magistrates, i.e. those who did not apply the law as the SRM demanded, were identified as problems to be overcome by the SRM, as they were in part responsible for the vice as a consequence of their inactivity. These are identified as 'ill magistrates', 'Magistrates ... unfaithful to their office', 'vicious Examples of Magistrates' and even 'corrupt and unfaithful Magistrates'. Just as the population of Britain, in the eyes of the SRM, was divided into the generators of guilt and those who suffered the burden of that guilt, so the magistracy was divided by the SRM into those who were part of the answer to the problem and those who were part of the problem itself.

Penalties is a much more straightforward keyword to analyse. The discussion of penalties in the text is focused exclusively on the penalties to be exacted in retribution for specific sins. The imposition of penalties is presented as the principal action to be taken against sinners, with a comprehensive discussion of the penalties to be extracted 'arising from the breach of . . . Statutes and Laws' undertaken with a desire expressed that sinners should 'have the Penalties of . . . Laws levied upon them in the Sight of their Neighbours or their Country' as a means of punishing and discouraging sin.

The categorisation of *oath* as a corrective action needs a little explanation, as *prima facie* it would appear that *oath* should probably be in the object of offence category. However, an examination of the use of *oath* in the SRMC reveals that *oath*, while it does occur as an object of offence, is also associated with the legal act of swearing an oath when giving evidence against a sinner in court. The SRM identifies the 'Necessity of a Solemn Oath Before a Magistrate' as a key to the process of securing the prosecution of sinners. Hence *oath*, much as *magistrate*, is both a problem and a solution. Oaths, in the right context, i.e. the court room, are part of the solution to the problem of vice that the SRM was fighting against. However, it is the oath used outside of a religious and legal context that is problematised, with one of the writers complaining that: 'the Children are infected: The Boys of seven Years old, that in my Time did not think upon an Oath, are now full of their God-Damn-You's and God-Damn-Me's at their Sports and Plays!?'

Note that while I list *men* as a corrective action here, the word will be discussed in the scapegoat section.

Desired outcome

Given that there were problems identified by the SRM and solutions that they proposed, what was the desired outcome of their campaign? On one level it was clearly the desire to stop the actions they disapproved of, in order to avoid the negative consequences which they thought flowed from such actions. But were there any other consequences of an absence of vice? Table 6.8 shows the one keyword which seems to reveal the positive effects that they believed their campaign would bring about is the word *virtue*. The suppression of vice was not simply an act of moral neutrality for the SRM, it promoted virtue. This in itself presents an interesting view of virtue which was one which anti-SRM campaigners such as Sacheverell had argued against[495] – that virtue was a neutral state which, in order to flourish, had to have the overlying skin of vice which obscured it peeled away. The vice of a sinner is argued in one case to have 'destroyed the Virtue and good Manners perhaps of his whole Family', with virtue represented clearly as a thing destroyed not simply by the commission of sin, but by mere proximity to it. Sin is destructive, and 'Sins, rob us of our Reason, deface the Impressions of

Table 6.8 Desired outcome keyword

Word	Frequency	Collocates in SRMC	Collocates in Lampeter B	Collocates in Lampeter A
virtue	101	retrieving, preservation, distinguish, piety, famous, royal, despised, pretence, reflection, rank	prince, chap, god's, stage	divine, claim, makes

Virtue, and extinguish the Remembrance of GOD's Mercies and our own Duty'. Consequently, with the elimination of sin, the erosion of virtue will cease and, ultimately, England would witness 'the Advancement of Piety and Virtue, and the public Good both of Church and State'. As guilt has negative private and public consequences, conversely the elimination of sin and the promotion of virtue would have positive private and public consequences. The private consequences of virtue were the province of the naturally virtuous – this question will be returned to later when we consider the nature of the victory over vice as represented by the SRM. For the moment, it is sufficient to note that virtue was a desired consequence of the SRM campaign.

Moral entrepreneur

The moral entrepreneurs (see Table 6.9) are represented in the text by a reflexive pronoun, *ourselves*. It is this pronoun in the text which is used to refer to those Christians who have embarked on a process of cleansing society of its evils, often by setting an example to others. Consider the examples in Figure 6.4.

Ourselves refers to a Christian group (example 1) who are committing themselves to a course of action in a religious spirit (example 2) in order to combat the sins of their age (example 3). In example 3 we see them acting as moral entrepreneurs, encouraging the implementation of a corrective action

Table 6.9 Moral entrepreneur keyword

Word	Frequency	Collocates in SRMC	Collocates in Lampeter B	Collocates in Lampeter A
ourselves	92	something, renders, relate, acquaint, principal, righteousness, others, dangerous (3.09)	clergymen, among (5.12)	deny, easily, among, prove, each, we (3.50)

1   We profess <u>ourselves</u> to be Christians, Followers of that JESUS, in whose Mouth no Guile was ever found;

2   That we will daily exercise <u>ourselves</u> in Self-denial, Mortification, taking up of our Cross and following Christ, Watchfulness, Acts of Dependence on God, by holy Ejaculations, Self-examination and Self-judging; endeavouring to have always a good Conscience towards God and towards Man.

3   To the Worthy Magistrates concerned in this Cause of God. In disclosing my own Thoughts with Reference to <u>ourselves</u> I may safely as well as seasonably say, that all Wise and Good Men do too sadly own, That the Growth of Impiety, Profaneness and Immorality in this Nation, where the Light of the Gospel has Shined for many Ages, but in late Years with a brighter Lustre, is a Blot in our Fame and a Discredit to our Kingdom, and will prove our Unhappiness and Ruin, if the Contagion be not Prevented.

Figure 6.4 Concordances of *ourselves.*

(the application of laws against immorality by magistrates) and speaking as a group through the voice of the author (*my own Thoughts with Reference to ourselves*).[496]

Ourselves also serves another purpose, however. As a first person plural reflexive pronoun it is capable of blurring the line between the author and the reader, making the author's concerns at times appear to be those of the reader also. Such a use of the first person plural pronoun in English is hardly novel. This does not mean it is any less effective in insinuating the concerns of the writer into those of the reader, however.

Object of offence

The objects of offence in the keywords (see Table 6.10) vary from the specific (*profaneness, oath, swear, swearing, drunkenness*) to the general (*vice, sin, offences*). In each case in the text, the action is presented as problematic and undesirable, as the sample concordance for *swearing* in Figure 6.5 shows.

A notable feature of these items is their interconnectedness – both the collocates and the links in the 'object of offence' category show that these keywords are at times collocated and/or linked together. I will not discuss the objects of offence in any more detail for the moment, as they will be returned to as a set shortly (see pages 173–181).

Table 6.10 Object of offence keywords

Word	Frequency	Collocates in SRMC	Collocates in Lampeter B	Collocates in Lampeter A
profaneness	88	*immorality, debauchery, immoralities, suppressing, blasphemy, vigorous, vice, impiety, statutes, execution, increase*	*english, view, short, stage, much*	No collocates of *profaneness* with an MI greater than 3
swear	58	*falsely, charged, creatures, precept, disciples, curse, saith, head, saviour, shalt*	No collocates of *swear* with an MI greater than 3	*letters, against*
swearing	77	*cursing, lewdness, damning, profanation, parliament, excessive, examined, common, blasphemy, dismal*	*cursing, blasphemy, lewd, stage*	No collocates of *swearing* with an MI greater than 3
drunkenness	92	*rioting, excuses, profanation, drunken, lewdness, cursing, pernicious, benefit, consequences, excuse*	No collocates of *drunkenness* with an MI greater than 3	No collocates of *drunkenness* with an MI greater than 3
vice	122	*irreligion, boldly, addicted, fruits, maintenance, discouraging, profaneness, suppressing, commonly, keeping*	*lewdness, encouraged, apt, chap, stage, most*	*immorality*
sin	164	*aggravations, object, mock, voluptuousness, provoking, sodom, heinous, folly, prevailing, crying*	*original, death, without, own*	*mortal, remedy*
offences	79	*supra, month, quarter-sessions, disturb, warrant, sureties, rogues, prosecuted, forfeitures*	No collocates of *offences* with an MI greater than 3	*private, public, persons*

to this Sin of common Swearing, even when the Parents
Drunkenness, Profane Swearing and Cursing, and all oth
Blasphemy, Profane Swearing and Cursing, Lewdness,
Jer. xxiii. 10. Because of Swearing the Land mourneth. It w
ourselves. First, Profane Swearing is a Dishonour to God.
Blasphemy, Profane Swearing and Cursing, Lewdness,
in the late times Profane Swearing and Cursing, Drunkennes
Adulteries; and because of Swearing the Land mourneth: Beho
Warrants against profane Swearing and Cursing, Drunkennes
us, as Lewdness, Profane Swearing and Cursing, Drunkennes

Figure 6.5 A sample concordance of *swearing*.

Scapegoat

The two keywords, *men* and *offenders*, represent the scapegoats of the moral panics (see Table 6.11). However, with the scapegoat category more than any other category so far explored, a consideration of the collocates of these words is necessary to appreciate the true nature of the scapegoat identified by the SRM.

To begin with, however, let me focus back on the texts via concordancing. With reference to *men*, the first thing to note is that the term at times appears to refer to humankind rather than those who are males by sex. While the use of *men* to refer either to males or to the human race is not a unique property of early modern English, in the texts of the SRMC the term more often means *males* than *humans*. The reasons for this reading of the concordance lines for *men* from the SRMC is illustrated by the examples in Figure 6.6.

These examples show the different ways in which it is possible to classify uses of *men* as male-specific. In the first example this is possible because *men* is being contrasted with a female-specific term, *wife*. In the second example the roles associated with *men* are those typically held by men in late-seventeenth/early-eighteenth-century society. It is deeply unlikely, given the context, that *men* in such an example could be said to easily encompass females. The third example is longer, as it is an example of how a discussion which is specific to a single, abstract, male can be generalised to cover all men, i.e. males. While it is possible that *men* could apply to all people in this example, I think the natural reading of it is as part of a referential chain: *man–him–he–men–they–they*. The later, gender-neutral part of the chain inherits the meaning 'male' over 'person' from the gender-marked pronouns higher up the chain. While it could still be argued that the pronouns in this

Table 6.11 Scapegoat keywords

Word	Frequency	Collocates in SRMC	Collocates in Lampeter B	Collocates in Lampeter A
magistrates	113	*subordinate, unfaithful, brief, unfaithfulness, negligence, governors, worthy, ministers, reign, obligation*	No collocates of *magistrates* with an MI greater than 3	*ministers, whom*
men	406	*wisest, lower, election, ranks, promotion, distinguish, bargains*	*plots, virtuous, united, understanding, skill, mere, flood, useful, orders, write*	*sett, landed, elect, council, quarantine, natures*
offenders	51	*warrants, notorious, exemplary, principal, bringing, legal, hardened, punishment, informations*	No collocates of *magistrates* with an MI greater than 3	*ensuing, sessions, presented, trial, next, law*

1   Wife, <u>Men</u> and Christians are not so much afraid of ill Names, as of wicked Actions.

2   And since the Examples of <u>Men</u> in High and Public Stations, have a Powerful Influence upon the Lives of others; we do most humbly beseech . . .

3   What a mean and unworthy Reflection it is upon a Man of any tolerable Capacity to say of him, that he can find no other Employment but Drinking? What Pity it is, that such Powers and Perfections should be bestowed, and he not know how to use and improve them. Besides, this Plea is generally as false as it is mean. Because <u>Men</u> not only pursue this Vice when they have nothing else to do, but often to the Neglect of their proper Business and Calling, in which they may find sufficient Employment, and in which they are obliged to be constantly industrious, as they tender their Ease, Innocency, and Happiness.

4   That either these Bargains must be made before <u>Men</u> are disordered with Drinking, or afterwards.

Figure 6.6 Four examples of *men* meaning *males*.

case are generic, i.e. not gender specific, weighing against this would be an argument similar to that made for example two – the role being described in the text is one typical of males, not females, in the period in which the texts were written. Yet, further evidence can be gathered for an interpretation that *men* refers to male in the third example if we consider the fourth example. In the fourth example, as in the third, the men in question are drinking. In the corpus texts, drinking is an activity identified as being masculine. One might say that the verb DRINK has a preference for a male subject in these texts. The collocates for women in the text are typically very positive and reflect very much the late-seventeenth-century view of women as outlined in Chapter 4 (pages 114–115) – for example, the node *her* collocates with *patience* and *gracious*, while the node *women* demonstrates the perceived relationship between men and women at the time by collocating with the genitive pronoun *thine*. The one fault consistently related to certain women in the corpus is that of sexual wantonness, with *she* collocating with *lust* and *women* collocating with *lewd*.[497] By contrast, drunkenness is presented as a male vice – the node *man* collocates with *drinks*, for example. Given that these sins in the corpus can be argued to be associated with sinners of a particular gender, we have grounds to interpret example four as gender specific, and we are also furnished with further evidence which allows us to view example three as such.

So, it is actually males, by and large, who are seen as the scapegoats in the corpus. With the sole exception of sexually promiscuous women, it is males who are identified as the main perpetrators of sin. It is at this point that returning to consider the collocates of *men* is profitable. Not all men are viewed as scapegoats. There is a contrast in the corpus between those males who are viewed as good (the collocates *wisest*, *ranks*, *promotion*, *distinguish* mark them out), and those who are wicked (the collocate *lower* marks them out). The good men are actually viewed as part of the corrective action – it is through the actions of such men that the SRM is to be established and vice extinguished. Just as the public was split into offenders and the victims of offence by the discourse of the SRM, so men are divided into those of worth – high social class, educated – and those who imperil the very nation by their wrongdoing – those of low social class and, by implication, low education. The issue of social rank and the scapegoats/objects of offence in the SRMC will be returned to shortly with reference to spirals of signification. However, for the moment, consider the following example in Figure 6.7, which brings together corrective actions and scapegoats. All keywords bar those in the unclassified category are underlined.

In this example, the followers of the SRM are to pray for corrective action (good magistrates) to bring about the suppression of an object of offence (vice) in order to achieve a desired outcome (the maintenance of virtue). The scapegoats (magistrates who are lax in their duties) who permit an object of offence (profaneness) to go unpunished will imperil the very nation itself. Magistrates and men of quality should, rather, be part of the corrective

Indeed we cannot easily conceive how any Nation can be long happy without good <u>Magistrates</u>: So that 'tis with great Reason that our Church directs us to pray, That all that are put in Authority may truly and indifferently minister Justice, to the Punishment of Wickedness and <u>Vice</u>, and to the Maintenance of God's true Religion and <u>Virtue</u>; and that we esteem those that thus discharge their Duty as great Blessings to their Country, and may praise God for them; and, on the contrary, that we think that those unhappy <u>Men</u>, who under the Obligations of Oaths and Trusts have neglected or opposed the Execution of the Laws for the Punishment of Wickedness and <u>Vice</u>, and Maintenance of Religion, do deservedly lie under the dreadful imputation of having been a great Cause of the <u>Profaneness</u> and Debauchery of the Nation, and the fatal Enemies of it, since we may look on that Nation, whether it be our Own, or any other, to be in a very languishing Condition, and in manifest danger of Ruin, where the <u>Magistrates</u>, and the Generality of <u>Men</u> of greater Ranks, who have, by their being placed in higher Stations, as Stars in higher Orbs, so many Advantages to conduct the lower Ranks of <u>Men</u> by the shining Examples of virtuous Lives, to support the Reputation and Interest of <u>Virtue</u>, do, by the Abuse of their Authority, or by their vicious Behaviour, scatter a pestilential Infection whereever they come, basely make use of the Advantages they have above others to the Dishonour of God, by whose Permission they enjoy them; instead of being Patrons of Religion, help to debauch those about them, and ruin their Country.

Figure 6.7 The discourse of moral panic in action.

actions to sustain virtue. The implication being that the 'lower Ranks of Men' must be led away from the vice that the social betters of those men should shun.

Offenders as a scapegoat requires less justification, as the offenders are clearly those whom the SRM were campaigning against.[498] Yet the collocates of *offenders* help us to link this group back to the corrective action keywords, most notably through the collocate *punishment*.[499] Other collocates clearly link to the legal processes which will bring about the penalties the SRM wished to see imposed on the offenders (*warrants*,[500] *bringing*, *informations*, *legal*[501]). Also apparent in the list of collocates is the negative view taken by the SRM of offenders (*notorious*, *hardened*).

Moral panic rhetoric

In discussing the word *and*, I would like to recall that earlier in this chapter we saw that *or* appeared as a negative keyword when Lampeter A was com-

Table 6.12 Moral panic rhetoric keywords

Word	Frequency	Collocates in SRMC	Collocates in Lampeter B	Collocates in Lampeter A
and	6,005	No collocates of *and* with an MI greater than 3	No collocates of *and* with an MI greater than 3	No collocates of *and* with an MI greater than 3
etc	64	*rogues, warrant, levy, goods, forfeitures, church-wardens, sale*	*jure, apour, love, new, death*	*ores, flints, chalk, marble, serpents, communitat, clothing, astronomical, arches, teeth*
will	616	No collocates of *will* with an MI greater than 3	*thither, pardon, frequented, forsake, ungodliness, hurt, weaken, unlearned, secure, apt*	No collocates of *will* with an MI greater than 3

pared to Lampeter B, but was removed from the keyword list when the SRMC was compared to Lampeter A. *And* appears as a positive keyword irrespective of whether the SRMC is compared to either Lampeter A or B. I recall *or* here as it is clear that the coordinator *and* is strongly associated with the language of the SRMC. *Or* also, while not key, is not shunned by the SRMC, unlike Lampeter B, i.e. when Lampeter A is used as a reference corpus *or* is a negative keyword in Lampeter B, but it is not when the SRMC is compared to Lampeter A. Yet, the processes surrounding *and* in the SRMC are also those surrounding *or*. For the moment, I will leave this as an unsupported assertion, though it is discussed in detail in the following section on spirals of signification. I claim that the coordinators are used in the SRMC text as part of the discourse of a moral panic, in that they are used with the important function of linking objects of offence to form networks of offence. These networks of offence are often visible as collocational networks, though the collocation here might more reasonably be called colligation, or at least we may say that the collocation is shading towards colligation, as the networking is achieved in part not merely by proximity, but by grammatical coordination. The claim that such coordination exists is clearly a major one, and it is for that reason that the section on spirals of signification will deal with this matter at length. My discussion of this here is oriented towards justifying the inclusion of *and* in the moral panic rhetoric category. Given that spirals of signification are important to a moral panic discourse, the identification of a linguistic mechanism which may form such a spiral is clearly important, and is clearly linked to rhetorical effects sought by the writers of the documents in the SRMC. If my claim is supportable, then the moral panic is managed in the text by coordination to such a degree that coordination using *and* is so frequent that it becomes a salient part of the language of a moral panic, and *or* is used frequently enough for the word to lose its status as a negative keyword, a status one would predict given the religious register of the SRMC.

Before leaving the discussion of the word *and*, I would like to comment briefly on another possible approach that I could have taken to organising the keywords in the SRMC – using a 'stop-list' to filter out function words from the keyword list. The use of stop-lists to eliminate high-frequency, typically closed-class, items from corpus analysis is far from uncommon.[502] The practice troubles me, as I have often thought that it would be possible for such words to form an important part of an analysis under the right circumstances. In the case of *and* here, I believe we have just such a case.[503] While I concede that it may be the case that, on the majority of occasions, high-frequency items will not be key, it is a brave, or rather foolish, analyst who assumes that, in any given data set, the words are so unlikely to be key that they can be safely ignored from the very start.

The word *etc.*, I believe, also belongs in the moral panic rhetoric category. The use of the word *etc.* in the SRMC betokens a notable vagueness in the identification of scapegoats and objects of offence in particular. This vagueness is certainly reflected in the scapegoat category – all of the scapegoats are general (e.g. *men*) rather than specific (e.g. *Mr Williams of 22 Acacia Avenue, Hove*). It is also true of the keyword *ourselves*, as previously noted. In the use of vagueness in defining scapegoats and object of offence, the SRM is implying that beyond those objects of offence and scapegoats discussed in the text, there are others which are not discussed. Consider the examples in Figure 6.8

In each of the examples in Figure 6.8 there is a vagueness about the offences (examples 1 and 2) and the offenders (example 3) under discussion. While in the first and second examples, some specific offences are mentioned (*adultery, cursing, drunkenness, lewdness*) the effect of the *etc.* in each case is to imply that a much longer list of offences could be provided.[504] The SRM are merely presenting the most salient, perhaps the most offensive, behaviour in the text. Other behaviour was also a matter of offence to them – yet it is not mentioned. The effect of a list of offences, such as that in example two, is interesting. The list in example two goes a good way towards completing a list of the offences outlined by the SRM moral panic. Such lists, as will be shown in the next section, are common in the SRM texts. Why, having given such a precise list, does the writer conclude it with *etc.*? As already noted, one consequence is to imply that there are further offences. But I would also argue that the use of *etc.* here is implying that there are further offences far too numerous to mention – in short, the use of *etc.* here has the effect of exaggerating the range of sins to be combated, and hence amplifies the moral panic discourse. The country is afflicted with so many sins, bringing with them their attendant tidal wave of damaging infectious guilt, that to list them would be wearying. It is also arguable that by casting such a

1 If a Constable, <u>etc.</u> has Notice that a Woman is in Adultery, *etc.* with a Man, or that a Man or Woman of evil Fame is gone to a suspect house . . .

2 There is no doubt but the Gallows is a great Grievance to Murderers, the Discipline of Bridewell to Whores, the Pillory to the Perjured, and the Stocks to Drunkards: But such Grievances as these are, I conceive, of near as long standing as Government, and will not be thought proper to be laid aside whilst it lasts, or at least till there is not so much Occasion for them, since, as hath been proved, its Interest and chief Business is to cherish and support Religion, and, by consequence, to take care that it be not treated with any disrespect, particularly, that it be not made the Scorn of any Order or Body of Men, the common Subject of the Profane Play-Houses, or the Sport of Buffoons; and that the open Violations of it by Profane Swearing and Cursing, Drunkenness, Lewdness <u>etc.</u> be suppressed, as all wise Nations, I conceive, have ever done, and ever will do.

3 Officers remiss in Punishing of Rogues, *etc.*

Figure 6.8 Three examples of the use of *etc.*

wide and vague net over offenders and offences, the SRM's goal of achieving a 'just terror' was enabled.[505]

The final keyword I will discuss here is the last to join the category of moral panic rhetoric – *will*. This word can, of course, have a number of uses. However, in the SRMC, the word *will* is predominantly a modal auxiliary, and more specifically it is a marker of volition/prediction.[506] There are 616 examples of *will* in the SRMC. Of these, 596 occurrences are of *will* as a modal verb. The remaining 20 examples all refer to the abstract noun *will*, which overwhelmingly refers to the will of God (15 of the 20 examples).

A feature of the use of *will* in the SRMC relates to the passive voice. There is a high proportion of uses of *will* with the passive voice in the data. No less than 75 of the 596 (12.6 per cent) of the uses of the modal verb *will* are in the passive voice. Consider the examples in Figure 6.9.

The use of *will* in the passive voice is rare in modern English[507] – but what of late-seventeenth-century English? The number of passives in Lampeter B was investigated in order to determine whether the use of the passive voice with *will* in the SRMC was unusual for religious texts. In Lampeter B, from a total of 265 examples of *will* as a modal verb, 36 (13.54 per cent) are in the passive voice. In contrast, Lampeter A has 1,913 examples of *will* as a modal verb, of which 146 (7.6 per cent) are in the passive voice.[508] Interestingly, however, when the SRMC is compared to Lampeter B,

---

1   The notions of Good and evil <u>will be soon confounded</u> . . .
2   In the mean while, so long as his Profanation continues, he <u>will be punished</u> . . .
3   And neither of these <u>will be denied</u> the most intemperate Persons from the Wisest and Best of Men.

Figure 6.9 Will in passive constructions.

Lampeter B also has a higher proportion of passivised uses of *will* than the SRMC.[509] Yet when the SRMC is compared to Lampeter A, we find that the SRMC uses the passivised *will* much more often than is typical in general English.[510] Once again, however, we discover that the SRMC is much closer to the religious texts than to general English – the difference in the frequency of usage of the passive *will* in the SRMC is much less marked by comparison to religious texts than to general English.

In order to understand why both the religious texts and, more importantly, the SRMC use *will* in the passive voice more frequently than in general English, we must consider the effect of the use of the passive voice. The effect relates, once again, to vagueness – the passive voice 'is used to avoid explicit identification of the person who is obliged to act'.[511] Consider the examples in Figure 6.9. Who will confound the notions of good and evil? Who will punish the perpetrator of profanation? Who is the potential denier? The interesting combination here is the potential predictive certainty on the one hand of *will*, which has at least the appearance here of being predictive, and the notable vagueness regarding who is to act. Vagueness seeps from the verb *will* itself into the sentence and is deepened by the unusually frequent choice of passive constructions in the SRMC. It is on these grounds that I place *will* in the moral panic rhetoric category.

Spirals of signification

The previous section explored the way in which the SRM texts constructed a moral panic and the way in which that moral panic is coded in the texts of the SRMC. In demonstrating this, I made use of collocations, yet I did not explore the interconnection between collocates and nodes, i.e. how patterns of meaning might network. I also deferred part of the discussion of the keyword *and*. The reason for the postponement of the discussion of networks, and the node *and*, is that, in the SRMC texts, the two are closely associated, in that both are means of achieving what have been identified by researchers in moral panic theory as *spirals of signification* (or *signification spirals*), that is, the threat posed in the moral panic:

Increases the perceived potential threat of an issue through the way it becomes signified.[512]

Significantly, signification spirals draw links between activities in order to amplify a threat through a process of convergence:

> Convergence occurs when two or more activities are linked in a process of signification as to implicitly or explicitly draw parallels between them.[513]

Moral panics can occur in clusters, or have concepts clustered within them.[514] *And* is a keyword because it is intimately associated with forcing convergence in the text – bringing together objects of offence in a grammatical structure, a noun phrase exhibiting coordination, for example. This process of convergence at the grammatical level is mirrored by a convergence at the level of the collocational network, I will argue. This in turn contributes to a signification spiral within the discourse of the SRMC.

Coordination and convergence

For the moment, let me focus on the use of phrasal coordination to achieve convergence. Table 6.13 shows how often, as a proportion of the total number of occurrences of each keyword, an object of offence keyword occurs as part of a coordinated phrase in the SRMC and Lampeter B.[515]

What is clear from Table 6.13 is that there is a relationship between most of the objects of offence and coordination in the SRMC, which is not typical of religious texts written in English at the time. With the exception of *offences* and *oath*, all of the object of offence words coordinate together much

Table 6.13 Coordination of objects of offence in the SRMC

Word	SRMC		Lampeter B		Sig. (log-likelihood) of coordinated occurrences
	Frequency	Coordinated occurrences	Frequency	Coordinated occurrences	
drunkenness	92	20	1	0	22.70
offences	79	0	2	0	0.00
profaneness	94	81	11	5	62.16
sin	164	23	18	5	8.20
swear	58	5	1	0	5.68
swearing	77	16	6	4	4.84
vice	122	34	10	4	19.71
oath	54	1	0	0	1.14
Total	740	180	49	18	

more frequently in the SRMC than they do in Lampeter B. This is further evidence of a process of convergence in the SRMC focused on *and*.

Given that there is evidence for a process of convergence in the text, governed by *and*, which should properly be called a colligation, what is converging in the SRMC? Table 6.14 gives, for each keyword which is coordinated in the corpus, a list of the words with which it is coordinated. Figures in parentheses following words give the frequency of words coordinated with a keyword where that word coordinates more than once.

Table 6.14 picks up at least one feature captured by the MI scores already: the strong mutual link between *vice* and *profaneness*. There is clearly a powerful convergence of these two ideas in the SRMC. Yet what of the other keywords? There are examples in Table 6.14 of words colligating strongly with negatively marked words, i.e. exhibiting negative semantic prosody. But what is truly remarkable is the ragtag of negatively loaded words associated with the object of offence keywords with low frequency. To take *swearing* as an example, this has a strong link to a number of negatively loaded collocates through the MI score; *cursing, lewdness, damning, profanation, common,* and *blasphemy* are all collocates of *swearing* (see Table 6.10) that appear coordinated with it also. Yet the words coordinated with *swearing* which do not collocate

Table 6.14 Words coordinated with keywords in the SRMC

Word	Coordinated with
drunkenness	backbiting, chambering, contention, cursing (6), excess, fornication, gluttony, injustice, intemperance, lewdness (5), lying, murders, perjury, practices, profanation (6), rapines, rioting (5), sabbath-breaking, slandering, surfeiting (2), swearing (8), tipling, treachery, vices, wantonness, whoredoms (2)
profaneness	blasphemy (3), debauchery (31), immoralities (4), immorality (19), impiety (3), irreligion, oaths, religion, ribaldry, vice (25)
sin	danger, excess, fear, filthiness, folly (4), guilt (2), helplessness, horror, illness, inhumanity, luxury, mischief, misery, nature, odiousness, punishment, sense, shame, sight, vanity, wickedness
swear	blaspheme, curse (4), damn, game, hector, rant
swearing	backbiting, blaspheming, blasphemy (2), chambering, contention, cursing (16), damning (2), dancing, drinking (4), drunkenness (5), fiddling, gaming, injustice, intemperance, lewdness (4), lying, perjury, profanation (5), rioting, sabbath-breaking, slandering, thieving, wantonness, whoring
vice	debauchery, immorality (2), irreligion (3), profaneness (25), ruin, virtue (3), wickedness (3)
oath	words

with it according to the MI measure I have used, make sense if we allocate them to one of four semantic fields, grouping the words under the broad categories of *malefaction, merriment, sex*[516] and *verbal acts*. The category of malefaction covers *injustice, intemperance, lying, perjury, rioting, sabbath-breaking, slandering* and *thieving*. Merriment covers *dancing, drinking, drunkenness, fiddling* and *gaming*, while sex covers *chambering,*[517] *lewdness, wantonness* and *whoring*. The verbal acts are: *backbiting, blaspheming, blasphemy, contention,*[518] *cursing, damning* and *profanation*. While I concede that these categories are broad, impressionistic and susceptible to subdivision, they do at least allow us to begin to make sense of the process of convergence that occurs in the SRMC. For example, the word *swearing* is being systematically associated with other disapproved of verbal acts, lawlessness, frivolous pursuits and sexual activity. Swearing on its own may be objectionable, but with such convergence in the text between swearing and other sins, a signification spiral is established in the text in which single offences converge, a strong negative semantic prosody is generated and a panic is amplified.

These categories can also be applied to the other objects of offence, with the notable exception of the word *sin*. *Sin* contains two further converging semantic fields which I will term *opprobrium* and *peril*. Table 6.15 lists which word forms in which semantic fields are associated with which objects of offence. In the third column of the table I have listed the convergent semantic fields for the object of offence. I have used a rough rule-of-thumb cut-off to determine convergence, with a field being convergent if at least five examples of the word forms in that field are found in the coordinated phrases represented in Table 6.15.

Given that convergence exists, it is clear that it is not linked straightforwardly to objects of offence. One object of offence, interestingly, is excluded from the process of convergence: *oath*. *Oath* is, of course, distinct from the other objects of offence in another way: it is the only object of offence which is also categorised as a corrective action. A plausible explanation of *oath*'s failure to converge is that, if this happened, then *oath* in its more positive sense may become associated with the process of convergence. Assuming that this explanation is sufficient to explain the exclusion of *oath* from the process of convergence (it is at least plausible), what of the other words? Across this set, convergence is still not homogenous. Two categories – opprobrium and peril – are associated with *sin* alone. The number of semantic fields converging around a given keyword varies between one to four. There is no one semantic field on which all of the keywords converge. The rank order of the semantic fields, based on the number of 'object of offence' words converging on them, are malefaction (5), verbal (5), sex (4), merriment (3), opprobrium (1), peril (1). So, if we take it that the fields on which each of the objects of offence converge is indicative of the basis of the signification spiral, then we can see malefaction, verbal acts, sex and merriment combining together in the discourse of the SRMC in order to generate associations between objects and actions.

Table 6.15 Convergence in the moral panic

Word	Distribution across categories	Word convergent with
drunkenness	**Malefaction**: *injustice, intemperance, lying, murders, perjury, rapines, rioting* (5), sabbath-breaking, treachery, vices **Merriment**: *excess, gluttony, surfeiting* (2), *tipling* **Sex**: *chambering, fornication, lewdness* (5), *wantonness, whoredoms* (2) **Verbal**: *backbiting, contention, cursing* (6), *profanation* (6), *slandering, swearing* (8) **Other**: *practices*	Malefaction, merriment, sex, verbal
profaneness	**Malefaction**: *immoralities* (4), *immorality* (19), *impiety* (3), *irreligion, vice* (25) **Merriment**: *ribaldry* **Sex**: *debauchery* (31) **Verbal**: *blasphemy* (3), *oaths* **Other**: *religion*	Malefaction, sex, verbal
sin	**Malefaction**: *inhumanity, mischief, punishment, wickedness* **Merriment**: *excess, luxury* **Opprobrium**: *folly* (4), *guilt* (2), *horror, misery, odiousness, shame* **Peril**: *danger, fear, helplessness* **Other**: *filthiness, illness, nature, sense, sight, vanity*	Malefaction, merriment, opprobrium, peril
swear	**Merriment**: *game* **Verbal**: *blaspheme, curse* (4), *damn, hector, rant*	Verbal
swearing	**Malefaction**: *injustice, intemperance, lying, perjury, rioting, sabbath-breaking, slandering, thieving* **Merriment**: *dancing, drinking, drunkenness, fiddling, gaming* **Sex**: *chambering, lewdness, wantonness, whoring* **Verbal**: *backbiting, blaspheming, blasphemy, contention, cursing, damning, profanation*	Malefaction, merriment, sex, verbal
vice	**Malefaction**: *immorality* (2), *irreligion* (3), *wickedness* (3) **Merriment**: **Sex**: *debauchery* **Verbal**: *profaneness* (25) **Other**: *ruin, virtue* (3)	Malefaction, sex, verbal
oath	**Verbal**: words	Not convergent

Collocation and convergence

While fruitful, so far my search for patterns of association has been limited to coordination focused on colligations around *and*. What of the collocates of the words? Do they provide further evidence of convergence and a signification spiral? In order to explore this point, I would like to establish a collocational network from the collocates of the two nodes, *swearing* and *drunkenness*, largely because these words converge in a very similar way, and one would hope that this convergence would be mirrored in the collocational networks around the nodes.

In order to explore these collocational networks, I will first construct two directional collocational networks, one for *swearing* and one for *drunkenness*. The networks are shown in Figures 6.10 and 6.11.[519]

In constructing the network, I am simply linking the collocates and nodes. The direction of the link depends on whether the node or the collocate has the higher proportion of all cases of its occurrence accounted for by the collocation. In the graph, to the right of each node I will give the total number of occurrences of the node in the SRMC.

The graphs are interesting in that they partly reflect the way in which convergence occurs in the corpus. For swearing, it is possible to place six collocates in the convergence semantic fields by placing *excessive* in merriment, *lewdness* in sex, and *cursing*, *damning*, *profanation* and *blasphemy* in verbal acts. Note that in each of these cases a process of collocation is reinforcing what is in essence a process of colligation driven by *and*, which, in turn, is bringing about convergence for some of these words through coordination anyway. For *drunkenness*, it is possible to place *drunken*

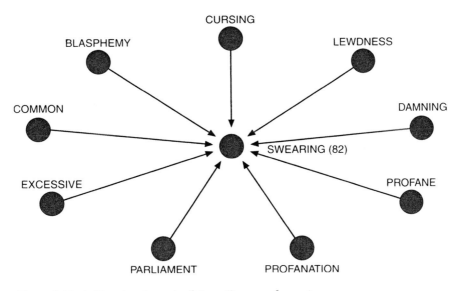

Figure 6.10 A directional graph of the collocates of *swearing*.

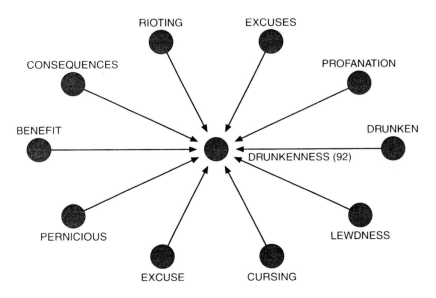

Figure 6.11 A directional graph of the collocates of *drunkenness.*

in merriment, *rioting* in malefaction, *lewdness* in sex, and *cursing* and *pro-fanation* in verbal acts. This leaves a sub-set of collocates which are not associated with the convergence semantic fields: *profane, parliament* and *common* for *swearing* and *benefit, consequences, excuse, excuses* and *pernicious* for *drunkenness.*

The fact that there is some commonality between the colligation and collocation is reassuring – association is being used to both colligationally and collocationally associate the objects of offence with negatively loaded words. Yet, at the collocational level at least, something else is happening. In the case of *swearing*, we have three unclassified words, two of which do not readily map to an existing convergent semantic field. *Profane*, of course, could. It does not coordinate with *swearing* as the parts of speech of the two words differ, one being an adjective and the other a gerund or verb in the coordinated structures examined earlier. However, with the addition of an appropriate suffix, we see *profanation* quite happily coordinating with *swearing*. *Parliament* is as easily explained as *profane* – in each of its collocations with swearing it is in the phrase 'Act of Parliament against Swearing and Cursing', i.e. it is a link between the objects of offence and the corrective action proposed by the SRM. The most interesting example here is *common*, though in part the reason for its failure to coordinate with swearing is just the same as for *profane* – part of speech. I shall set aside the discussion of this collocate for the moment, and focus on it in the next section when I consider bad language alone. For the moment, it is sufficient to say that the discussion of the attempts of the SRM to force a distinction between the middle and lower orders in society, in part by a focus on the use of bad language by the lower orders, seems to provide a compelling explanation for this collocate.

Drunkenness has a higher number of collocates unaccounted for by the semantic fields identified with the coordinated structures surrounding the objects of offence.

Pernicious can be dealt with immediately by noting that in collocation, but not in colligation, the node *drunkenness* is associated with the semantic field of peril. The words *benefit*, *excuse* and *excuses* can be accounted for by a rhetorical device 'The [nth] Excuse for Drunkenness upon the Account of Benefit, is to . . .' used repeatedly in the SRMC. This device accounts for all of the associations of these three words with *drunkenness*.

Before discussing the representation of bad language in the SRMC, I would like to consider the links between the collocation graphs. As well as coordination bringing about convergence, I would argue that collocational networks do also. Words share collocates. In sharing collocates, some degree of convergence, one could argue, must be forced. I have connected together the graphs in Figures 6.10 and 6.11, minus frequency information, in Figure 6.12 to illustrate this point, with links formed by joint collocates. Nuclear nodes, which for this purpose are nodes with one or more inward arcs, i.e. the direction of collocation is towards them, are emboldened.

Collocational networks, as well as coordination, specify a set of properties that objects of offence share in common. Both *drunkenness* and *swearing* are linked, by collocation, to *cursing*, *lewdness* and *prophanation*. I will call collocates such as these, which link two nodes, 'linking collocates'. Each of these linking collocates is also linked to *drunkenness* and *swearing* by colligation. Further words are shared by the two by virtue of common colligation only: *backbiting*, *chambering*, *contention*, *injustice*, *intemperance*, *lying*, *rioting*, *sabbath-breaking*, *slandering*, *wantonness* and *whoring*. Concepts are busily brushed together in the SRMC in just the way that sociologists have claimed happens in a moral panic, resulting in a spiral of signification: swearing is not simply the uttering of an offensive word. It associates the speaker of that word with a host of negative acts which have been connected to that act by the discourse of the SRM.

Associations are occurring in the moral panic at a number of levels, and convergence is clearly observable. It is this process of convergence that, I claim, was being used by the SRM to construct modern attitudes to bad language. Figure 6.13 gives a pared-down view of the whole network, focusing solely on the object of offence keywords and collocates shared by two or more nodes.

It is no mistake that I placed *swearing* at the centre of Figure 6.13 – in terms of convergence through collocation, I would argue that *swearing* does very much sit at the centre of this collocational network. It is linked directly by one linking collocate to three of the four other nuclear nodes in this diagram. As connectivity in this case can be said to translate to convergence,

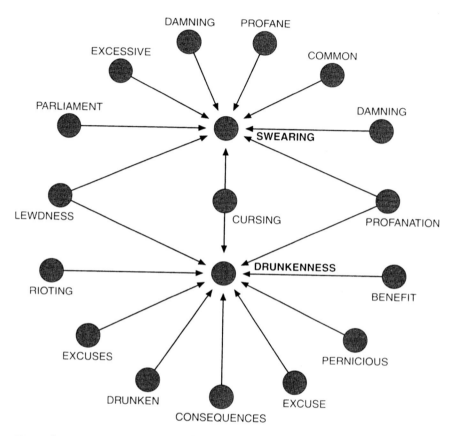

Figure 6.12 Two graphs joined to form a network.

one may also say that no other nuclear node in this diagram is as prone to the process of convergence. Even if we dismiss the nuclear node *swear*, as *swearing* is merely a variant form of that word, there are no other nuclear nodes better connected than *swearing*. If there is a process of convergence at work in the SRMC, as I would argue there is, then *swearing* is a focal point for the convergence – it has the single largest number of words coordinated with it by colligation[520] and is the focus, I would argue, of the collocational network in which the objects of offence in the SRMC may be placed. Given this, it is now time to consider the representation of bad language in the SRMC in a little more detail. Before I do so, however, I would like to briefly consider convergence in the SRMC with reference to Lampeter A and B.

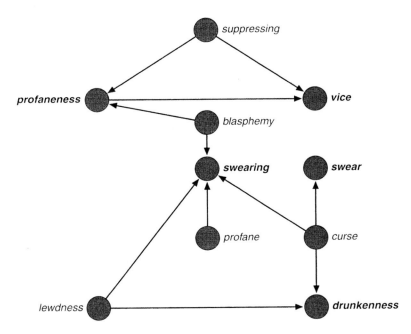

Figure 6.13 Objects of offence and their linking collocates.

Convergence in the SRMC

One of the main arguments put forward, currently backed up largely by the historical study of the SRM undertaken in Chapter 4, is that it was the SRM which generated, or at least popularised, the type of convergence of negative ideas around bad language that we have seen in the previous sub-section, through the medium of a moral panic as explored earlier in this chapter. Textual evidence can also be drawn from the SRMC, Lampeter A and B to support that claim. The process of convergence described here is largely absent from Lampeter A and B. While the objects of offence discussed in the SRMC are mentioned in Lampeter A and B, they do not converge with one another and other negative concepts. This does not happen by a process of collocation, and it certainly does not happen through a process of colligation. Words which are focus points for convergence in the SRMC sometimes lack any collocates at all in Lampeter A or B. *Profaneness* and *swearing* have no collocates in Lampeter A. *Swear* and *offences* have no collocates in Lampeter B. Most markedly *drunkenness*, an important focus for convergence in the SRMC, has no collocates in either Lampeter A or B (see Table 6.10). *Swear*, which has collocates in the SRMC and Lampeter A only, is clearly used primarily in its legal sense in Lampeter A, unlike the SRMC. *Offences*, which also has collocates only in the SRMC and Lampeter A, has an entirely different set of collocates in both corpora. *Profaneness* and *swearing* have collocates in Lampeter B and the SRMC. No collocates are shared by the SRMC and Lampeter B, and the semantic fields we saw converging on *profaneness* in the SRMC are absent from the collocates of Lampeter B (*english, much, short, stage, view*). However, the collocate *stage* is of interest in Lampeter B, as it is a linking collocate between *profaneness* and *swearing*. Indeed, *swearing* in the SRMC and Lampeter B seems to be the only word where a similar process of convergence is at work in both corpora, with the collocates *cursing* and *blasphemy* being associated with *swearing* in both. However, the word *stage* is a clue as to why this is the case. All of the examples of the word *swearing* in Lampeter B bar one come from the same document – a document from 1730.[521] This file, coming from late in the period, has arguably already been affected by the moral panic discourse of the 1690s. There is text-internal evidence for this – the text is concerned with bad language on the stage, and as such is part of a tradition of discourses about bad language on the stage, leading back to the very roots of the SRM with Collier's attack on the stage (see pages 85–86). The text actually identifies itself with Collier's attack on the stage:

> Those Plays, (Love for Love, and Tunbridge-Walks, etc.) which were justly exposed by Collier, at the first Attack upon the Stage, as most scandalous for Swearing, Cursing, Smut, Burlesquing the sacred Scriptures, and all other Sorts of Profaneness, continue still to be acted with the same Applause as formerly.

In short, this text appears to have a similar pattern of convergence to the SRMC texts, as its source of inspiration is the ideas encoded in the SRMC texts.

For those words which have collocates in all three corpora (*vice, sin*), Lampeter A clearly differs in its patterns of collocation from the SRMC – the pattern of convergence in the SRMC is not present in Lampeter A. The same is true for the word *sin* in Lampeter B; its collocates in Lampeter B do not indicate a convergence similar to that in the SRMC. With *vice*, while the pattern of convergence is not the same, one could note that it appears that *sex* shows some sign of converging with *vice* in Lampeter B, through collocation with *lewdness*. However, as *sex* is not one of the fields of convergence for *vice* in the SRMC, we can certainly say that the pattern of convergence in the SRMC is not shared by Lampeter B. We can say a little bit more than this, however. All examples of *vice* collocating with *lewdness* come from one text – the same text in which *swearing* shows a similar pattern of convergence as in the SRMC.

While not conclusive, this study does at least provide persuasive evidence for one of my claims about bad language – that the SRM was responsible for beginning the process whereby bad language came to be associated with a wide range of negatively loaded concepts in British society.

Very bad language

It should be apparent from the preceding section that bad language – profanation, swearing, cursing, damning, blasphemy – is presented in a very negative light in the writings of the SRM. It is a focal point of convergence in this moral panic discourse. As such, it is linked to malefaction, licentious merriment and sex. Yet there is a key collocate of bad language in the SRMC which I have, so far, only considered very briefly: *common*. This word must now be examined in detail. Figure 6.14[522] shows the collocational network in the immediate vicinity of *common*.

Common is second as a collocate only to *swearing* – the direction of collocation is towards *common* in all other cases where it collocates with a word. It is possible to group the collocates of *common* into four semantic fields – two semantic fields previously used in this chapter (opprobrium and verbal acts) and two new semantic fields, distinction (words used to denote a group in society on secular grounds) and religion (discussion of religion which may include the possibility of defining a group in society on religious grounds). The words collocating with *common* group as follows:

- Distinction: *civility, genteel, ordinary*
- Opprobrium: *heinous*
- Religion: *christianity*
- Verbal acts: *discourse, opinion,*[523] *swearing, swearer, conversation*

The semantic fields, more so in this case than in previous cases we have considered in this chapter, are associated with specific meanings of the word

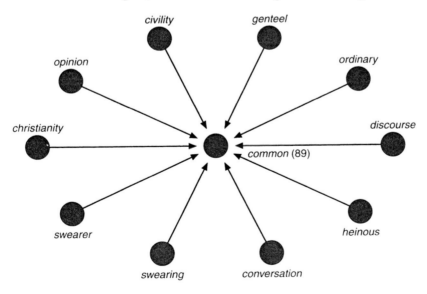

Figure 6.14 Collocates of *common*.

common.[524] *Common* is used with two specific senses in the SRMC: (i) something shared by all; or (ii) something that is usual. Figures 6.15 and 6.16 give examples of both meanings of *common*.

The first meaning of *common* covers all of the collocations of *christianity* and *common*. In total, the word *common* appears with this sense 24 times in the corpus. The word is used to create an 'in' group and an 'out' group, in much the same way as *public* and *offender* as keywords set up an 'in' and 'out' group in the exploration of moral panic discourses earlier in this chapter. The in-group is typified by common goals that are identifiably good by the standards of the SRM – *'body of christians'*, *cause*,[525] *'cause of christianity'* (twice), *'cause of religion'*, *'duties and virtues'*, *duty*, *'friend and protector'*, *good* and

---

1   I ask leave therefore, in this <u>common</u> Cause of Religion, humbly to apply myself.

2   Robberies, Fires, and other Villainies, that have been done in drunken Fits, make Drunkenness a <u>common</u> Enemy to human Society.

3   This is the Voice of Interest, for the <u>common</u> Good of the whole Society, Rulers and Ruled.

4   With these Encouragements they prosecuted their Business, increasing their Number by the Addition of Persons of considerable Note, and of the best Character; some of whom, though they were of different Opinions from those of the Established Church, as to some Points concerning Religion, were willing to unite their strength in the <u>common</u> Cause of Christianity, and engage in so Noble a Design, that had done so much Good . . .

Figure 6.15 Common meaning something shared by all.

---

1   In truth, I think 'tis much to be feared, but being very unwilling to fall under the too <u>common</u> Error of not duly considering Human Frailties and Prejudices . . .

2   It is their <u>common</u> Diversion and Entertainment.

3   Repeated Curses are indeed the rash, but yet too <u>common</u>, Returns, when we unseasonably check a Profane Swearer and Blaspheming Wretch.

4   Because they want Society and Company, or good Fellowship, the <u>common</u> Plea that is usually pretended and generally made.

Figure 6.16 Common meaning something that is usual.

'*reason of mankind*'. The out-group, on the other hand, is referred to in terms of how the in-group identifies them: *enemy, enemies* (twice), *nuisance*, and the consequences of the actions of the out-group for the in-group if it does not act, *guilt*[526] means that those failing to act against the out-group will become tainted by the actions of the out-group and will become, in essence, a member of the out-group.

While the word *common* in its first sense is largely concerned with establishing the universality of the concerns of the in-group and contrasting them with the out-group, the second sense of *common* is reserved for the out-group. The usual, the ordinary and the typical are locuses of sin. It is in this sense that *swearing* collocates with *common*. With it are a host of other negatively charged words, all converging on this meaning of *common*. *Common* in this sense is the most frequent use of *common* in the SRMC, occurring 65 times. It is strongly associated with bad language in everyday speech, modifying *conversation* (7), *discourse* (4), *profanation, returns* (cursing), *swearer* (2), *swearing* (20) and *to hear* (bad language) (2). No less than 36 of the 65 uses of *common* in the sense of everyday/ordinary are associated with bad language. I will return to discuss this point shortly.

The remaining uses of *common* are related to the out-group (*disturbers, 'profane Play Houses', whore-masters, soldier, seaman*), its actions (*covetousness, vice, practice* (3)[527]), and the consequences of its action (*effect, error, consequences, fate*). Set against this group are a number of words typical of the in-group such as *christians, civility* and *honesty*. However, these words are negated in the examples – they are being used to distinguish the out-group as not possessing these qualities. For example, consider the following example where the devil is being discussed:

> Nay, so far is he from entertaining his Stranger or Friend in a Friendly Manner, that he does not shew him <u>common</u> Civility.

Lined up with the devil as the negation of the common good promoted by the SRM are sinners, who burden the good with public guilt, negating the shared nature of such features as honesty in the nation:

> I do not easily conceive how wife and good Men should either take much Pleasure in Living otherwise than in Obedience to the Will, and for the Glory of God, and the working out their own Salvation, or in the Thoughts of leaving a Posterity behind them in a Nation where there is no more Religion, or even common Honesty; I intended, I say, having done this, in the next place to offer some Arguments against those Vices that are most reigning among us, as Lewdness, Profane Swearing and Cursing, Drunkenness, etc. in hopes that the Representation of the Baseness, the Folly and Beastiality of those Sins, together with the various and great Mischiefs they bring upon the Public . . .

The out-group is the negation of the values of the in-group, as can be seen in the following example:

> So that common Swearing is a very Uncivil, as well as dangerous, Vice; an Offence to the Religious, as well as a Temptation to the Unwary.

What is happening around *common* is a process of distinction – the in-group is being identified with a set of positive values, while the lack of those values is being used in part to identify the out-group. The out-group is in turn being identified with a set of negative actions, which themselves are the negation of the in-group. The identity of the in-group is, at least in part, obvious from the words associated with them – they are those Christians who agree with the SRM. Yet the in-group is something a little more than that. They do not identify themselves with the mass of society, in that their actions/values are common in the sense of universal rather than typical/ordinary. Similarly, they do not identify themselves with the upper echelons of society. They exhort their followers to approach this group and chide such figures as magistrates for not prosecuting sinners. The references to members of the establishment are not in the first or second person. The texts are not addressed to the upper tier of society. Following is a typical third-person reference to the upper classes:

> if Men of a Superior <u>Rank</u> have Money enough to maintain their Famil-
> ies, and discharge their other Obligations, and to spare, and they have
> no better Inclinations than to carry it to those Houses, they have time
> enough to spend it in them on the other six days of the Week, without
> doing it upon the Lord's-Day, to the Neglect of their Duty to their
> Families, and the manifest Danger of the Ruin of their own Souls.

The lower classes are certainly part of the out-group – they are the source of the common behaviour that the SRM is fighting against. To be from the lower ranks is such a sure sign of being in the out-group, that on the only occasion in the SRMC that the lower classes join the SRM in its crusade, in this case in Ireland, it is a point worthy of note:

> I may satisfy my self, at present, with saying in general, of my own
> Knowledge, That the Transactions of Reformation here having been
> near Two Years since laid before some few Persons in Ireland, and most
> of those (I must again observe) private Persons, and of the lower <u>Rank</u> of
> Men, with proper Consideration to move them to unite in the same
> Design, and Methods to pursue it with Advantage.

More typically, the lower class was identified with all of the common acts that the SRM objected to, and hence by association the lower class was pushed into the out-group:

Persons of a lower <u>Rank</u> ... submitted to be reckoned Disturbers of the public Peace, Imprudent and Hypocritical Persons...

Indeed the identification of the lower classes with the out-group, to a much higher degree than the upper classes, is made explicit in the following statement which comes after a discussion of the need to enforce the law against immorality:

If these were duly executed upon proper Objects (and it is an Injury to our God, to our Country, and to the Poor, when they are not) a heavy Burthen would probably be felt, especially by those of an inferior <u>Rank</u>, who by this means might be brought under the happy Necessity, either of forsaking the Sin, or of losing their Substance.

The upper classes are targeted by the SRM in their efforts to ensure the laws against immorality will be imposed. The lower classes are the intended object of those laws; those sitting between the lower and the upper classes are those calling for the laws to be enforced. Chief amongst the crimes of the lower classes that are identified is swearing and other forms of bad language. It is in the use of *common* in the sense in which it is used by the SRM of swearing that a final convergence takes place around bad language in the SRMC – the convergence between low social class and bad language.

The SRM over time

One issue I have not touched on so far is how the discourse of the SRM changed over time. When one plots the dispersion of the keywords over time, while different topics come into focus in the texts from time to time, making the plot clump at certain points as the keyword is used frequently in a specific passage/section, on the whole the keywords are well dispersed. Thus, if one can take the keywords as a proxy for the moral panic as this chapter has argued is possible, the moral panic did not change its form noticeably across the 50 years represented in the SRMC.

Conclusion – distinction and moral panic theory

The SRM, through the use of a moral panic, focused a process of distinction on a number of activities, notably, for this chapter, BLWs. The discourse of the SRM represents a classic moral panic. The discourse roles of the moral panic are easily identified in the SRMC and the obsessive, alarmist and moralistic tone of the discussion is evident, in part from the collocations in the corpus, but mainly through its keywords.

In using a moral panic to generate distinctions in speech, the SRM created an out-group, so that the in-group they also generated could be clearly defined. As is typical of such events, the SRM largely define the in-group by implication, being much more specific about the out-group and implying, therefore, that the in-group were the polar opposites of the out-group.[528] If the out-group swear, are of low social class and endanger the nation, then the in-group is defined, by implication, as those who do not swear, are of higher social class and who defend the nation. The process of forging these distinctions is aided by a key component of a moral panic discourse – spirals of signification. Embedded within the moral panic discourse, these spirals work to generate a process of convergence, bringing together objects of offence and scapegoats, binding the offence to the offender and generating associations in their discourse which, while they are present in modern English, had little presence in the English of the time. It was this discourse, introduced by the SRM and propagated through the schools by the SPCK which, I argue, generated the set of distinctions around BLWs in English which persist to this day. While individuals undoubtedly shared those attitudes prior to the advent of the SRM, it was the widely publicised discourse of the SRM, spread through the villages, towns and cities of the English-speaking world, as well as the equally widespread schooling provided over a much longer period by the SPCK, which naturalised these distinctions within English.

In the next chapter I will look at another moral panic in which bad language figured, that associated with Mary Whitehouse and the VALA. In doing so, I will argue that what was established by the SRM was exploited and maintained by the VALA.

7 Mutations

The National Viewers' and Listeners' Association moral panic

Introduction

In this chapter I will use the analytical framework established in Chapter 6 in order to investigate the moral panic encoded in the writings of Mary White-house in the 1960s and 1970s in Britain. In doing so, I will once again be using keywords as a way of focusing on the aboutness of the moral panic, and a study of patterns of colligation and collocation to explore convergence in the MWC. Towards the end of the chapter, I will return to the issue of bad language and consider how bad language was represented by the VALA (pages 124–126). The chapter will consider throughout how the moral panic in the MWC compares to that in the SRMC. To begin with, however, let us return to the question of moral panics and the use of keywords to explore them.

Keywords and moral panic

A comparison of the MWC and the LOB corpus produces a significantly larger set of positive keywords than the one produced by the comparison of Lampeter and the SRMC. Table 7.1 outlines the keywords derived from comparing LOB and the MWC.

The MWC, LOB and FLOB

Before considering the keywords derived from a comparison of the MWC and LOB, I would like to consider the issue of the comparability of the MWC and LOB. I do not believe that the differences that I am looking for between the LOB corpus and the MWC are such that the differences in the sampling frame of the two should matter much. In order to explore this, I compared the MWC with the FLOB corpus. If the list of keywords is relatively stable across the comparisons, then my hypothesis has some weight. If the list is radically different, then my hypothesis is in serious doubt. Table 7.2 shows the keyword list derived from the comparison of the FLOB and MWC corpora. The similarity between the keywords in Tables 7.1 and 7.2 is quite remarkable and certainly adds weight to my

Table 7.1 Keywords of the MWC when compared with the LOB corpus

Positive keywords	*Negative keywords*
bbc, sex, television, broadcasting, sexual, programmes, programme, pornography, children, public, violence, tv, whitehouse, people, our, viewers, censorship, we, society, greene, campaign, film, intercourse, abortion, listeners, denmark, governors, freedom, education, women, ita, who, permissive, radio, danish, obscene, manifesto, moral, director-general, responsibility, standards, corporation, humanist, child, obscenity, vala, debate, clean-up, pornographic, hugh, what, birmingham, rape, films, legal, parents, media, report, normanbrook, responsible, to, masturbation, my, morality, association, advisory, mrs, fpa, screen, laws, i, that, us, press, rang, crime, young, religious, postmaster-general, which, very, school, sexuality, contraception, concern, lobby, me, shewn, trevelyan, book, daily, itv, decency, dr, its, meeting, liberation, corrupt, viewer, homosexual, phone, porn, hoggart, calder, fox, law, parliament, sixties, support, interview, copenhagen, jury, human, letter, homosexuals, abortions, christian, audience, drama, wrote, of, relationships, girls, cosmo, publication, sexually, speak, opinion, prosecution, believe, homosexuality, kenneth, broadcast, about, reaction, invited, charter, adults, licence, series, listener, family, exploitation, medium, producer, compassion, dpp, buckland, anti-censorship, four-letter, creative	*company, car, s, de, french, eyes, percent, two, looked, n't, water, ll, him, you, pound, his, her, she, he*

hypothesis that, in this case, the mismatch in sampling frame is largely irrelevant, or at least is as relevant to a corpus (LOB) sampled some seven years before the first text of the MWC as a corpus (FLOB) sampled 11 years after the last MWC text was written. For example, the LOB/MWC comparison yields 151 positive keywords, 109 of which are shared with the FLOB/MWC comparison, and 42 of which are unique to LOB/MWC (27.8 per cent of the total). The FLOB/MWC yields 145 positive keywords, 109 of which are shared by both corpora and 36 of which are unique to FLOB/MWC (24.8 per cent of the total). It is arguable that the 109 keywords may be the best focus of this study – in effect, one is triangulating on the keywords in the MWC by using a pair of reference points,

were my intended goals in carrying out these analyses? First, I wanted to see how the key-keywords organised themselves in terms of the moral panic categories – are the key-keywords spread evenly across the categories? Second, I wanted to see what the key-keywords were across the whole MWC (i.e. which key-keywords are keywords across all of the texts in the MWC) and which keywords drew their strength from particular subsections of the MWC, as small as a single chapter perhaps. The first goal is methodological to some extent, as it allows us to explore the question of whether or not key-keywords can give us sufficient data to allow us to populate the moral panic discourse model. Yet, it is also related to the content of the corpus data. The key-keywords we find at the corpus level, i.e. shared between all four books in the MWC, highlight enduring themes of the MWC. Certain other words, while keywords in the whole corpus, may have their keyness attributed to just one book, or perhaps even one chapter. In short, we will be able to differentiate relatively transient keywords (those appearing, say, in the first book but not in later books) from those which are permanent, i.e. key across the whole corpus. In turn, when we then consider these transient and permanent key-keywords in terms of the moral panic discourse categories, we may discover that a pattern emerges, e.g. scapegoats being more transitory and consequences being more permanent. We may see that part of the moral panic is prone to being more static than other parts.

Figures 7.1 and 7.2 give the results of the key-keyword analyses for all three texts and all 57 chapters in the MWC respectively. Following that, in Tables 7.4 and 7.5 the data from the two tables are placed in the moral

---

television, broadcasting, bbc, sex, i, programmes, whitehouse, programme, sexual, pornography, tv, children, viewers, cannot, our, violence, we, people, greene, society, censorship, me, campaign, intercourse, my, vala, obscenity, public, phone, permissive, clean-up, women, pornographic, ita, parents, masturbation, freedom, film, sexuality, listeners, corporation, education, meeting, abortion, director-general

Figure 7.1 Words which are key-keywords in five or more chapters of the MWC.

---

broadcasting, television, bbc, sex, i, programmes, whitehouse, programme, sexual, pornography, tv, viewers, our, violence, censorship, children, we, people, greene, campaign, society, me, public, intercourse, my, vala, obscenity, permissive, phone, women, school, ita, pornographic, mrs, masturbation, freedom

Figure 7.2 Words which are key-keywords in all of the MWC texts.

Table 7.4 Words which are key-keywords in five or more chapters of the MWC mapped into the moral panic discourse roles

Category	Positive keywords in that category
Consequence	*public, violence, children, people, society, freedom, corrupt, education*
Corrective action	*censorship, debate, parents, report, responsible, meeting*
Desired outcome	*decency*
Moral entrepreneur	*whitehouse, viewers, listeners*
Object of offence	*sex, sexual, violence, sexuality, abortion*
Scapegoat	*television, broadcasting, programmes, programme, greene, radio, director-general, humanist, report, film, corporation*
Rhetoric	*our, we, who, what*
Unclassified	none

Table 7.5 Words which are key-keywords in all of the MWC texts mapped into their moral panic discourse roles

Category	Positive keywords in that category
Consequence	*public, violence, children, people, society, freedom, women*
Corrective action	*censorship, campaign, ita, school, phone*
Desired outcome	none
Moral entrepreneur	*whitehouse, viewers, vala*
Object of offence	*sex, sexual, violence, pornography, intercourse, permissive, obscenity, pornographic, masturbation, school*
Scapegoat	*bbc, television, broadcasting, programmes, programme, tv, greene*
Rhetoric	*our, we, my, me, i*
Unclassified	*mrs*

panic discourse categories. In the figures and tables that follow, I have only listed the key-keywords which were key in all of the MWC texts (Figure 7.1 and Table 7.4) and key-keywords that were key in five or more chapters in the MWC (Figure 7.2 and Table 7.5). In Figures 7.1 and 7.2, the words are ordered in descending order of key-keyness.

Table 7.6 shows, for each moral panic category, which key-keywords are moral panic keywords when key-keywords are calculated both by book and chapter, as well as solely by book or chapter.

Table 7.6 The distribution of chapter only, text only and chapter and text key-keywords across the moral panic discourse categories

Category	Book-based key-keyword only	Both book- and chapter-based key-keyword	Chapter-based key-keyword only
Consequence	*women*	*children, freedom, people, public, society, violence*	*corrupt, education*
Corrective action	*campaign, ita, phone, school*	*censorship*	*debate, meeting, parents, report, responsible*
Desired outcome			*decency*
Moral entrepreneur	*vala*	*viewers, whitehouse*	*listeners*
Object of offence	*intercourse, masturbation, obscenity, permissive, pornographic, pornography, school*	*sex, sexual, violence*	*abortion, sexuality*
Scapegoat	*bbc, tv*	*broadcasting, greene, programme, programmes, television*	*corporation, director-general, film, humanist, radio, report*
Rhetoric	*i, me, my*	*our, we*	*what, who*
Unclassified	*mrs*		

Table 7.6 in particular is interesting as it shows that transience of key-keywords is observable. In this table, however, transience is relative, as even the most transient keyword is key in at least five chapters. This transience would become more profound if the cut-off of five applied to key-keywords in this experiment was reduced further. Transient keywords will be returned to on pages 223–225.

Having calculated the chapter and book-based key-keywords, I would now like to consider the key-keywords in Table 7.6 and discuss how they act as moral panic key-keywords in each category of the moral panic discourse model. However, rather than following the format of Chapter 6, where I explored each category word-by-word, I will simply present the fully populated model here and then address particularly important/surprising cases in a general discussion. My reason for doing this is that Chapter 6 was used, in part, to demonstrate how the model could be populated in this way. Given that the method was applied as easily to the MWC as to the SRM corpus, albeit with a shift of emphasis to key-keywords, I do not see any need to discuss the results on a case-by-case basis with the goal of justifying the method.

The key-keyword populated model

In this section, I will present the key-keywords, placed into moral panic categories and divided into semantic fields, where appropriate.[530] See Table 7.7 for the populated model. I will then present a series of more detailed discussions of the key-keywords and, to a lesser extent, the keywords. For the detailed discussions I will give the collocates for the words discussed, showing where those collocates are link collocates (emboldened, MI strength for link collocate plus the keywords linked to in parentheses after the MI

Table 7.7 The key-keyword populated model

Semantic field	Key-keywords
Consequence	
People	*public, children, people, women*
Acts	*violence, corrupt*
Abstractions	*society, freedom, education*
Corrective action	
Agitation	*campaign, debate, meeting, phone*
Organisational	*school*
Public	*parents, responsible*
Self regulation	*ita*
Research	*report*
Statutory	*censorship*
Desired outcome	
–	*decency*
Moral entrepreneur	
–	*whitehouse, viewers, listeners, vala*
Object of offence	
Crime	*violence*
Obscenity	*obscenity*
Pornography	*pornography, pornographic*
Scapegoat	
People	*greene*
Research	*report*
Broadcast programmes	*programmes, programme, radio*
Media	*television, tv, film, broadcasting*
Media organisations and officers	*bbc, director-general, corporation*
Groups	*humanists*
Moral panic rhetoric	
Pronouns/determiners	*our, we, who, what, my, me, i*
Unclassified	
–	*mrs*

score). Where the link collocate is also a keyword, the word is underlined. So, for example, the entry **clean-up** (6.38, *tv*) for the key-keyword *campaign* indicates that *clean-up* is a collocate of *campaign*. It is also a keyword. The words collocate with an MI score of 6.38, and the word *tv* is a keyword which shares the collocate *clean-up* with *campaign*.

The MWC and the SRMC

The panics in the SRMC and the MWC show striking similarities and dissimilarities. For example, the consequences encoded in the discourse of the MWC are similar, yet also different, from those encoded in the SRMC (see Table 7.8). They are similar to the extent that the consequences will be felt by the *public*, i.e. the victims will be people who did not carry out the acts (*public, children, people, women*). To this extent, as with the SRMC, the MWC identifies a range of victims of the actions of others, as shown in the *people* semantic field in the consequence category.

Yet, the MWC differs from the SRMC in that it also identifies a range of actions that will arise from the broadcast of material disapproved of by the VALA. This set of actions can reasonably be assumed to be another consequence that *people* can be expected to endure.

In addition to people suffering as a consequence of the distribution and broadcast of certain material and the further consequence of the negative behaviours that this material will provoke, the MWC also links the consequences of this material to broader, more abstract, concepts than specific classes of people. Here it is once again similar to the SRM which saw the *public* as a major victim of the actions of sinners in the late seventeenth century. In the case of the MWC, however, there is a range of abstract targets which mostly link to properties of human society rather than human

Table 7.8 Consequence keywords

Word	Frequency	Collocates in the MWC
public	361	*prosecutions,* **library** *(4.37, meeting), decency, opinion,* **sections** *(4.05, laws, obscenity), disregard, disorder, bemused, accountability,* **libraries** *(3.79, school)*
children	404	*benefit, unsuitable, wear, rings, reasoned, hero,* **classroom** *(3.79, invited), safely, indicate, collect (3.62)*
people	589	*educated, types,* **teacher's** *(3.34, young), confuse,* **ordinary** *(3.27, viewer, listener), coloured, hundreds, stimulated, proud, disturbance (3.08)*
women	162	**housewives** *(5.30, association), unlike, lib, compose,* **capitalist** *(5.20, society), middle-aged, eminent, differences, men, virtue (4.72)*

society itself. So, while society will indeed be a victim of the actions condemned by Whitehouse, there is also specific mention of one aspect of society that would suffer – *freedom*. Freedom would be damaged by the corrosive effect of the broadcast and distribution of offensive material. The specific freedom that would be damaged was negative in nature – the freedom not to see or hear something. This is encapsulated perfectly in the following quote from the MWC: 'Public sex is a restriction of our private freedom.' Freedom in the MWC is a private affair – where freedom is associated with public acts which Whitehouse disapproves of, it becomes an intrusion into private space within which the only accepted form of freedom exists. It is in this sense that Whitehouse claims that freedom is in jeopardy. By restricting the notion of freedom to the private domain, and then insisting upon her right to defend her own private domain, she was able to assert the need to curb public freedoms. Whitehouse's desire to repress the public expression of what she disapproves of means that she accepts, tacitly at least, the possibility that those acts could occur in private. This reflects both on comments on her attitude to swearing made in Chapter 5 and the late SRM attitude to moral reform (see Chapter 4, pages 109–110). As such, freedom is not absolute, as 'real freedom can only be exercised in an atmosphere of responsibility'. Freedom, for Whitehouse, must be defined, limited and, on those terms only, defended.

A further notable contrast between the discourse of the SRMC and the VALA is apparent in the scapegoat category. In the MWC, this contains keywords and one key-keyword that are the names of people that she specifically blames for the ills of society.[531] While the targets of the SRM were groups, the VALA, while focusing on groups, also scapegoated individuals, typically those who exercised power in a way that they claimed undermined the moral and social settlement that they were defending. While there is a partial parallel with the attitudes of the SRM to magistrates,[532] the identification of individuals as scapegoats is not a major feature of the discourse of the SRM.

How to lobby without lobbying

The words in the corrective action category speak strongly of the day-to-day lobbying that the VALA was engaged in, particularly in the agitation field (see Table 7.9). Letters are written, phone calls made, public debates undertaken, meetings held and interviews, typically in the media, are given. Throughout, there is an attempt to garner and maintain support from a range of organisations, such as the police federation.

The agitation that the VALA was engaged in seems to be a blueprint for other lobbying organisations. However, interestingly, the keyword *lobby* does not belong in the corrective action category at all. As shown in Table 7.3, *lobby* is most certainly a scapegoat category word.

Lobby in the MWC is a word with a powerful negative semantic prosody.

Table 7.9 Corrective action keywords

Word	Frequency	Collocates in the MWC
campaign	143	***clean-up*** (6.38, *tv*), *supporter*, **represent** (5.12, *clean-up, tv*), *mount, begun, discredit, specifically, launched*, **tv** (4.51, *clean-up*), *swizzlewick* (4.38)
debate	80	*parliamentary, opening*, **roy** (4.96, *obscene*), *lords, dealt, continuing*, **bill** (3.84, parliament), **annual** (3.69, *ita, report*), *union, result* (3.51)
meeting	143	*anniversary*, **library** (5.12, *public*), *brighton, interruption, arrange, hall*, **sponsored** (4.71, *pornography*), *demanded, holding*, **town** (4.52, *itv*)
phone	43	*ringing*, **calls** (7.06, *hoggart*), *feb, call, stopped, hardly*, **rang**, **received** (4.58, *letter*), *down, next* (3.55)

As will be shown later (Figure 7.3), *lobby* links into a negatively loaded collocational network, with the words *homosexual* and *permissive* being its immediate link nodes. Its collocates (*anti-censorship, myths, tactics, permissive, claim, humanist, homosexual*), are linked to groups or concepts Whitehouse was opposed to (*anti-censorship, permissive, humanist, homosexual*) or represent a negative evaluation of the lobby concerned (*myths*). These lobbies make

---

1 The fact that the Postmaster-General met us in the middle of the postal strike of 1964 was an indication, in the words of one M.P., that 'this campaign is regarded as the expression of the will of serious and responsible people in the country'.

2 As far as censorship is concerned it is quite clear to me that the people most likely to create a backlash are those in the arts who refuse to listen to the modulated voices of responsible opinion.

3 We may well agree with the Head of Religious Broadcasting when he says 'We must go on trying to see that every responsible Christian viewpoint is given fair expression within the whole spectrum of religious broadcasting in television and radio'.

4 The FPA was founded fifty years ago to alleviate the child-bearing problems of women in countries all over the world, but it has travelled a long way since then, and not always to the satisfaction of those responsible people who worked so hard and selflessly for its orginal aims, or to the credit of those who have been involved in its change of emphasis and policy in recent years.

Figure 7.3 The responsible.

claims and use tactics. *Claim* and *tactics* are in turn words in the MWC with notably negative collocates. CLAIM in its verbal form collocates with *lobby*. This verb is a marker of epistemic modality – a degree of uncertainty is being attributed to the statement made. It is hardly surprising, then, that when we explore the verb LOBBY, we discover that claims are typically made by those groups with whom Whitehouse disagreed. Those who are claiming they are 'the secularist lobby', 'advocates of permissiveness', 'the new populists' and 'the anti-censorship lobby'. *Tactics* is another word which is coloured in a negative fashion in the MWC. Tactics are used by 'the permissive lobby', 'the anti-censorship lobby', 'the progressive left', 'the New Left' and 'the new morality wing of the Anglican church'. They are 'communist' and 'revolutionary'. In short, from Whitehouse's perspective, lobbies are bad – they are the encapsulation of all that she opposes, and their pronouncements lack certainty. In this way, Whitehouse generates an in- and an out-group. People who campaign for a cause which she approves of, such as her own group, are not lobbies, and do not collocate with *lobby* – those people who campaign in exactly the same manner for things that she disapproves of are lobbies. The word *lobby* is in effect a snarl word in the MWC. So while Whitehouse undoubtedly lobbied, the word is not in the corrective action category, and is not a key-keyword, as the word was taken to embody the activities of the groups to which she was opposed.

Schools

One key-keyword, *school*, is of interest as it is both a corrective action key-keyword and a scapegoat keyword. Certain schools and schooling practices were viewed as not merely acceptable by Whitehouse, but a means of combating changes she did not welcome in society. Those schools which adopted progressive schooling practices, or which failed to regulate children in a manner which Whitehouse found to be acceptable were, however, a significant object of offence for Whitehouse. The contrast between the two types of school in the MWC is stark. An almost Enid Blyton picture of hyper-normality is painted of the 'good schools'. There is talk of a 'school choir', children attending art classes bringing with them 'little bags and boxes of samples of sand, bark and tea'. These schools are populated with children who always 'wear gloves when in school uniform' and 'carry a clean hankie' in their pockets. By contrast, the progressive school is interested in launching 'a campaign to persuade girls to carry condoms in their school satchels', is not 'terrified of thirteen-year-olds starting sexual intercourse', wishes there were 'several contraceptive machines in every school'. It may also take children to visit 'a sex show club in the course of their studies'. It is a place where 'boys were chasing the girls round the school playground punching them in the stomach'. If this were not bad enough, 'filthy books of no literary merit are to be found in school libraries' at this kind of establishment.

The contrast could not be starker – between an idealised version of British childhood and an appalling hell on Earth. The contrast in itself underlines the innate conservatism of Whitehouse's approach. She lionises an approach to education based on an idealised version of schooling in the 1950s. Only the good is emphasised in this argument, with the class bias inherent in the system ignored and the brutal treatment meted out to children in such schools overlooked.[533] Anything that deviates from this idealised norm is subversive, and all attempts are made to suppress any good aspect of the alternative, and to highlight and dramatise any possible negative aspect of it. The only people who could possibly agree with such schooling were, in Whitehouse's view, the constitutionally irresponsible. For example, in an echo of her approach to swearing, she claims, only children themselves could approve of such libertinism:

> This is, admittedly, not in agreement with the wish of Swedish parents, 70% of whom would wish the school to exercise its authority to promote the ideal of youthful abstinence, but on the other hand in full accord with the wish of schoolchildren, 95% of whom are reported to share the view of their radical school authorities.

Whitehouse's was the responsible view. That of those who agreed with the 'radical school authorities' the childish one. Schools were key in promoting the responsible view for Whitehouse – hence their appearance as a corrective action key-keyword also. Much as with the voluntary school movement of the early eighteenth century, schools were to play an important role in the imposition of a new moral order, especially in the area of sex education. However, unlike in the early eighteenth century, in the 1960s and 1970s widespread national schooling was established, as was an approach to schooling which ran counter to the views of the VALA. The classroom in which the *Little Red Schoolbook* could be used was not one in which Mrs Whitehouse wanted to place children. Consequently, *school* is cross-posted to both the corrective action and scapegoat categories. Those schools which Mrs Whitehouse approved of were part of her corrective action (grammar schools, for example). Those which she disapproved of were one of the many scapegoats targeted by the VALA. Two examples from the MWC show how Whitehouse saw schools participating in her corrective action, in this case with regard to sex education:

1   This made me realise that the true function of the school is to help parents educate their own children, and this is what the majority of parents want to do.
2   Just as in my sex education work at school I worked from the very strong belief that the school's job in this matter was not to remove the privilege and responsibility from the parents, so I believe the TV screen should help the parent and not rush in to tell all without restraint.

Schools which were approved of by Whitehouse did not impose any morality other than that imposed in the assumed Christian home of the child by the child's parents.[534] In seeking to impose that morality Whitehouse would, where convenient, appeal to published or informal research, as the next section discusses.

Reports and research

The use of the key-keyword *report* in the MWC is usually focused on advisory or research reports commissioned by either a public or private body. The key-keyword does occur in the context of press reportage, but given that only seven of the occurrences of *report* occur with this sense, the key-keyword *report* in the MWC can reasonably be viewed as almost exclusively referring to commissioned reports. One thing that is clear from looking at the collocates of *report* is that reports are often identified by their chairmen – hence, frequent references to the Newsom and Pilkington reports, both commissioned by the UK government, generate the collocates *newsom* and *pilkington* for the key-keyword *report*[535] (see Table 7.10).

The Newsom report was published in 1963 and made recommendations for the future of secondary schooling in the UK. The Pilkington report was published in 1960 and was tasked with determining the future development of the BBC and the ITA. Given the importance of *school*, as a corrective action and a scapegoat, and television output as an object of offence, the prominence of these reports in Whitehouse's writings is hardly surprising. The surprise wanes yet further when one observes that these reports broadly support the position that Whitehouse was taking. It was the desire of Whitehouse to see the concerns of reports such as Newsom and Pilkington taken into account that places the key-keyword *report* in the corrective action category. These reports are cited as support by Whitehouse for her own position. Talking of the concern generated by media output felt by the mass of citizens that Whitehouse claims she represents, Whitehouse asserts:

> 'It cannot be dismissed as the unrepresentative opinion of a few well-meaning but over-anxious critics, still less as that of cranks. It has been represented to us from all parts of the kingdom and by many organisations of widely different kinds'. So wrote the authors of the Pilkington Report in June 1960. 'Disquiet,' they said, 'derived from an assessment

Table 7.10 The keyword *report*

Word	Frequency	Collocates in the MWC
report	127	**newsom** (6.39, *education, religious*), *pilkington, revealing, debated,* **council** (5.56, *advisory, listeners*), **annual** (5.34, *debate, ita*), *biased, authors,* **secondary** (4.66, *school*)

which we fully accept' that the power of the medium to influence and persuade is immense; and from a strong feeling, amounting often to a conviction, that very often the use of the power suggested a lack of awareness of, or concern about the consequences.

The Newsom report produced conclusions in line with Whitehouse's own, leading her to cite it as a source of evidence and a guide for legislators:

> The fundamental questions by whom should sex education be given? when? and to what end? – have been increasingly submerged in a culture which, by its very nature, negates the basic privacy essential to healthy mental and emotional growth and deals with this most personal of matters in a conformist and impersonal fashion. It was an awareness of this growing threat that caused the compilers of the Newsom Report, *Half Our Future*, published by the Ministry of Education, 1963 (still the most recent government report on secondary education), to declare that sex education must be given on the basis of 'chastity before marriage and fidelity within it'.

The summation of a position that it is claimed Newsom supports, the assertion of the recency, and hence one assumes authority, of the report and the use of a quotation from the report that is very supportive of Whitehouse's views on the dangers presented to society by moral relativism, allow Whitehouse to take upon herself the authority of the report, claiming that her views were 'not simply my own, but also those set out in the Newsom Report'. While taking support from such reports, Whitehouse also supports them, presenting the reports as a good guide to corrective action. In a discussion of a case where parents in the Knapmann family withdrew their children from schooling because of what they saw as progressive sex education,[536] Whitehouse is quick to point out that the corrective action taken was in line with the Newsom report, and quotes Exeter local education authority as recommending the Newsom guidelines on spiritual and moral development as offering 'excellent guidance'. These guidelines, Whitehouse notes, coincide with those of the VALA in so far as 'For our part we are agreed that boys and girls should be offered firm guidance on sexual morality based on chastity before marriage and fidelity within it'.

The finding that reports are used as support by Whitehouse raises a vexatious issue. In Chapter 5, I noted Whitehouse's stated opposition to certain forms of academic research. Yet the Newsom and Pilkington reports were based on research. A related issue links to another collocate of *report – biased*. It is clear from the references to reports such as Newsom and Pilkington that Whitehouse does not merely see these as the positive results of research, she sees them, especially Newsom, as blueprints for corrective action. Yet she also clearly sees some reports as biased. In order to begin to discover whether this split occurs with *report* only, I also decided to look at a clearly related word – *research*. Does a similar split occur there also, or is research viewed exclusively negatively?

The word *research* occurs 59 times in the MWC. If one distinguishes the cases where research is reported in positive terms from those in which it is presented in negative terms, the picture is somewhat surprising. Whitehouse's references to research are overwhelmingly positive – 50 out of the 59 cases see Whitehouse presenting research positively, typically in support of her own views. Collocates allow us to begin to see how the division between positively evaluated research and negatively evaluated research may be drawn. For positive mentions of research, *audience* collocates nine times, *own* six times and *my* four times. For the negative mentions of research, two collocates, *academic* and *sexual* occur twice each in complementary distribution. These results are broadly in line with what was said about Whitehouse's views of research in Chapter 5 – the research she cites is either her own (*own*, *my*) or that derived from viewers (*audience*). Academic research (either by academics in general or sexologists in particular) is marginalised in the sense that it is referred to fleetingly, and when it is referred to, it is referred to negatively. There are only two co-occurrences of *academic* and *research* and both of these cases present research negatively. Does the same divide – research based on the views of non-academics being good, research undertaken by academics being bad – apply to the reports? The answer to this question is no – the reports referred to by the VALA are almost exclusively produced by organisations, whether they be public or private, and are not linked to academic or non-academic research sources explicitly.

In order to investigate the split between the positive and negative uses of *report*, I categorised each use of the word in the same way as I had categorised *research*, either as a positive or negative use of the word. As with the word *research*, the number of positive references to a report far outweighs the number of negative references, with counts of 98 and 24 respectively. Mentions of Parliamentary reports (10), the Pilkington report (8), the Newsom report (5) and police reports (4) predominate. Other reports mentioned include those from religious organisations (e.g. the Church of Scotland) and medical authorities (e.g. the British Medical Association). There is an interesting link here between the source of the reports and the corrective action category. Parliament, as the ultimate source of the Newsom and Pilkington reports, is an important focus for corrective action, and its reports are presented as such. The religious nature of corrective action is underlined by the reference to religious reports also. Yet what of the reports which are presented as problematic? In the case of these reports, it was the presentation of views with which Whitehouse disagreed that caused the negative evaluation. However, the sources of these reports form as coherent a group as the positive reports. Rather than linking to the corrective action category, though, they link to the scapegoat category. The negative reports are produced by such scapegoats as *bbc* (3), *bha* (1), *hoggart* (1),[537] as well as other organisations which, if they are not scapegoat keywords in the MWC, are certainly organisations which would fall into that category, such as the Greater London Council and the National Council for Civil Liberties. It would obviously be foolish to claim that the word *report* is at times used positively by Whitehouse because she collocates it with a corrective action keyword. It would be similarly foolish to make that claim with reference to negative uses of report and scapegoat keywords. However, the relationship between the word *report* and the authors of the report is shown clearly by the collocates here. Those reports written by organisations which Whitehouse approves of, giving advice she agrees with, are evaluated positively. Those produced by organisations she disapproves of, espousing views she disagrees with, are evaluated negatively. The negative evaluation of the reports Whitehouse disagrees with is further intensified by evaluative terms being attached to the word *report* – these reports display 'ideological bias',[538] are 'biased', 'tendentious'[539] and display a mastery of 'half-truth'.[540] By contrast, the reports Whitehouse approves of are typically presented with modifications that amplify the panic Whitehouse is trying to exploit, or are used to strengthen the credibility of the report. For example, Whitehouse states that 'Recently the Chief Medical Officer to the Ministry of Health, Sir George Godber, presented a report on the disturbing increase in venereal disease among young people and called for "an all-out attack" on the problem'. Whitehouse cites this as evidence in support of her own solution to the problem – sexual abstinence before marriage. No evidence is provided regarding Sir George's own proposed solution, nor is there any discussion of the possible source of the increase – whether it was an increase in the report of the diseases, or an actual increase in the rate of infection. The quotation is interpreted within a framework established by Whitehouse to give maximum support to her position. Another report used for this purpose is the British Medical Association's 1955 report on Homosexuality and Prostitution. This is described by Whitehouse as a 'famous' report. The report describes how homosexuality may be 'cured' and Whitehouse uses this evidence to support her own view that homosexuality is an aberration which should be treated both physically and mentally. No major medical authority in the world now agrees with this position, and even in 1977, when Whitehouse was writing, she was not quoting from current research, and was citing a position that the medical profession had retreated from.[541] Nonetheless, such matters were overlooked and the report lionised as 'famous'.

The use of research and reports by Whitehouse is complex. Research from non-academic sources is welcome. Academic research – which tends to disagree with her 'common sense' research – is shunned and vilified. Reports which are in tune with her own thinking, especially by agents of corrective action, are used to support her view, and are granted her approbation, even when this means endorsing out-of-date and discredited research which forms the basis of a report. On the other hand, reports which disagree with her positions, notably those produced by scapegoats, are dismissed as being biased. In looking at what Whitehouse thought of those organisations producing such biased reports, we find her describing a practice which could just as well be attributed to her as to any of those individuals and organisations she is complaining about:

> So do big doors hang on little hinges – not because of the strength of the hinges themselves but because the intellectually committed believe what they want to believe, see what they want to see, and do their best to ensure that the rest of us see it their way too.

In-groups and out-groups – parents and responsibility

In the corrective action category, the key-keyword *parents* and *responsible* are interesting as they generate in- and out-groups as two key in-groups are those who may be viewed as *responsible* and *parents*. There is also an assumption of considerable overlap between these two groups, though not all people represented as responsible by Whitehouse are parents (e.g. Pope Paul VI) and not all parents discussed by Whitehouse are assumed to be responsible, with Whitehouse being clearly condemnatory of divorced parents, or, as she puts it, those who 'run to a cigarette or a drink or out through the front door whenever there is trouble'.

Yet, these two groups are generally held up by Whitehouse as a crucial source of corrective action. It is parents working with such professionals as educationalists who can offset such undesirable practices as teachers who 'use pornographic books'. Parents, in Whitehouse's view of society, are the force which will anchor the moral absolutist position in the face of the floodtide of moral relativism. For Whitehouse, *parents* are typical of the 'ordinary decent-minded people, who are so cruelly offended and worried' by moral revolution. As such, they, and other responsible people, i.e. those opposed to this change in British society, represented the 'silent majority' that Whitehouse claimed to speak for.[542] Whitehouse was very clear on the point that her view was responsible, and those who supported her view were of necessity responsible also, as shown in Figure 7.3.

The quotations in Figure 7.3 are illuminating, as they define an in-group, the responsible, while also setting up a series of potential oppositions which define an out-group. The in-group is serious (1), reasonable (2) and selfless (4). By contrast, one may imagine that the out-group is defined by the reverse of these qualities. Similarly, it is established that there are responsible Christian viewpoints as well as ones which are not responsible (3). In terms of this particular delineation of the in-group, the quotation in (3) (Figure 7.3, above) continues to clearly impose the in/out-group distinction based on religious conservatism (Billy Graham, Cardinal Heenan)[543] in the in-group versus religious liberalism (Dr Robinson, Werner Pelz)[544] in the out-group:

1   But when he translates that unexceptionable principle into personal terms one cannot but shudder: 'We must find room for Billy Graham as well as Dr Robinson, for Werner Pelz as well as Cardinal Heenan,' he tells us.

Porn, pornography and enclitics

Given that pornography was a major source of offence for the VALA, its appearance in the object of offence category is hardly surprising.

What is interesting, however, is that its shortened form, *porn*, while a keyword, is not a key-keyword. On closer investigation, one discovers that there is a marked difference between the collocates of *porn* (*harmless, pleasure, pictures, industry*) and those for *pornography* and *pornographic* (see Table 7.11). While the collocates of *pornography* and *pornographic* are broadly the type of words which one would expect to imbue these words with a negative semantic prosody, the collocates of *porn* do not merely not represent a failure to associate the word with a negative semantic prosody – it associates the word with a positive semantic prosody through collocates such as *harmless* and *pleasure*. However, an exploration of the concordances of *porn* reveals an explanation – *porn* is a word Whitehouse rarely uses, though she does report the use of it in the speech of others. In the 22 examples of the word in the MWC, 14 occur in quotation. It is in these examples, where Whitehouse is quoting from those who oppose her views, that the word collocates with *harmless* and *pleasure* and has a positive semantic prosody, as shown in the examples in Figure 7.4.

In both examples, *porn* is a word used by others, and the word itself becomes a marker of approval for pornography, being associated with a positive view of pornography to the extent that Whitehouse avoids the use of the word (using it herself only eight times) in favour of *pornography* (which is used in quotation by Whitehouse 17 times and by Whitehouse herself 180 times in the MWC). In quotation, *pornography* has a negative semantic prosody just as it does out of·quotation. The word *porn* itself, it could be argued, is shunned by Whitehouse, and hence fails to become a key-keyword, as she was aware of the positive semantic prosody of the word, and wished to avoid it,

Table 7.11 Collocates of *pornography* and *pornographic*

Word	Frequency	Collocates in the MWC
pornography	197	**presidential** (5.07, *obscenity*), *freely, sell, sale, pictorial,* **deviant** (4.66, *sexual*), **commission** (4.52, *obscenity*), **sponsored** (4.24, *meeting*), *proof, link* (4.24)
pornographic	56	*enterprise, gross, sight,* **blasphemous** (5.60, *obscene*), **pictures** (5.47, *porn, intercourse*), **explicit** (5.25, *sexually*), *cheap, erotic, magazines, material* (4.65)

1   'But,' says the book, 'there are other kinds,' and it goes on to describe, in concrete terms, bestiality (in the specific sense of that term) and sado-masochism. The book's general comment on what it has thus described is as follows: '<u>Porn</u> is a harmless pleasure if it isn't taken too seriously and believed to be real life'.

2   The 'soft' essence of the trendy churchman was encapsulated by the Reverend Chad Varah when, writing the Encounter, he used 'a great deal of language that most people would call simply filthy' and went on: 'In Soho, the soft <u>porn</u> is kept in the front room and the hard in the back ... In Denmark, thanks to the enlightened Danes' abolition of censorship it's all in the shop ... The best <u>porn</u> is not only therapeutic but appeals to our sense of wonder.'

Figure 7.4 Porn is good.

instead favouring its full form, as the semantic prosody of the full form better reflected her own views towards pornography. However, there is another possible explanation for her avoidance of the word *porn*. Whitehouse is a formal writer as, amongst other things, she tends to avoid enclitic forms. Note the presence of the enclitic forms *'s, 'll* and *n't* in the negative keyword list given in Table 7.1. Enclitic forms are markers of speech and informal writing,[545] and the presence of these enclitics in the negative keyword list indicates a more formal register for Whitehouse's writings. The formal style of her writing is one of its most notable features. However, a discussion of the enclitic forms begs two further questions which must be addressed before we can proceed. First, are there genres in LOB which are more similar to the MWC in terms of their use of enclitics and second, with reference to the form *'s*, is it a negative keyword as an enclitic verb form, a genitive marker or both? In the MWC, *'s* occurs as a genitive 597 times, and as an enclitic form of the verb *be* 140 times. Tables 7.12 and 7.13 compare the distribution of genitive and enclitic forms of *'s* in the MWC and LOB. While a description of the LOB categories is included in Chapter 1 of this book, I have included a description of each category in Table 7.12 for ease of reference.

This table shows two things quite clearly. First, the form *'s* is a negative keyword for the MWC irrespective of which of the sub-sections of LOB the MWC is compared to. Second, LOB H is the sub-section of LOB which, in terms of its usage of enclitics, matches the MWC most closely. Given that it is argued here that avoidance of enclitics is an indicator of formality, it is interesting to note that the LOB H category is composed of very formal texts indeed, largely government documents and official reports. It is also notable that those texts which use a wider variety of enclitics – such as LOB

Table 7.12 Enclitics which are negative keywords in the MWC when the MWC is compared to the sub-sections of LOB

LOB section	Category description	Negative keywords enclitics when the MWC is compared to the LOB section
Lob A	Press:reportage	*n't, s*
Lob B	Press:editorial	*n't, s*
Lob C	Press:review	*n't, s*
Lob D	Religion	*n't, s*
Lob E	Skills, trades and hobbies	*n't, s*
Lob F	Popular lore	*n't, s*
Lob G	Belles Lettres, biographies, essays	*n't, s*
Lob H	Miscellaneous	*s*
Lob J	Science	*m, s*
Lob K	General fiction	*m, d, ll, n't, s*
Lob L	Mystery and detective fiction	*m, re, ve, ll, d, n't, s*
Lob M	Science fiction	*ll, n't, s*
Lob N	Adventure and western	*re, ve, d, ll, n't, s*
Lob P	Romance and love stories	*m, d, re, ve, ll, s, n't*
Lob R	Humour	*ve, ll, n't, s*

Table 7.13 The relative frequency of genitive *'s* forms and enclitic *'s* forms in the MWC compared to the sub-section of LOB

Section	Frequency of genitive 's	Frequency of enclitic 's	MWC v LOB genitive 's LL score	MWC v LOB enclitic verb LL score
LOB A	608	52	240.89 (−)	0.39 (+)
LOB B	222	16	24.80 (−)	10.58 (+)
LOB C	327	30	272.86 (−)	2.01 (−)
LOB D	124	30	7.26 (−)	2.15 (−)
LOB E	215	34	0.12 (−)	3.95 (+)
LOB F	364	128	33.77 (−)	41.12 (−)
LOB G	800	41	137.15 (−)	29.04 (+)
LOB H	173	0	0.40 (−)	67.87 (+)
LOB J	435	20	0.03 (+)	68.31 (+)
LOB K	233	155	18.22 (−)	133.23 (−)
LOB L	279	168	85.24 (−)	195.70 (−)
LOB M	49	31	5.03 (−)	34.05 (−)
LOB N	260	248	32.16 (−)	313.24 (−)
LOB P	276	242	44.08 (−)	302.30 (−)
LOB R	75	28	8.99 (−)	13.93 (−)
LOB total	4,440	1,223	127.06 (−)	57.75 (−)
MWC	597	140	−	−

L and LOB P – are clearly more informal genres, composed of popular fiction. Importantly, these are also genres in which representations of speech occur most frequently. However, given the fact that *'s* is a negative keyword for the MWC, irrespective of the sub-category of LOB it is compared to, the question of exactly what the *'s* in the corpora is – a genitive, an enclitic or both, becomes all the more pressing.

In Table 7.13, the last two columns give a log-likelihood score which tests the significance of the difference in frequency between the MWC and sub-sections of LOB for the occurrence of the genitive *'s* form (column four) and enclitic *'s* form (column five). Following each log-likelihood score is a + or a – in parentheses. A plus indicates that the relative frequency of the form is greater in the MWC, a minus indicates that this relative frequency is higher in LOB. The log-likelihood scores have been emboldened where these figures exceed the 99.9 per cent significance level.

Table 7.13 shows that, with few exceptions, it is both the genitive and enclitic form of *'s* which is a negative keyword for the MWC. Both overall and in ten of the 15 sub-sections, singular genitive marking is used significantly less frequently in the MWC than in LOB. Similarly, overall and in eight of the 15 sub-sections, the enclitic *'s* form is used significantly less frequently in the MWC than in LOB. However, the enclitic *'s* form does differ somewhat from the singular genitive – in three of the genres, LOB G, H and J, the enclitic form occurs significantly more frequently in the MWC than in LOB. One infers, therefore, that in Table 7.13 it is the effect of the combination of the genitive and enclitic form of *'s* which makes *'s* a negative keyword when compared to LOB G (Belles Lettres, biographies, essays), H (miscellaneous) and J (Science). When the different types of *'s* are separated, the formality of LOB G, H and J with reference to enclitic forms is underlined – it is even more formal than the MWC.

Given Whitehouse's general avoidance of enclitic forms and the resultant formal style, the avoidance of the abbreviated form *porn* may simply be explained by her tendency to formality. However, I do not believe that the two explanations for her preference of *pornography* over *porn* are antagonistic. Rather, they are complementary in that, together, they give an even stronger impetus for Whitehouse to use *pornography* rather than *porn*.

Bad sex

Given the history of the VALA, the presence of a cluster of keywords associated with sex in the discourse of the MWC is hardly surprising. Nor is the rather negative semantic prosody of the words in this cluster, with its emphasis on what Whitehouse would view as deviance (*homosexual, torture*), transgression (*offences, pre-marital*) and indulgence (*fantasy, gratuitous, titillation*). The collocates are revealing. Two out of the four link to the keyword *homosexual*, generating a link between *homosexual* and *masturbation* via *intercourse*, and *homosexual* and *minorities* via *sexual*. *Sex* is linked to *violence* through the collocate *gratuitous*. *Masturbation* is linked to *abortion* via *prior*. Then a link is made to the pornography semantic field of the objects of offence through the link collocate *pictures*. The impact of such links will be discussed in more detail on pages 216–222. For the moment it is sufficient to say that the 'sex' semantic field is tied to the scapegoat category (*homosexual*) and another 'object of offence' semantic field (*pornography*).

Bad programmes

Words relating to the broadcast of programmes on the television and radio appear in the key-keyword scapegoat list (see Table 7.14).

The discussion of these broadcasts almost always identifies the broadcast as a problem, and the act of broadcasting the material as a problem leading to negative consequences. The collocate *excellent* for *programmes* may lead us to assume, however, that not all programmes are identified by Whitehouse as having negative consequences. However, a closer inspection of the examples where *excellent* programmes are discussed shows that it is indeed those programmes to which Whitehouse objects that are being discussed – they are being accused of driving excellent programmes off the air or negating their positive effect, as in the following example from the MWC: 'What a great pity it is to spoil these excellent programmes and the excellent shewing we get from the BBC by distasteful programmes.'

As well as blaming individuals for the objects of offence and consequences outlined by Whitehouse, the media, broadly conceived, is accused by Whitehouse of broadcasting and distributing the object of offence. Hence collocates with a negative semantic prosody such as *horrible*, *suffer*, *blue* and *x* occur with the key-keyword *film* and the keyword *films*.[546]

Table 7.14 The collocates of *programme* and *programmes*

Word	Frequency	Collocates in the MWC
programmes	237	*olds, types, satirical, excellent, preview,* **screened** (4.39, *programme, television*), *intervals, affairs, related,* build (4.17)
programme	282	*catholics, transmitted, complained, talkback,* **screened** (4.14, *programmes, television*), **falling** (4.14, *tv*), *braden, finished,* **thames** (3.73, *broadcast, tv*), *night's* (3.73)

Table 7.15 The collocates of *film*

Word	Frequency	Collocates in the MWC
film	191	*censors, russell's, makers, horrible, cole's, distributed, glc,* **management** (4.29, *director-general*), *exceptional, critic* (4.09)

Such collocates clearly form a bridge to the objects of offence category, as they are emblematic of the bad language, sex and violence Whitehouse objects to. It is hardly surprising, therefore, to see a link to the corrective action category: *broadcasting* and *television* are linked to the corrective action category by the use of language associated with the proposed regulation of the media, resulting in the collocates *accountable* and *accountability*.

Yet, if particular broadcast programmes are often presented as the scapegoat by Whitehouse, she is also clear that the decision to broadcast material is often the decision of individuals within a media organisation, and the individuals, or a reified organisation, may also be represented as scapegoats. As was demonstrated earlier, individuals are indeed represented as scapegoats in this way. But what of those bodies and groups associated with the decision to broadcast? As can be seen from the media organisation and officers field of the scapegoat category, media organisations are identified as scapegoats by Whitehouse, and as such we could say that, for her, the scapegoating process encompassed the entire organisation. The principal organisation that was the subject of her disapproval is indicated by the key-keyword *bbc*. As well as criticising the corporation itself, specific individuals associated with those different layers may be singled out for signal blame, e.g. Hugh Greene. The process of Whitehouse moving between levels in an organisation while criticising it is a feature of Whitehouse's approach to attacking scapegoats, and the BBC in particular.

The fragile nature of decency

The desired outcome identified in the MWC is the advent of a society in which *decency* reigns.

A form of Christian values based on absolute morality were intimately linked to decency and compassion for the MWC, as noted in Chapter 5. This link to Christianity becomes explicit for *decency* via the link collocate *faith*. However, it must be noted that in linking Christianity and decency, there is

Table 7.16 The collocates of *television* and *broadcasting*

Word	Frequency	Collocates in the MWC
television	399	*screens, dimension, **consumers** (4.23, radio, broadcasting), **accountable** (4.23, broadcasting, parliament), **independent** (4.05, ita), correspondent, __radio__ (3.92, broadcast, jury), **myths** (3.90, lobby), companies, **screened** (3.64, programmes, programme)*
broadcasting	277	***accountable** (5.49, broadcasting, television), **consumers** (5.17, radio, television), accountability, range, exempt, authorities, overall, affirm, **urges** (4.17, corporation), temple (4.17)*

Table 7.17 The collocates of *decency*

Word	Frequency	Collocates in the MWC
decency	29	*offend, taste,* **petition** (6.01, *parliament*), *calling, good, against, feeling,* **faith** (4.52, *christian*), **public** (4.32, *opinion*), *standards* (3.23)

the implicit denial that those who oppose the MWC are either *christian* or *decent*. Those people identified in the scapegoat category must be those trying to frustrate this outcome and, hence, cannot be Christian and cannot be decent. Indeed, they are responsible for the state of the media that needs to be cleaned-up. Consider the examples in Figure 7.5.

The examples in Figure 7.5 claim that the public wanted decency restored, implying that it was under threat and in decline (1). Those who sought to defend decency would have to suffer attacks from those that wanted to attack it (2). The enemies of decency represent an out-group who are opposed to decency, amongst other things, and those who wish to defend decency (2 and 3). Decency can be maintained or restored through the work of moral entrepreneurs who will persuade the government to institute changes to the law to enable the curbing of the out-group that wants to attack decency (1 and 4). Much as *virtue* was for the SRM, *decency* is a fragile object for the VALA. It is also under attack and must be defended by

---

1 On a point of information, 1.1 million people signed the 1973 Nationwide Petition for Public <u>Decency</u> calling for more effective controls – 85% of those who had the opportunity to sign.

2 While they try to discredit with a yell of 'fascist' those who defend <u>decency</u> and culture, they themselves launch an assault upon the senses and freedom of the individual which is the essence of the worst kind of dictatorship.

3 She isn't afraid of being called a moral busy-body, a pedlar in cant, a prude, a hypocrite, or any of the other verbal weapons in the arsenal of those who despise taste, ridicule good manners, resent <u>decency</u>, applaud blasphemy and generally espouse the litter louts of the arts.

4 It was with this warning in mind that National VALA, with the support of the Festival of Light, launched a Petition calling upon the Government so to revise the Obscenity Laws that they become an effective and workable instrument for the maintenance of public <u>decency</u>.

Figure 7.5 The call for the restoration of decency.

individuals and, ultimately, the State. Those seeking to attack *decency* are those 'who despise taste, ridicule good manners, resent decency, applaud blasphemy and generally espouse the litter louts of the arts'. In terms of presenting an out-group negatively, this is a powerful example, and echoes the way in which out-groups were generated by the SRM.

Be vague – moral panic rhetoric

The presence of first person singular pronouns (*i, me, my*) as key-keywords in the MWC texts is to some extent not surprising, as the texts in this corpus are largely written from the point of view of Mary Whitehouse herself. However, the fact that the corpus also has a first person plural pronoun (*we*) and the first person plural determiner *our* as key-keywords makes the choice of the first person singular point of view an interesting one, as through the predominance of singular and plural first person pronoun/determiner forms the author is able to blur the distinction between the views which she holds, those which she and her supporters hold, and those which are held by a larger group, including both the author and the reader. First person plural pronouns/determiners are vague.[547] Consider the use of *we* and *our* in the manifesto of the VALA as shown in Figure 7.6 (the examples in Figure 7.6 have been given superscript letters by me to facilitate a discussion of the pronouns).

The letters a and b clearly encompass only those people who sat down to write the manifesto. However, c encompasses a larger group, as not all of the Christian women of Britain sat down to write the manifesto and not all British women are Christians. Much as in the writings of the SRM, an in-group and out-group is set up here – the in-group being the Christian women of Britain who agree with the manifesto, the out-group being those women of Britain (whether they view themselves as Christian or not) who do not agree with the manifesto. The letters d, e, f, g and h may or may not refer to the groups identified by a, b and c or to some other group. These pronouns/determiners have a sweeping and vague scope that is difficult to determine with certainty from the text. As well as exploiting the vagueness of the plural first person pronouns/determiners and generating in- and out-

---

So we put <u>our</u>[a] heads together and produced <u>our</u>[b] manifesto. THE MANIFESTO 1. <u>We</u>[c] women of Britain believe in a Christian way of life. 2. <u>We</u>[d] want it for <u>our</u>[e] children and <u>our</u>[f] country. 3. <u>We</u>[g] deplore present day attempts to belittle or destroy it and in particular <u>we</u>[h] object to the propaganda of disbelief, doubt and dirt that the BBC projects into millions of homes through the television screen.

Figure 7.6 Pronoun use by the VALA.

groups, these word forms can also be used to imply that the reader shares the views of the VALA, as shown Figure 7.7.[548]

Examples a, b and c in Figure 7.7 assume that the reader is a Christian. While this may indeed have been true for many readers, it is not axiomatic that those who would read Whitehouse's works would be Christian. However, given the central role of a variety of Christianity based on absolute morality in the campaigns of the VALA, it is clear to see why Whitehouse wanted to assume that readers would be Christian, as she was claiming that she was representing the views of the silent Christian majority, who abhorred the switch away from absolute moral positions driven along by groups and individuals, such as the humanists or Hugh Greene, as shown in the examples in Figure 7.8.

Whitehouse's tactic when claiming that Britain was essentially Christian

---

The philosophical concept of the spontaneous apprehension of absolute good has lost all credence in a day when the entire concept of good is challenged, and we[a] need to be aware that it is largely our[b] Christianity and nothing else that has taught us[c] of goodness, justice, love, truth and beauty. And this is not something just for a reluctant Sunday.

Figure 7.7 The assumption of Christianity.

---

1   The Churches – as indeed had happened in other European countries where the pornographer Thorsen had tried to get his film made – not only came vigorously to life but united, one with another, under the leadership of the Queen, the Archbishop of Canterbury, Cardinal Hume of Westminster and the Prime Minister. And they united with those lay people in the country who had been fighting pornography for years. The people spoke with one voice – all except, that is, for some pathetic bleats from some of the anti-censorship lobby whose gods are, of course, those same pieces of silver which betrayed Christ in the first place. This seemed to me the most wonderful thing. No longer could the publicists of the 'God is dead' school, or the hot gospellers of the secularist lobby, claim that we live in a post-Christian era. We may not all go to church, but we care.

2   There is at the heart of the nation a sound Christian core. Parents who know what they value for their children and are prepared to see that they get it.

Figure 7.8 Speaking up for the silent majority.

was to argue that, while the population was not visibly Christian, they were, so to speak, closet Christians. This may or may not have been true. What is true is that having adopted this position, the writing of Whitehouse is then bound to reflect that view, and that view in itself is crucial to the argument Whitehouse is putting forward. If Britain was not full of closet Christians, then Whitehouse's arguments would have no force. Her battle would be lost before it began. Hence, in the use of first person plural pronouns and determiners to encompass groups in society larger than Whitehouse can rationally claim she was representing, Whitehouse was implying a support for the moral panic that she was promoting that she may – or may not – have had.

Again, there is a notable link between the SRM and the VALA here. Within the moral panic rhetoric category, both the SRMC and the MWC contain words connected to vagueness. Vagueness seems to be a key feature shared by both discourses, and vagueness is used for similar purposes in both corpora.

The *wh*-keywords in the MWC (*who, which, what*) merit some discussion, as they signal another important rhetorical device used in the corpus: the use of questions.[549] While not all of the uses of the *wh*-forms discussed here are questions, in the MWC 131 examples of *what*, 37 examples of *which* and 59 examples of *who* are questions. It is their importance as interrogative clause markers in the MWC that has led to their inclusion as *wh*-interrogatives in this discussion. What is the purpose and nature of questions in a discourse of the sort encoded in the MWC? The examples in Figure 7.9 illustrate the role of these *wh*-interrogatives well.[550]

In all three cases in Figure 7.9, a question is used as a rhetorical device to allow the writer to provide the answer that they prefer – the lunatic fringe consists of the critics of the VALA, not the VALA itself (1), censorship is the responsible choice (2), and Mary Whitehouse is the person who can stand watch over the nation's morals (3). By posing and replying to questions, the texts give a semblance of debate, while remorselessly pursuing an agenda of moral absolutism in a context in which the answers given to questions, and the outcome of a supposed debate, will be in harmony with the views of the VALA.

Convergence

Following from the analysis undertaken so far, is there any evidence for convergence in the MWC? More specifically, are the mechanisms of convergence, link collocates and nominal coordination in evidence in the MWC? Link collocates are certainly present, as has been noted in the discussion of the MWC so far. The following diagram shows the major set of linked keywords in the grouping 'permissive society', in the 'objects of offence' category.

Two minor networks occur in this category, a network in which the keywords *sexuality* and *liberation* are linked via the collocate *human*, and a

1   When the Viewers' and Listeners' Association was formed Sir Hugh Greene that evening called it a 'lunatic fringe'. <u>What</u> does this so-called lunatic fringe consist of? Among its members are an Anglican Bishop, the head of the Roman Catholic Church in Britain, a high official of the British Medical Association, many chief constables and many Members of Parliament. I submit that the lunatic fringe who ought to look at their own misconduct are the minority to whom I have referred not the people who are trying to get things put right.

2   A month earlier the Managing Director of STV the BBC's Scottish rival had attracted a good deal of attention by announcing that he intended to act as a censor himself 'to fight some kind of rearguard action against progressive loosening of moral standards'. <u>Which</u> is the more responsible attitude? The BBC has always prided itself on exercising its own controls and gives this as a reason for rejecting any control from outside. In *The Listener* Sir Hugh Greene re-stated the theory: 'We have (and believe strongly in) editorial control ...' That is exactly what all this protest is about. Some simple clear principles must be defined.

3   But <u>who</u> has the time for eternal vigilance? Mary Whitehouse, whom I first knew as a teacher in a School in my Diocese and had met at her parish Church, decided to give herself entirely to this new task and with great courage resigned from her teaching post.

Figure 7.9 The use of wh-interogatives by the VALA.

Table 7.18 Object of offence keywords

abortion	83	*reform* (7.32, *association, homosexual, law*), *venereal* (6.11, *crime, homosexuality*), *achieve, addiction,* <u>*homosexuality*</u>*, prior* (5.24, *masturbation*), *divorce, disease* (5.03, *homosexuality*), <u>*contraception*</u>*, associated* (4.89)
permissive	49	*lobby* (6.01, *homosexual*), *turning, trend, society, created, increasingly, highly, publicity, behaviour* (3.12, *contraception*)
school	209	*grammar* (6.16, *girls*), *red* (5.63, *book*), *libraries* (5.16, *public*), *approved, comprehensive, secondary* (4.94, *report*), *hygiene* (4.84, *copenhagen*), *drove, corner, choir* (4.57)
sexuality	33	*deepest, own, human* (3.02, *liberation*)

network where the keywords *homosexuals* and *sexual* are linked via the collocate *minorities*. The major network, however, focuses on the keyword *homosexual*. This is the network shown in Figure 7.10. In this figure I have only shown the nodes and their link collocates. Where a node being linked to is outside of the 'permissive society' group, I have underlined the node.

One notable feature of this diagram that we have not seen in the analyses so far is a near synonym acting as a collocate of a keyword – in this case *gay* as a collocate of the keyword *homosexual*. This collocate, in effect, is a variant of the word *homosexual* used in preference to homosexual when linked to *masturbation*, *intercourse* and *liberation*. Homosexual links, via the link collocates *acts*, *lobby* and *reform*, to the keywords *obscene*, *permissive* and *abortion* respectively. In turn, the keyword *contraception* is linked to the keyword *permissive* via the collocate *behaviour*. The weight of negatively loaded words in this network allows one to hypothesise with some confidence that the overall semantic prosody of *homosexual* is negative in the MWC, and, through a process of convergence, *homosexual* is linked to a host of negative concepts not necessarily related to homosexuality, namely *abortion, contraception, intercourse, liberation, masturbation, obscene* and *permissive*. Beyond that, if we link to the 'sexual acts' category via the keywords *intercourse* and *masturbation*, then *homosexual* may be linked to keywords such as *pornographic*. At the level of collocation, convergence is clearly visible in the MWC.

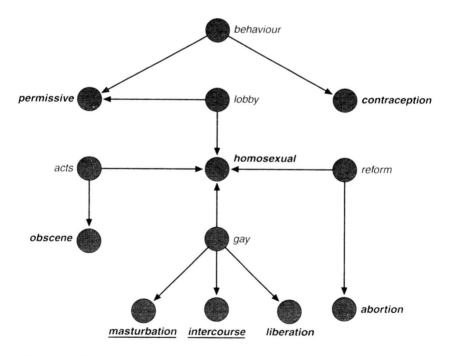

Figure 7.10 The major collocational network in the 'permissive society' grouping.

However, one keyword which is not the subject of collocation-driven convergence at all is *four-letter*. Indeed, an exploration of the keywords of the MWC finds *four-letter* as the sole bad language keyword, an isolation made all the more profound by the failure of *four-letter* to link to any other keyword whatsoever via link collocates. But may it be the case that *four-letter*, and other keywords for that matter, are subject to a process of convergence through coordination as was observed in the SRM texts?

The first thing that must be noted is that *and* is not a keyword in the MWC texts; nor is it a collocate of any of the keywords of the MWC. However, it still seems worthwhile exploring coordination in the MWC, as this mechanism for forging convergence – even if not present to the extent that *and* is turned into a keyword – may be a property of the text.

The nouns participating in the coordination differ markedly between LOB and the MWC. Tables 7.19 and 7.20 give the top-20 nouns appearing as part of a head-noun coordination in a noun phrase in LOB and the MWC.

Tables 7.19 and 7.20 show a clear trend in the MWC data. While the use of *and* is no more frequent in the MWC than LOB, the likelihood that certain nouns will be subject to noun phrase head coordination is much greater in the MWC than LOB. The top-20 coordinated nouns in the MWC are coordinated much more frequently than the corresponding top-20 from

Table 7.19 The most frequently coordinated nouns in LOB

Rank	Most frequently coordinated nouns in LOB	Frequency as a coordinated head noun per 100,000 words
1	*men*	4.8
2	*women*	4.4
3	*others*	3.7
4	*time*	3.2
5	*children*	2.8
6	*england*	2.7
7	*britain*	2.4
8	*food*	2.3
9	*knowledge*	2.3
10	*john*	2.2
11	*life*	2.2
12	*girls*	2.1
13	*music*	2.1
14	*science*	2.1
15	*water*	2.1
16	*friends*	2.0
17	*boys*	1.9
18	*mother*	1.9
19	*power*	1.9
20	*body*	1.8

Table 7.20 The most frequently coordinated nouns in the MWC

Rank	Most frequently coordinated nouns in MWC	Frequency as a coordinated head noun per 100,000 words
1	*viewers*	25.89
2	*men*	23.58
3	*radio*	14.79
4	*television*	14.33
5	*association*	12.43
6	*sex*	12.02
7	*listeners*	7.86
8	*violence*	7.86
9	*council*	6.47
10	*bbc*	6.01
11	*broadcasting*	6.01
12	*obscenity*	6.01
13	*parents*	6.01
14	*time*	6.01
15	*boys*	5.55
16	*ideas*	5.55
17	*life*	5.55
18	*women*	5.55
19	*taste*	5.08
20	*crime*	4.62

LOB. When one examines the top-20 of LOB, one sees the types of nouns that one would expect and which, largely, accord with reported accounts of which nouns are prone to such a form of coordination,[551] notably so called relational pairs such as *men/women* and *boys/girls*.[552] The top-20 list for the MWC does contain a relational pair – *men/women*.[553] Yet it also contains a number of other frequent pairings: *radio/television* (44 examples), *sex/violence* (18 examples), *BBC/ITA* (17 examples), *obscenity/pornography* (14 examples), *taste/decency* (9 examples) and *parents/teachers* (7 examples). What are the relationships expressed here? Three pairs are worth commenting on in some detail: *sex/violence*, *obscenity/pornography* and *taste/decency*. There are certainly two examples of the signification spiral in action – *sex/violence* and *obscenity/pornography* are forcing an equivalence between words. Interestingly, these are moral panic keywords. This gives further evidence for the use of coordination as a mechanism by which a signification spiral is formed in the text. A similar process links two positives together: *taste/decency*. This pair forces an equivalence between two concepts that is not necessary – taste may be indecent, and, aesthetically speaking, one may imagine circumstances under which decency may be tasteless.[554] Yet, by linking taste and decency, I would argue that decency serves to limit and define taste. Taste must be equivalent to decency and decency must therefore define taste. The decency in question in the MWC is the decency prescribed by Mary Whitehouse, and it was a decency which was to take precedence over any question of artistic taste and values:

> Instead of dismissing complaints as the work of a disgruntled puritanical minority, the corporation chiefs should try to appreciate the cause of public unease. They should seek to uphold standards of decency – even at the risk of ruffling artistic temperament.

Whitehouse's application of her view of what constituted decency was taken as one held by all. Her brand of decency is not given any detailed explanation in her works, rather it is appealed to as a given. However, attempts to impose any other definition of the word are attacked:

> Why should not the Governors decide for themselves whether a particular programme or person has offended against public feeling and make it clear that such standards are unacceptable? Those who are not prepared to accept their interpretation of what constitutes good taste and decency could be told that the Governors no longer have need of their services in the Corporation. The fact that they never seem to do so is perhaps due to their fear of a head-on clash with the Director-General and the Board of Management.

In this case Whitehouse is attacking another person's interpretation of decency – that of Sir Hugh Greene, and those who supported him – as being out of line with the views of the general public. Yet given the primacy of decency in Whitehouse's attitude to broadcasting, and her objections to the definition of decency by others, it remains curious that she never actually defines the term herself. One is almost tempted to suggest that the above paragraph could be turned around to say 'Those who are not prepared to accept Greene's interpretation of what constitutes good taste and decency could be told that the Governors would no longer listen to them'. Whitehouse would doubtless have found this mirror argument to be unacceptable. But it merely highlights the strength of her own commitment to the undefined notion of decency, and underlines the moral absolutism of her position. She could demand of the Governors that they take action against Greene in a way which, if applied to her, would be quite unacceptable, because of her blind belief in the absolute moral rectitude of her position. As such, it is easier to view Whitehouse's arguments as being based on faith, rather than rational belief.

There is little doubt, then, that convergence is just as active in the MWC texts as in the SRMC. Both colligationally and collocationally, convergence is being forced in the texts and signification spirals are being initiated. However, the claims made so far in this discussion, and the claims put forward in the previous chapter, rest to some extent in the validity of the general patternings extracted from the texts. These patterns have been extracted on the basis of lexis and, via a process of concordancing, the lexis has been assigned to broad semantic fields. If one does not accept the broad semantic fields outlined in this and the previous chapter, one could argue that the discussion presented may at best be subjective speculation. While I would argue that all linguistic analyses are to some degree subjective, I believe that the semantic field analyses presented here are generally valid. With reference to early-modern English it is difficult to test the relative subjectivity of the findings. Yet with modern English, the possibility exists to present the MWC to an automated semantic tagging system to see whether the same results, broadly speaking, for the semantic field analysis of the MWC can be derived automatically. This is exactly what I did in order to test the analysis undertaken in this chapter.

Semantic tagging

For the purposes of experiment, the MWC texts were run through a semantic tagger.[555] The semantic tagger assigns words to the broad semantic field in which they occur in a given example. This process entails assigning a unique semantic field code to a polysemous word to reflect its meaning in the context in which it occurs. Hence, to use a hackneyed example, in the utterance 'I robbed the bank' one would want *bank* to be placed in the semantic field of *financial institution* rather than *location* in this example. If the utterance were 'I sat on the river bank and fed the ducks', we would want the reverse decision.

My aim in applying the semantic tagging to the MWC was to discover whether, given a system which used a set of semantic fields not designed by me and a field assignment system not devised by me, a similar result to mine in terms of the identification of the preoccupations of the MWC could be achieved.[556]

In order to discover the key semantic fields in the MWC, I also tagged LOB and compared the frequency of the different semantic fields in each of the corpora. I used a log-likelihood score to rank the fields in descending order of significant difference. Table 7.21 gives the top-ten key semantic fields for the MWC compared to LOB.

I would argue that the results in Table 7.21[557] are broadly consonant with the findings presented in the sections on pages 194–195. The focus of the MWC on television, radio and cinema is reflected in the presence of that semantic field (Q4.3) in the top slot in the table. Similarly, the focus on people in general (semantic field ranked 5), males over females (semantic fields ranked at 4 and 7) and the family (semantic field rank 8) is also clear. The salience of discussions of sex (semantic field rank 3) and violence (semantic field rank 6) and the exhortations of the VALA to the government to act against sex and violence (semantic field rank 9) by criminalising activities and particular broadcasts (semantic field rank 10) are reflected in the

Table 7.21 Top-ten key semantic fields in the MWC

Rank	Semantic field	Frequency of field in MWC	Over (+) or under (−) represented	LL score	Description of the semantic field
1	Q4.3	3,687	+	6,680.19	The Media: TV, Radio and Cinema
2	Z8	23,710	+	6,633.12	Pronouns etc.
3	S3.2	1,098	+	3,579.39	Relationship: Intimate/sexual
4	S2.2	904	+	2,506.40	People: Male
5	S2	1,816	+	1,948.26	People
6	E3−	1,168	+	1,935.26	Violent/Angry
7	S2.1	622	+	1,787.04	People: Female
8	S4	1,290	+	1,399.10	Kin
9	G1.1	1,473	+	1,173.69	Government etc.
10	G2.1−	551	+	1,135.92	Crime, law and order: Law and order

semantic fields. Finally, the keyness of certain pronouns in the MWC leads to the appearance of pronouns (semantic field rank 2) in this table.

In terms of the analysis undertaken in this chapter, I would argue that the similarity of the results derived by semantic tagging and those arising from a keyword analysis is such that if not proved, in some abstract sense, to be right, one's faith in the keyword approach is strengthened by another process producing results compatible with the findings of the keyword analysis.

Transient key-keywords – the transient nature of the objection to bad language

What of those keywords which are 'transient', i.e. key in sub-parts of the corpus, but not in the corpus as a whole? A good example to look at are three keywords which are key in just one chapter of the MWC – *alf*, *bloodies* and *garnett*. These keywords, as well as allowing us to focus on the topic of transient keywords, also bring this discussion squarely back to the objections of Whitehouse to bad language. With reference to bad language, the most remarkable feature of both the keywords and key-keywords in the MWC is the near absence of any lexis clearly related to bad language in them. One keyword – *four-letter* – does occur. Yet, it is only when keywords are explored at the chapter, rather than the corpus or even the whole book level, that further bad-language-related keywords emerge. The reason for the appearance of *alf*, *bloodies* and *garnett* is obvious, in the light of the review of Whitehouse's campaigning in Chapter 5 – these keywords all arise in one chapter of one book (Chapter 9 of *Whatever Happened to Sex?*) where she writes about *Till Death Us Do Part*. The chapter is a discussion of White-house's campaign against the show, in particular focusing on the use of the word *bloody* in the programme. The topic of the chapter itself clearly explains the existence of the three transient keywords in question. Yet, the transient nature of the keywords calls for a return to an issue raised in Chapter 5: if Whitehouse was offended by bad language on television, why does the only swear word to appear as a keyword in her writing occur in a context where it is both transient and related specifically to one programme? If *Till Death* were the only programme using such language on the televi-sion, or if it was using it with an exceptionally high frequency, then the transient nature of the keyword *bloodies* may be understandable. However, Case study 1 in Chapter 5 showed this to be doubtful. The explanation put forward in Chapter 5 for Whitehouse's attack on *Till Death* seems to fit the evidence here – the complaint about bad language on television was princip-ally focused on this programme. There was not a general objection to such language in Whitehouse's writing, simply a specific objection to the way that this particular programme used it. As the attack on bad language, and particularly *bloody*, was solely in relation to *Till Death* for Whitehouse, the keyword *bloodies* is a transient keyword.

Might it be the case that the apparent salience of the attack on the lan-guage of *Till Death* is caused by Whitehouse's general objection being to four-letter words (hence the keyword *four-letter*), while *Till Death* generates a transient keyword *bloodies*, as it was this swear word, rather than any others, which was used with unusual frequency on the show? *Four-letter* is a keyword in two sub-divisions of the MWC; it is key in two books (*Cleaning Up TV* and *Who Does She Think She Is?*). In *Cleaning Up TV*, the phrase is key because it is used repeatedly with reference to a specific person on a specific programme – Kenneth Tynan, who used the word *fuck* on a late-night TV show.[558] In *Who Does She Think She Is?* the phrase is used repeatedly by Whitehouse to draw a dividing line between what she views as decent and what those that she opposes view as decent, as shown in Figure 7.11.

Four-letter becomes key for much the same reason that it is key in *Who Does She Think She Is?* and *bloodies* is a transient keyword when Alf Garnett is discussed. Bad language is used as the negation of the right of a person to be heard (example two), or the approval of its use is seen as a mark of member-ship of an out-group (example one). In the case of Garnett and the Yippies (example one), a four-letter assault on authority is just another example of things getting 'political'. Tynan's use of bad language associated him with the indecent out-group in just the same way as Avril Fox's defence of bad language makes her a member of that out-group. The Fox example is a particularly interesting one as it shows Whitehouse using bad language as a litmus test of membership of the out-group – Fox is asked for her opinion of the use of four-letter words in part to define a clear difference between the two speakers, but in large part to clearly identify Fox with the out-group

1 Mrs Whitehouse smiled. 'I suppose you'd approve of the <u>four-letter</u> word being bandied around the screen every night. Even in the news . . .,

Mrs Fox smiled back. 'You mean **** Why not? Modern English has no better word for sexual intercourse. In Saxon times **** was respectable. Now it's obscene because people tie dirty meanings to it.'

2 The host Headmaster to the Essex Sixth Form Conference on Censorship was discussing with the panel – the playwright, Wolf Mankovitz, Harold Nicholson the publisher, someone from the Religious Department of the B.B.C. whose name eludes me, and myself the order and general content of our contributions, when Mankovitz declared that he proposed to settle the censorship question once and for all by using the <u>four-letter</u> word! Obviously embarrassed, the Head said he would prefer a more academic approach to the matter, but Mr Mankovitz insisted. 'Then,' I intervened, 'if you say that in front of the children, I will walk off the platform.'

3 Decided to stay up and watch The Frost Show, very glad I did, Most extraordinary affair. Group of 'Yippies' led by the American Jerry Rubin, a defendant in the famous 'Chicago Six' trial, quite literally 'took over' from David Frost. The 'Yippies' – hippies turned political – squirted a water pistol in Frost's face, flung '<u>four-letter</u> words' about and smoked what they said was marijuana.

Figure 7.11 Four-letter assaults on authority.

and, thus, much in the same way as has been discussed previously in this book, to imply that her voice should not be heard and that her views are immoral.

It is also interesting to note the keywords that never appear, even in a transient fashion. Racist, sexist and homophobic terms in *Till Death* are never complained about by Whitehouse to the extent that they become salient. To some degree this is unsurprising – sexist and homophobic language was certainly not something which Whitehouse saw much reason to complain about. The absence of racism from the keyword lists is more notable, especially as racism was nominally a focus of complaint for Whitehouse.

Conclusion – distinction and moral panic theory

The use of bad language as a focus for complaint by Whitehouse is very much that predicted in Chapter 5 of this book. Bad language is objected to where it is being used as part of a four-letter assault on authority, as seen with the keyword *four-letter* and the transient keyword *bloodies*. But bad language as such is not a central concern for Whitehouse and the VALA. It only becomes a concern when the discourse of power is threatened. Bad language use which conforms to the discourse of power (e.g. the lower classes using bad language, but refraining from its use in the presence of their social superiors – see Case study 1, Chapter 5) is not a cause for concern. Whitehouse was defending a discourse of power that had already been established in the seventeenth/eighteenth century. The moral panic of the SRM set in train a process of distinction. The discourse of panic propagated a view of bad language which became entrenched in British public life to the extent that bad language became an active marker of distinction, as seen in Chapters 2 and 4 of this book. This established bad language as, for example, a token of low social class. To do so, the moral panic of the SRM had to foreground bad language in its discourse, as the distinctions associated with bad language were not, at that time, widely accepted. They became so as the moral panic which began with the SRM was carried forward by others, notably the SPCK, and the distinctions inherent in the discourse of the SRM became naturalised.

By the late twentieth century, the discourse surrounding the use of bad language, as represented in the writings of the VALA, was different. Importantly, the discourse did not need to work to establish distinctions. These distinctions had been established for centuries by the time that Whitehouse wrote, and consequently she could simply appeal to these distinctions as a given. There was no need to argue that the distinctions should be established, merely maintained. Another difference between the SRM discourse and the VALA discourse relates, however, not to the originators of the discourse as such, but rather to their reactions against the discourse of others. The SRM was using a moral panic discourse to subvert the current language of power – they were problematising the language-use of the lower classes, of those members of the middle classes who did not conform to their vision of how the middle classes should act, and of those members of the upper classes over which the SRM could claim moral, if not social, superiority. The SRM established a discourse of power with reference to their own language use. In doing so, they faced no serious opposition for some years. Whitehouse, on the other hand, faced a group which was trying to act as the SRM had done in the seventeenth century – revolutionaries who, through four-letter assaults on authority, wished to overturn a discourse of power in order to establish a new discourse of power that they would control via the four-letter assault on authority. Whitehouse reacted against that group and in doing so faced a more organised opposition, with an alternative discourse of power. Whitehouse appealed to the distinctions and discourse of power established by the SRM in order to combat a group who had, one could argue, similar abstract aims to the SRM, though their discourse was a competing one. So, in the late twentieth century we can see the primacy of a discourse of power, the discourse of purity, established centuries before by middle-class moral revolutionaries, defended against a new set of political, typically leftwing, revolutionaries who wished to subvert and supplant that discourse.

What was the outcome of that conflict? In some ways, the answer to that question would beg a whole new book – looking in detail at the use of bad language in the media and society from 1980 onwards. However, I would argue that ultimately Whitehouse was successful in defending the purity of the discourse of power. The distinctions established in the discourse of the SRM are very much observable in the BNC data gathered in the early 1990s. Interestingly, if one watches an evening of television in the UK, one will find bad language used in abundance, certainly after the watershed. Yet, the use of bad language on television conforms to the discourse of power. In much the same way as *Steptoe and Son* conformed to that discourse, and hence was not complained about, so comedy programmes and the like which use bad language today conform to the discourse of power: one will find bad language in shows on which the powerless are shown at play – not on the news or political debating programmes. The likes of Alf Garnett are not seen on British television so clearly nowadays – there is little in the way of an effort to subvert the language of power on contemporary British television. Indeed, I would argue that, much as was the case with the Steptoes, when one sees bad language on TV that conforms to the expectations of the discourse of power, then the distinctions underpinning that discourse are strengthened. Almost perversely, the increase in the abundance of bad language on television has served to strengthen the purity of the discourse of power.

Bad language has clearly been subjected to a successful process of distinction, fuelled by moral panics about bad language, for centuries. In the twenty-first century, Bourdieu's claim that the disempowered are 'at the mercy of the discourses that are presented to them'[559] takes on an added dimension when one considers that one of the discourses being presented to the disempowered is the discourse of disempowerment itself, i.e. a discourse which contains BLWs. One could argue that not only do the disempowered have to acquire the 'pure' discourse in order to wield power, they now have to resist the non-pure discourse that is increasingly being presented to them as something which it is accepted that they may use amongst themselves in everyday speech not focused on 'serious' subjects. Worse still, attempts by the disempowered to use the language of power may be actively lampooned, with their attempts to accommodate to the discourse of power being represented as a token of servility, a servility which, once again, is accepted. Acceptance of this sort is not to be welcomed where purity and power are still linked. The situation is vexatious. I am certainly not suggesting that the disempowered should be taught, from an early age, to accept the purity of the discourse of power. Such a suggestion would condone educational practices established in the eighteenth century which have enforced the purity of the discourse of power and the moral ascendancy of the middle class. It would also, in all likelihood, perpetuate the system rather than bring about change. Yet, it is difficult to suggest that purity, language and power should be disentangled – Chapters 5 and 7 show, quite clearly, how interest groups are able to defend the linkage of the three. So I can only finish this book on a somewhat aspirational note. The purity of the discourse of power is discriminatory and maintains an established hierarchy of power which disadvantages the disempowered further by problematising their language use. While I do not believe that the relationship between language, purity and power can be changed by one book, I do believe that this book has begun a process whereby speakers of English can begin to critically re-examine the relationship between these three factors. Through critical re-examination may come change, and that is something I for one would welcome.

Postscript

Readers may have read parts of this book thinking that the issues raised are firmly in the past. To conclude this book, I thought it would be interesting to reproduce parts of recent news stories to show that, while the times may have changed, issues have not. Following are a series of excerpts from news stories. The heading in each case relates to issues in this book which I think the news article relates to.

Convergence (BBC News Online, Tuesday, 2 April 2002, 19:53 GMT, 20:53 UK), in a discussion of Anti-Social Behaviour Orders (Asbos):

> Known as Asbos, the orders are designed to prevent theft, intimidation, drunkenness, violence and other nuisance behaviour. Asbos, available to police and local councils, often bar people from entering a geographical area or shop and can include bans on specific acts, such as swearing in public.

The Purity of the Discourse of Power (from *Delete Expletives?*,[560] a press release from the Advertising Standards Agency), in a discussion of results showing where people thought that the use of bad language was unacceptable:

> At the top of the pyramid of high public expectations was BBC1 because it was paid for by the licence fee and, therefore, expected to be more 'responsible'.

Skeat and Morrison Ride Again (BBC News Online, Friday, 1 October 2004, 12:47 GMT, 13:47 UK):

> Police in Russia's western Belgorod region are imposing fines on people who swear in public – and local officials say the campaign is very popular. The officials say young people have been minding their language since the ban was introduced in July. Any person caught uttering profanities in public can face fines of up to $50.[561]

Convergence in Belgorod (ABC News Online, Wednesday, 20 October 2004, 9:49 AEST):

> Soviet-style morality brigades are also busy at work across the town cleaning swear words from walls and replacing them with propaganda posters and stickers decrying the practice. The man leading the war of the words is local official Pavel Bispalenko, who says Russia's future is at stake. 'Swearing is a moral disease, a social illness,' he said. 'Scientists have proved that people who use bad words turn into bad people, so the aim of our campaign is to improve the health and the moral standing of our nation.'

A Masculine Pursuit (Ananova News, October 2004):[562]

> Too much swearing can make men impotent and women develop male characteristics including facial hair and extra muscles. According to research by Russian scientist Gennady Cheurin and his team at the Centre for Ecological Safety and Survival in Yekaterinburg, the research was based on the popular belief that water has a type of 'memory' that can be influenced by positive and negative forces. Cheurin said that his team had sworn at a glass of water for several hours and then poured it over wheat seeds. Only 48 per cent of those seeds which were watered with the 'foul' water sprouted as opposed to 93 per cent of seeds watered with holy water taken from natural springs. Cheurin said: 'We then looked at heavy swearers and others who never used bad language, and found whenever men use these words in their daily life, this immediately leads to sexual dysfunctions, i.e. impotence. If a woman uses these words in her daily speech, she slowly begins transforming into a man, getting more hair and muscles.'

Unsuitable Entertainment (ABC News Online, 31 January 2003):

> Even in this age of raunchy rap and tasteless television, high school drama coach Ruth Ridenour warned students trying out for 'Les Miserables' that it contained swear words. Three, precisely: 'hell,' 'bitch' and 'bastard.' The students were all right with that, but some parents were not. Several complained, and administrators are now preparing to consider whether the musical – four weeks into rehearsals and set for an April 11–13 run – is too raw.

The Flood Never Ends (BBC News Online, Tuesday, 23 September 2003, 09:49 GMT, 10:49 UK):

> A study of the major broadcast networks by the Parents Television Council found a jump in profanity on 'virtually every network'. It called

on the TV industry to reduce what it called 'the flood of vulgarity'. The results mirror the findings of a similar UK survey in July which found that the use of bad language was also increasing on British TV. That report – by Mediawatch-UK – said that the 'f-word' was used almost 1,500 times in films on the five terrestrial channels during the first half of 2003.[563]

The Purity of the Discourse of Power (BBC News Online, Wednesday, 3 March 2004, 03:18 GMT):

Top referee Stuart Dougal has been given an unprecedented fine and reprimand for swearing at Rangers midfielder Christian Nerlinger. A Scottish FA spokesman said: 'The committee decided that Mr Dougal should be fined £200 and severely censured.

'The committee interviewed Mr Dougal and decided that he had been guilty of using foul language.' Dougal, who was caught on BBC cameras during a league match against Partick Thistle, is considering an appeal. 'I'm very disappointed by what has happened,' Dougal said. 'A fine of £200 and an official censure amounts to a double punishment in my eyes. I accept I may have used language unbecoming of a referee and I was not surprised to be called in front of the disciplinary committee.'

Notes

1 Bad language, bad manners

1 Though see Crystal (2001: 173) for a contrary view. The one way in which I would concede that swearing may be special is neurologically. There is certainly evidence, gathered from Tourette's syndrome sufferers exhibiting coprolalia as a symptom, that the organisation of and/or connections forged by swear words in the mind may be quite distinct from those formed by general lexis. See Jay (1999). In addition, readers interested specifically in swearing in America should refer to Jay's earlier work, Jay (1992).

2 Thompson (1998) provides an accessible overview of the competing models of moral panic.

3 For readers interested in seeing and hearing some contemporary reporting of these events, look at: http://news.bbc.co.uk/onthisday/hi/dates/stories/may/18/newsid_2511000/2511245.stm.

4 Note that the media are an essential component of moral panic theory, as noted by Sindall (1990: 29).

5 Cameron (1995: 82).

6 Beaumont, cited in Thompson (1998:3).

7 I use the past tense here as the Association has changed its name to Media Watch. In that guise it still campaigns against such things as bad language on the television.

8 I do not want to give the impression that I am the first linguist to use moral panic theory, or even to use moral panic theory to look at panics related to the appropriate usage of the language. Neither claim would be true. Cameron (1995) is an example of a linguist who has used moral panic theory to explore 'good' and 'bad' language. The analysis presented in this book can best be seen as complementary to that of writers such as Cameron. While those writers have considered such matters as grammaticality and the notion of standard English (see also Milroy and Milroy 1985), they have not considered bad language as such. This book is hence expanding the scope of the debate set in train by Milroy and Milroy, and furthered by Cameron.

9 Bourdieu (1984: 176–177).

10 Bourdieu (1984: 194).

11 Bourdieu (1984: 226).

12 Bourdieu (1984: 255).

13 Bourdieu (1984: 461–462).

14 Bourdieu (1984: 462).

15 Bourdieu (1984: 462).

16 The distinction between forms of language that are approved of and legitimised in society in general (overt prestige) as opposed to non-overtly prestigious forms

that may be approved of in groups, especially disempowered and marginalised groups, within society (covert prestige).

17 Labov (1966a) and Trudgill (1972) can reasonably be viewed as the studies which established the concepts of overt and covert prestige in sociolinguistics. Both are still rewarding reads. For modern research using these concepts, almost any introduction to sociolinguistics will cover this topic, e.g. Trudgill (2000).

18 One might argue that the Lancaster Corpus of Abuse, which is an annotated subset of the spoken BNC, is not a corpus as such, but is rather either an extract of a larger corpus or simply a set of annotations which should be reincorporated into the BNC. As the corpus has been constructed with a specific research question in mind, within the so-called problem annotated corpus paradigm, I am quite happy to call the LCA a corpus. For those readers who would rather call it an annotated extract or somesuch, I suggest that for 'corpus' they read 'annotated extract' (or whatever pleases them) when they see the LCA referred to as a corpus.

19 I am indebted to the Faculty of Social Sciences, Lancaster University, for a small grant which enabled me to construct this corpus. I would also like to thank Dan McIntyre, who undertook the bulk of the corpus construction work under my supervision.

20 I am indebted to the Faculty of Social Sciences, Lancaster University, for a small grant which enabled me to construct this corpus. I wish to thank Matthew Davies who built this corpus under my supervision.

21 The Penn (1745) tract is an extract from an earlier Penn work from 1679. However, as it was published in 1745, I assume it is part of the discourse of that time, even though it was originally part of an earlier discourse, albeit in a different form.

22 See Schmied (1994) for more details of the corpus.

23 In using the corpus in this way I am assuming that the corpus can be viewed as a reasonably balanced and representative sample of English in the period. Given that other authors have fruitfully taken this view, e.g. Claridge (1997), I do not view this assumption as particularly controversial.

24 See Johansson *et al.* (1978) for more details of the corpus.

25 See Hundt *et al.* (1998) for more details of the corpus.

26 Chapter 4 of this book discusses the SRM in depth.

27 Note that this argument, once again, applies to the MWC corpus.

28 See Mair *et al.* (2002) for an example of such a study.

29 Scott (1999).

30 I will not, however, discuss the calculation of keyness. This is done by using the log-likelihood measure (see Dunning 1993) to determine when the frequency of a word between two corpora differs significantly. Interested readers are advised to refer to the help system of WordSmith for a description of the way in which keyness is determined in the program.

31 Such as Scott (1999, 2000, 2003), Tribble (1999) and Baker (2004). My use of the term 'keyword' here relates expressly to the work of Scott. However, Scott's notion of keyword does have clear parallels in the work of other corpus linguists who do not necessarily use the term 'keyword', notably Rayson (2003). See Baker (2004) for a critical appraisal of the strengths and weaknesses of keywords.

32 For the study in this chapter, I set the p-value threshold to 99.9999999999999 per cent, i.e. a very high significance threshold was used, well beyond the 99.9 per cent level of significance used in many studies as a threshold for significance.

33 Readers interested in the use of the log-likelihood test in this book in preference to the chi-squared test are referred to Dunning (1993).

34 See Baker (2004) for a further discussion of this point.

35 I make this statement based on how WordSmith calculates key-keywords. There is no reason, in principle, if given a suitably mark-up aware concordance package, and an appropriately marked-up corpus which could carry out a key-keyword analysis, one could not change the textual unit one wanted to explore key-keywords within (e.g. paragraphs, chapters, documents) dynamically, i.e. the mapping of file structure to text structure could be avoided. However, as I am not aware of any such program being commercially available, I will tailor my remarks to WordSmith.

36 Phillips (1985). Note, however, that while my approach is clearly inspired by Phillips, and I gratefully acknowledge his intellectual contribution to the work done here, I do not follow his methods. I want to present an analysis here which can be replicated, or at least emulated, using a commercial software package, in this case WordSmith. If I had chosen to follow Phillips' methods exactly, that would not have been possible.

37 Firth (1957), with whom the idea is often associated, drew inspiration from Wittgenstein. Similar concepts had also been developed in the Prague school in the 1930s (see McEnery and Wilson 2001: 24 for further details). In addition see Kennedy (1998) for a further history of the collocate.

38 See, for example, Hoey (1991) and Stubbs (2001).

39 This is a fairly standard span for studies of collocation, following from the exploration of Sinclair *et al.* (1970) into optimum span settings.

40 See Sinclair (1966).

41 In corpus linguistics, as in this book, lemmas are conventionally written in small capital letters.

42 This example is taken from Phillips (1985: 147).

43 The following description is brief and technical, and is largely intended for readers already familiar with the work of Phillips (1985). For those readers requiring a fuller description of that work, I suggest they refer back to Phillips.

44 I am in fact using the squared variant of mutual information in this study. While I would have preferred to use the cubed variant in light of the findings of Daille (1995), the cubed variant is not available in the WordSmith package.

45 I accept that this is a relatively arbitrary level at which to set the MI score. However, as is common with heuristic measures of this sort, this score was determined by me and set at a level which gave rise to useful collocates in my data. Below 3, the quality of the proposed collocates declined markedly, while setting the level above 3 seemed to delete good collocates. However, I am not suggesting that 3 can be viewed as a standard cut-off when using the MI^2 association measure. I believe this varies depending on the size and nature of the data set to which the measure is applied.

46 Note that Phillips used the chapter as the largest interval for his technique. While I accept that the chapter is a useful interval, I see no necessary reason why the whole text, or even the whole corpus, may not be used as the interval for Phillips' technique. While I concede that the result of focusing the technique on each of these levels may be rather different, I believe that valid results can be achieved at each of these levels, and that these results may interact usefully when derived from the same data set at multiple levels simultaneously.

2 'So you recorded swearing': bad language in present-day English

47 This part shares its name with a talk of the same title given by me at King's College London. I am indebted to Willard McCarty for this splendid, concise, title.

48 The quotation in the title is taken from a speaker, Andrew, in the spoken BNC in file KPA utterance 3,635.

49 The corpus was originally constructed as a set of annotations based on concor-

dances from the spoken BNC. These concordances were later reintroduced to those BNC spoken files in which the swearing had occurred to form the LCA itself.

50 A major problem with the construction of the LCA was the poor markup of such information in the first version of the BNC. When initially released, the spoken section of the BNC had significant errors in its metadata. Most notably, the social class of speaker information in the spoken corpus was so unreliable as to be unusable. The LCA was initially based on that faulty markup. However, the LCA has now been updated using the corrected metadata encoded in the BNC World Edition. With that said, it would be a brave analyst who would say that they were convinced that the metadata in the BNC World Edition is entirely reliable. I do assume, however, that this new metadata is accurate enough to produce results that are not likely to be invalidated by future versions of the BNC.

51 These words are (Hughes 1998: 208) *arsehole, bastard, bitch, bugger, cow, cretin, cunt, fart, fucker, idiot, imbecile, moron, pig, pillock, prat, prick, shit, sod, sow, swine, tit, turd, twat.* See McEnery *et al.* (2000) for a corpus-based evaluation of Hughes' claims.

52 There are categories absent from the corpus at present, for example, terms of abuse based on disability. I hope to expand the corpus to cover such terms in the future.

53 For example McEnery *et al.* (2000).

54 See, for example, Oftedal (1973), Bailey and Timm (1976) and Head (1977).

55 See Coates (2003) for example.

56 The log-likelihood score is used in this chapter to determine the significance of observed pairwise differences. The critical value for statistical significance at $p < 0.05$ is 3.8. The critical value for statistical significance at $p < 0.01$ is 6.6. Comparing male and female usage of BLWs using the log-likelihood test gives rise to a significance score of 0.96, which is not significant, even at the 95 per cent level. So while there are slightly more male than female examples of bad language in the LCA (3,876 v. 3,790 respectively), the observed difference is not significant.

57 This finding leads me to reflect on Lakoff's (1975: 10) claim:

> Consider (a) 'Oh dear, you've put the peanut butter in the refrigerator again.'
> (b) 'Shit, you've put the peanut butter in the refrigerator again.'
> It is safe to predict that people would classify the first sentence as part of 'women's language', the second as 'men's language'.

If people did draw this conclusion, at least in Britain in the early 1990s, they would have been quite wrong. Given that *shit* is used in a Gen type utterance here, the grounds for ascribing utterance (b) to a female are twofold – *shit* is a typically female word and Gen type utterances are typical of females (see Table 2.6).

58 The data in this table are derived from the BNC World Edition. The normalised figures given are based on raw frequencies derived from the 3,267,444 words of data marked as spoken by females and the 4,920,742 words of data marked as spoken by males in the spoken corpus.

59 I have combined here the findings of Millwood-Hargrave (2000) and the British Board of Film Classification Guidelines to the certification of films in the UK. I am indebted to Margaret Ainsley for providing me with the latter. I would encourage readers to explore these classifications because in large part the statements made in this chapter about BLW strength rely on the credibility of these studies.

60 I have excluded *pissy* from this table as I could not reliably locate the word within the reports used to construct the scale of offence used in this chapter.

61 Males are the target of BLWs 1,094 times, females 653 times, yielding a log-likelihood score of 112.54.

62 For simplicity, I have excluded here cases where the frequency count of gender direction was one.

63 Here I am discussing only examples where the word appears as something other than a Literal type.

64 The BLW *bitch* is directed at females 36 times and males six times in the LCA. One could argue that in switching the direction of the BLW from a female to a male, one is implying femininity in the male at whom the word is directed. I would not dispute that claim. What I would note is that *gay* – and other gender exclusive terms – do not appear to be used in this way even though they, in principle, could be. The exclusivity of the direction of the BLW at one gender or another is the issue here, not what effects are achieved when BLWs with apparently gender-exclusive direction are directed at either sex, interesting though that question is. Another way of approaching some of the words is to note differences in the meaning of different words directed at males and females, e.g. sexual inadequacy/dissidence being an important concept behind male-directed words (e.g. *bastard, gay, wanker*) and animal words being typical of female-directed words (*cow, bitch*). Given that such topics have been discussed by authors such as Hughes (1998) and Montagu (1973) I will note, but not discuss, such features here.

65 In the LCA, this word is directed by females once at a female and twice at a male.

66 I accept that there is a possible flaw in my method here. I assume that the five categories of the scale used so far are each weighted equally, i.e. each covers one-fifth of the dimension of offence. If this is not true, the results based on this assumption may be at fault. Additionally, I assume that the scale of offence is linear, i.e. there is a steady increase in offence as one moves up the scale, with words in category five being, roughly, five-times as offensive as those in category one. If it is in fact the case that the scale is not linear, and, for example, words in category four are four-times as offensive as category one words while category five words are not five but ten-times more offensive than those in category one, then the results presented would change. However, this later problem is less worrying – the differences presented here would simply be exaggerated by the type of non-linear scale discussed, not fundamentally invalidated.

67 It should be noted that in calculating these figures, I used only the BLWs listed in Table 2.9 – I did not attempt to rate all words, relying instead on those weighted by reports such as Millwood-Hargrave (2000). However, as Table 2.9 covers all of the important BLWs in the LCA, I lost only 29 examples of female-directed BLWs and 30 examples of male-directed BLWs when calculating these figures. All told, 624 examples of female-directed BLWs and 1,062 examples of male-directed BLWs were used to calculate these figures.

68 Here the same equation is used as was used to calculate the average strength in the previous example. The result is based on 3,996 female and 3,952 male BLW. Examples selected as per the previous example.

69 Another question that would be well worth exploring would be whether a person who is the target of third-person BLW use is present or not when the word is uttered. Again, this would be close to impossible using the spoken BNC.

70 Note that I am not claiming that it is not possible to form a Gen with any of the words weighted 3 here – it simply does not happen in the data that I have.

71 When an LL test was used, with five degrees of freedom to test whether the

decline from U25 was significant across time it proved to be so, with a score of 2,515.4, giving a significance level of 99 per cent. On those grounds I will not discuss the slight (non-significant) difference between the U45 and U60 age groups.

72 Though a Gen may be generated even if the *Oh* is omitted, of course.

73 This search was done using BNC Web, using the search pattern (oh)_("!").

74 The differences across the age groups for different categories of BLW use when tested was statistically significant at the <0.001 level. Fisher's exact test was used because of sparsity in parts of the table used to calculate significance. The score achieved was 742.739 with 70 degrees of freedom.

75 An LL test, undertaken with three degrees of freedom, produced a score of 1,546.218 when BLW use across the four social classes of the BNC was considered. This gave a significance score of <0.001.

76 See Labov (1966b).

77 The use of the different categories of BLW use is statistically significant. Using Fisher's exact test, because of the relative sparsity of the data in some categories and social classes, the difference in the use of BLW categories for the different social classes were found to be significant at the <0.001 level (score FE = 478.59, 42 degrees of freedom).

78 The pairwise comparisons of male and female targeted BLW use by the different social classes yielded the following LL scores, all of which exceed the 0.001 significance level at 1 df: AB (25.39), C1 (84.60), C2 (443.89), DE (454.86).

79 I would like to thank Dr Damon Berridge, of the Applied Statistics Department, Lancaster University, for his help with the statistics used in this section.

80 For example, the groups use the frequent word form *bloody* 1.0 and 0 times respectively. This is low even by the standards of conservative non-BLW users such as the 60+ age group. For example, for males this group uses *bloody* 89 (AB), 47 (C1), 10 (C2) and 20 (DE) times. For females the word is used 8 (AB), 10 (C1), 4 (C2) and 31 (DE) times. The counts for the three groups under discussion are very low indeed.

81 If the BNC were balanced for age, sex and social class in combination, there should be roughly 208,333 words in each combined category (i.e. $(2 \times 4 \times 6)/10,000,000$ per category).

82 Lemmatisation might be a way of addressing this problem. However, for most of the word forms under investigation, there is little word form variation, e.g. *cunt/cunts* would provide CUNT with a frequency of 57. Combining word form frequencies into lemma frequencies hardly helps. Where there are a greater variety of word forms, it is also the case that some of the word forms on their own – notably *fucking* – are frequent enough to allow analysis to proceed without lemmatisation. Consequently I do not employ lemmatisation here.

83 When testing for significance in log-linear modelling, we are checking the difference in the mean counts across the number of count categories we have (in this case three, as three words are being investigated) to see whether those counts vary significantly. Significance is tested using the chi-squared statistic. In the case of age, a scaled deviance score of 952.6 (ten degrees of freedom) is achieved. For class, the score is 325.7 (six degrees of freedom) and for sex the score is 450.7 (two degrees of freedom). All scores are significant at $p < 0.01$. Note that, in this case, raw, rather than normalised frequencies were used because, although a scaling factor could be introduced to normalise the data, as the data were all drawn from the same sample space and the raw results are subject to the same scaling, the results with normalised data tended towards orthoganality with the raw results.

84 The reliability of the result is shown by the standard error scores produced by the model when the analysis is undertaken. The standard error figures become

inflated as data sparsity is encountered in the analysis of the interaction of age and class, indicating that the results of the model should not be trusted. The same effect is even more pronounced when age, class and sex are considered together.

85 This shrinkage could, of course, be a more general feature of 60+ speech. However, when I explored this question using the BNC there was no evidence to support this view. Using the number of types per million words uttered as a proxy for lexicon size, the 60+ group has by far the most varied lexicon – the number of types per million for the age groups are as follows: U15 (6,789.83), U25 (6,947.08), U35 (5,994.55), U45 (6,952.12), U60 (5,694.01) and 60+ (9,814.17). Using this measure seems to indicate that far from shrinking, lexical variation peaks in the 60+ group. Using other measures (e.g. a standardised type token ration) the peak in the 60+ group disappears, but no decline occurs. The standardised type token ratio results are U15 (29.66), U25 (30.09), U35 (30.81), U45 (31.16), U60 (30.57) and 60+ (30.97). Neither measure suggests that the lexicon in 60+ speakers shrinks. Hence the disappearance of BLWs from the productive lexicon with advancing age is all the more marked as it is not part of a general process of lexis deletion.

86 Apart from more data, we would also have to take the question of the words covered by the LCA much more seriously, as it may be the case that the corpus does not contain word forms which would, in fact, change this result if they were included. It may also be the case that euphemism may have an explanatory role to play here, i.e. there is an increase in euphemism as BLW usage declines. While I have little faith in either of these possibilities, I cannot dismiss them without a very thorough and painstaking revision of the data, which I have not undertaken as, after those problems are solved, the greatest problem, lack of data overall, will still remain.

87 See particularly Eiskovits (1998: 48–49).

3 Early modern censorship of bad language

88 The Dominican, Peter Bromyard, writing in the fourteenth century, called for swearers to be branded and placed in the stocks. Henry I imposed fines for swearing in his presence (Montagu 1967: 108–111).

89 In the Elizabethan era, for example, diocesan courts were charged with judging cases brought against the faithful which were crimes 'against the Pietie of god'. These included both blasphemy and swearing. For further details, see Cosin (1591). There is no evidence that the courts regularly tried such cases, and one must doubt the effectiveness of this sort of censorship. Indeed Capp (2003) argues such laws were largely used as a last resort in an attempt to sustain social harmony, not as a means of enforcing morality.

90 See Montagu (1967: 307–315).

91 It has been argued that modern attitudes to bad language have their roots in the courtly language adopted in Mediaeval Europe (see Coates 2004: 13–14, for a potted version of this argument). While not doubting the existence of courtly language, and its undoubted effect on some speakers of English, I would argue that courtly language had little impact on society as a whole. I doubt that it even had any long-term impact on the court itself. As an explanation of the existence of certain attitudes to bad language in Modern English, the courtly argument is not sufficient in itself as an explanation. The process whereby the language of the court became the language of the masses has not been explored. Indeed there is little evidence, as this chapter seeks to show, that the state itself ever set about trying to impose such a form of speech on society at large. Nonetheless, courtly language itself is an interesting early

flourishing of an idea which was to become potent around the end of the seventeenth century – that power and purity of language are linked.

92 See Kishlansky (1997: 72).

93 See Kishlansky (1997: 73).

94 Cressy (1977a, b, 1980) concludes that literacy levels surged in the late sixteenth century. At the beginning of the seventeenth century he concludes that one-third of the male population of England was literate. Literacy was not evenly spread across the population, however, and seems to have been closely associated with social status. Similarly, while book ownership increased in the early seventeenth century, it seems to have been the preserve of propertied males. Indeed, there is evidence that the prospect of women reading was seen as socially threatening and offensive; Bartholemew Dann of Faversham was so incensed whenever he found his wife reading that 'he would catch the book out of her hands and tear it to pieces or otherwise fling it away' (Clark 1976: 97).

95 While the Church Court of High Commission was ultimately responsible for this censorship, much day-to-day censorship was carried out by the clergy acting on its behalf.

96 This was possibly not the only time that a Star Chamber decree profited the Stationers. Lambert (1987) argues that the Star Chamber decree of 1636 escalating censorship was for the economic benefit of the Stationers' Company, not to meet the needs of the government.

97 Coward (1994: 98) sums up the situation nicely when he says, 'The pulpit was the most important means of disseminating government propaganda and information in the days before the development of other means of mass communication.'

98 The Church Court of High Commission had clear authority over all clergy in the period under discussion (Usher 1913).

99 Such was the power of print that it eventually supplanted the pulpit as the medium of mass communication when 'royalist pamphlets refuting the heresies of the radicals introduced their ideas to a much wider audience than itinerant preachers could ever have done' (Hill 2001: 344).

100 Hill (2001: 31) says that he is led 'to suspect, though I cannot prove, that there was silent censorship, usually self-imposed' in the period of Laudian censorship at least.

101 It was certainly successful as a means of extending the monopoly of the Stationers' Company. John Wolfe, one of those who had not been a member of the Company and had produced printed works before 1586 became 'an extremely loyal and leading member of the company' (Dutton 2000: 23) after the Star Chamber decree.

102 See Clegg (2001: 29).

103 In this the Elizabethan state was continuing a typically Tudor censorship policy pursued from the reign of Henry VII onwards, a policy where the major measures to control the press related 'directly or indirectly to the Crown's interest in ensuring a particular religious settlement' (Clegg 1997: 25).

104 Martin Marprelate was a pseudonym used to protect the identity of the author of four texts produced by radical protestants, *The Epistle* (1588), *The Epitome* (1588), *The Mineralls* (1589) and *Hay Any Worke for the Cooper* (1589). Death sentences were proclaimed on those suspected of having written the documents, and the first publisher of the tracts, Robert Waldegrave, fled in fear from England to Scotland. His fear was justified – the next printer of the tracts was captured and tortured.

105 See Neale (1957). Tellingly, Neale claims that the Puritans opposed any 'measure which would weight the scales more heavily against the clandestine Puritan press' (Neale 1957: 94–95).

106 Quoted from Greg (1967: 142). See also a proposed *Act to Restrain Licentious Printing* of 1580 which sought to hold back a 'Sea of wickednesse' emanating from the presses (Arber 1875, Vol. II: 75). The bill was neither presented nor enacted.

107 See Clegg (1997: 173–174) and Clegg (1997: 178).

108 I agree with Clegg (1997: 30) when she says that in the Early Modern period no 'monarch can truly be said to have inherited the government of his or her predecessor; shifting religious priorities made this impossible, especially in matters of press control and censorship.'

109 See Clegg (2001: 29).

110 A quote from a letter written in 1604 at the King's behest by Robert Cecil (Salisbury Manuscript 190.1, Hatfield House).

111 See Clegg (2001: 68–89).

112 James's greatest censorship campaign, in 1620–1621, encompassed censorship of both the printed word and sermons in an attempt to suppress opposition to his decision not to become embroiled in the war caused by the accession of the protestant Frederick to the throne of Bohemia. This war developed into the Thirty Years War.

113 I do not want to imply that the Gunpowder Plot led to a persecution of Catholics. It did not. It did, however, lead to a number of legislative measures aimed directly at ensuring the loyalty of English Catholics to the Crown, such as the Oath of Allegiance imposed on them in 1606.

114 See Bellarmine (1610) for an example of a Catholic response to *A Premonition*. To give an impression of the insulting nature of Cardinal Bellarmine's work, it accuses James of eating frogs and claims that he was party to the execution of his mother. James is also likened to a carrion crow.

115 While The Master of the Revels formally takes on the role of censor of plays from this date, the beginnings of the role lay in a decree of Elizabeth I's in 1581, which authorised Tilney, as Master of the Revels to license plays and players. However, the goal of this order seem to have been to ensure the quality of performances rather than to censor them (Streitberger 1978).

116 Sir Henry Herbert licensed plays for print from 1624 to 1640. This is in some ways surprising as the 1581 decree did not include this among the duties of the Master of the Revels. However, the licences for printing plays were issued and were dutifully noted in the Stationers' Register. However, attempts by Herbert to license non-dramatic texts between 1632 and 1633 met with resistance. Herbert was even summoned before the Star Court in 1632 to explain why he was issuing licences for such material. While he was not censured, one must expect that events such as this encouraged Herbert to restrict his licensing activities to drama. The end of his licensing dramatic texts for the press came in 1637, when a Star Chamber decree on printing made it clear that the responsibility for licensing works for the printing press lay in hands other than those of the Master of the Revels. This stopped Herbert issuing such licences, though after this decree he did issue one further printing licence, in 1640.

117 Notably, for example, with reference to Jonson's play *The Magnetic Lady*, Dutton (2000: 42–43).

118 As Charles II did in the case of *The Wits* by Davenant, where he over-ruled some of Herbert's decisions (Bawcutt 1996: 186, entry 281).

119 As Charles I did in the case of *The King and the Subject*, by Messinger, where he found part of the play to be 'too insolent, and to bee changed' (Bawcutt 1996: 204, entry 386a).

120 For a fuller discussion of this case, readers are directed to Clegg (2001).

121 Wither (1624: 66).

122 See Wither (1624: 43, 44, 54, 58 and 59).

123 Wither (1624: 44).

124 Wither (1624: 58).

125 To be fair, Wither (1624: 60–61) presents a defence of why the songs could be sung in church. However, he also accepts (Wither 1624: 56) that the hymns should be used with caution 'because sensuall men will turne that grace of God into wantonesse'. He also mounts a defence against a charge of blasphemy for his choice of language in presenting the songs (Wither 1624: 56–57).

126 This analysis of Wither's case follows Clegg (2001: 49–50).

127 Wither, G. *Withers Motto*, London, 1621.

128 By 1623–1623 the *Metrical Psalms* went through 80 editions (see Clegg 2001: 45).

129 See Clegg (2001: 45).

130 Throughout this chapter, where referencing Herbert's records, I use the edition of the records edited by Bawcutt (1996).

131 Bawcutt (1996: 182, 265b).

132 The plays being Shakespeare's *A Winter's Tale* and a play by an anonymous author entitled *The Peaceable King*. It was *A Winter's Tale* that Herbert did not examine at all. See Bawcutt (1996: 45).

133 Bawcutt (1996: 183, 265e).

134 Bawcutt (1996: 183, 265e).

135 Bawcutt (1996: 182, 265c).

136 Bawcutt (1996: 182, 265a).

137 Bawcutt (1996: 182, 265c).

138 See Bawcutt (1996: 52).

139 Bawcutt (1996: 183, 265c).

140 To be more precise, it is likely that the 1633 edition of the text represents the version licensed by Buc, while the 1647 edition is that censored by Herbert. See Bawcutt (1996: 60) for details.

141 See Bawcutt (1996: 54).

142 See Bald (1938: 296–299).

143 See Dutton (2000), Scott (1620) and Hill (2001: 395–396) for evidence of the prevalence of allegory as a device for making political comment in the Early Modern period. Scott is particularly interesting as his is a contemporary voice suggesting that this indeed happened. In discussing the use of allegory by early modern dramatists Hill (2001: 396) concludes, rightly in my view, that 'many of them wished to say things to which they knew the censor was likely to object, and so they adopted techniques calculated to avoid this attention – or they could not have published at all. Some at least of their readers would be aware of this fact.'

144 See Bawcutt (1996: 52).

145 See Bawcutt (1996: 73) and Bawcutt (1996: 154, 177c).

146 See Bawcutt (1996: 154–155, 117c).

147 Patterson (1984) and Yachnin (1991) are two good sources of support for this view. Patterson (1984: 7) sums up the attitude well when she says 'there were conventions that both sides accepted as to how far a writer could go in explicit address to the contentious issues of his day, how he could encode his opinions so that nobody would be *required* to make an example of him'.

148 This quote from the *Calendar of State Papers and Manuscripts Relating English Affairs, existing in the Archives and collections of Venice*, Vol. 11, no. 99, pp. 489–490. A similar sentiment is expressed in *State Papers* 14/121, art. 251, Public Records Office, London, regarding an obscene slander made in 'lewde and contemptuous words' against the King and Queen of Bohemia by one Edward Floyd. Floyd was dealt with leniently as 'the King thincks it better to

suppress such scandalous speeches than by his punishment to blase them further abroad'.

149 *The Tamer Tamed* case is far from unique. Dutton (2000) provides further examples. Also, see Smith (1995) for further support of the view that Herbert's censorship in this case was politically motivated. It should be noted that the other explanation current for Herbert's action – greed, as he wanted to maximise his fee income from licensing – is also consonant with the argument put forward in this chapter that political or economic interests abound in the censorship of bad language in the period in question.

150 See Bawcutt (1996: 52).

151 See Bawcutt (1996: 208, 413).

152 See Bawcutt (1996: 60).

153 This claim is similar to that of Heinemann (1980: 37), who argues that censorship in this period was 'almost exclusively' political.

154 See Hughes (1998: 118).

155 See Montagu (1973: 167).

156 There were rare performances of plays between 1642 and 1660, usually under some guise and the guidance of Sir William D'Avenant.

157 The Ranters were Antinomians, who believed that the saintly were beyond the reach of the law.

158 Abbott (1937–1947: Volume III, 437).

159 A line from an anti-Ranter poem, *A New Proclamation*, by 'J.F.' (1693).

160 See Coward (1994: 247) for further details of the Act of 1650.

161 Quotes in this paragraph drawn from Scobell (1658: 124–126).

162 See Clarkson (1659) for a lurid, and possibly exaggerated, account of the practices of the Ranters.

163 It should be noted, however, that even where opinions were clearly expressed in public, 'persons with distempered brains' were excluded from prosecution under the Act. This provision may be important in understanding the case of Abiezer Coppe (see pages 77–79).

164 Friedman (1987: 16).

165 The quotes in this paragraph are from the second *Flying Fiery Roll*, pages 17, 1, 10, 12 and 12 respectively (Coppe 1650).

166 See, for example, Friedman (1987: 92).

167 Coppe (1651a: 2).

168 Coppe (1651b: 4).

169 Coppe (1651b: 12–13).

170 Tickell (1651: 37–40).

171 Clarkson, while once a so-called Captain of the Rant, wrote the most sensationalist account of the Ranters after recanting, *The Right Devil Discovered*, in which he writes at length about the immoral lifestyle of the Ranters and the joy that they took in swearing (Clarkson 1659: 104). While Clarkson should be read with caution, it is undoubtedly the case that *The Right Devil Discovered* does offer an insider view, albeit somewhat sensationalised, of the Ranters.

172 I would like to acknowledge the support of the British Academy for my work on *Mercurius Fumigosus*, grant reference LRG 35423.

173 *Mercurius Fumigosus*, Issue 10, 1654.

174 *Mercurius Fumigosus* was licensed by Glibert Mabbott, the Commonwealth censor. See Ward *et al.* (1907–1921, Vol. VII, Chapter XV, sub-section 5).

175 See Bawcutt (1996: 101–103) for a discussion of *The Cheats*.

176 Note that once again economic interests were paramount in the introduction of this Act. The government appointed Sir Roger L'Estrange to enforce the licences issued under the Act. L'Estrange was 'a rancorous conversationalist with a financial interest in restricting printing' (Kishlansky 1997: 229).

177 Though it should be noted that Charles II himself was not much given to using bad language. See Fraser (2002: 237).

178 See Plum (1972: 59) for a brief description of the focus of Restoration censorship. Of particular note for the following chapter is the emergence of informers and agents provocateur in the reign of Charles II to secure the convictions of non-conformists. See also Keeble (2002: 148–154).

179 See note 81, this chapter.

180 See Kishlansky (1997: 29).

181 See Capp (2003: 84).

182 See Capp (2003: 89).

183 Pierce (1671: 22).

4 Modern attitudes to bad language form: the reformation of manners

184 Though it must be noted that, from William III onwards, some measure of official support was afforded to the religious societies, whether that be at the initiative of the monarch (as was the case with William III and Queen Anne) or through the interest of powerful figures in the establishment (such as Lord Townshend). See Isaacs (1982: 396) for details.

185 In this chapter I am referring to the middle classes, but in doing so I do not wish to imply that the post-Marx tripartite taxonomy of class, with its attendant narrative of class struggle, can be applied to the late seventeenth and eighteenth centuries. I do not believe it can. Nonetheless, I follow other authors in accepting the three-fold divisions of society current in this period, but relabel the three classes with the more modern terms of lower, middle and upper class. See Porter (1991: 53–54) for a good discussion of the class system of this period and Speck (1977: 31–61) for a splendid overview of class attitudes and classifications in England in the Georgian era.

186 See Speck (1977: 297–298) for a table contrasting the composition of English society in 1688 and 1760.

187 Porter (1991: 290–291).

188 This is a selection of trades from members of a society that met on the Strand in London in 1694 (Rawlinson Manuscripts 1694: 2).

189 Though that does not mean to say that the societies did not draw any members from the upper and lower classes. Rather, the bulk of the society's strength was drawn from the middle classes. For example, of the 254 names listed in Rawlinson (1694), only seven are gentry. Of these, none are nobility; five are clerks, one is an attorney and the final gentleman is a steward.

190 For example, the Bristol SRM was charging a ten-shillings-a-year membership fee in 1700. As Curtis and Speck (1976: 48) note, such subscriptions ensured that the SRMs were 'exclusive to gentlemen'. Such exclusivity is easily explained when one considers that, in the late seventeenth century, ten shillings represented a sizeable sum, well beyond the means of a labourer, for example, who could expect to earn £10 (200 shillings) per year. However, a shop-keeper, who earned on average £45 per year would have been able to afford such a subscription (estimates of income taken from Porter 1991: 48, 70).

191 A phrase used by John Tutchin to refer to the theatre in *The Observator*, March 1703 edition.

192 Letter to Viscount Cornberry, February, 1664–1665, reprinted in Bray (1827).

193 Collier (1688: 6).

194 Collier (1688: 57–58).

195 Collier (1688: 7).

196 Collier (1688: 7).
197 Collier (1688: 8).
198 Collier (1688: 58).
199 Collier (1688: 14–16).
200 See Krutch (1961: 104–105 and 117).
201 Collier (1688: 72).
202 Other critics shared this talent for the discovery of hidden offence, for example Bedford (1706), which is little more than a tedious catalogue of such dubious divinations of offence.
203 See Krutch (1961: 118–119).
204 Collier (1688: 57).
205 Atmore (1811: 158) is a good example here. He launches a fearsome attack on the early-nineteenth-century stage very much in the vein of Collier and Bedford, saying of the stage that 'in this amusement, whatever can corrupt the mind is set off to greatest advantage. Every lewd allusion receives strong emphasis from the actor's air and voice, whilst the greater part of the audience expresses aloud the filthy joy it gives them.'
206 See Krutch (1961: 157–158).
207 Horneck (1690).
208 The anonymous SRM pamphlet favouring the censorship of the stage, 'A Letter to A.H. Esq' (1698) is most likely addressed to Horneck. See Krutch (1961: 132).
209 Note that in my account of the history of the Society for Reformation of Manners, I am taking the line proposed by Woodward (1701) and Plum (1972: 90) that the Society for the Reformation of Manners grew out of the religious societies.
210 Woodward (1701), who witnessed the formation of the societies, seems to ascribe their formation to Horneck. However, considering that Horneck's biographer, Kidder (1698) does not do so, one must treat Woodward's claim with some caution.
211 Also, some religious societies later became branches of the SRM. See, for example, the SPCK correspondence archive, Cambridge University, letter number 261.
212 Kidder (1698: 14).
213 The secretive nature of the societies continued to be a source of concern for the critics of the later Society for the Reformation of Manners. See the SPCK correspondence archive, Cambridge University, letter 122.
214 Woodward (1701: 31).
215 Woodward (1701: 118).
216 Defoe (1702: 35).
217 Middlesex Records Office, Sessions Book 575, folios 46–47.
218 See Dunton (1696) for example.
219 Both quotes from Horne (1978: 5).
220 See Isaacs (1982: 392).
221 See Webb and Webb (1903: 15–48).
222 Swift (1709).
223 I am sceptical about the claims made by writers like Dennis (1726) that sodomy was an act 'the like of which has never been heard of in Great Britain before' (1726: 20) and that 'the sodomites are invading the land' (Bray 1709: 30). Given the evidence available in such books as Bray (1996), it is possible that, while Dennis and Bray may not have heard of this activity before, it had nonetheless been spoken of and practised by other Englishmen well before the early eighteenth century. Indeed, Woodward (1697) decries the practice. Similarly, with reference to the masque, it was attacked as a modern, foreign, innovation, yet masques had been held in England in the reign of Charles II

(Bahlman 1957: 5). The key point here seems to be that both sodomy and masques had not been known to the masses. The key change that occurs in this period is that sodomy is discussed and masques are held for the masses, not just for the Court. Bray and Dennis are reacting against their discovery of these practices, not the nation's.

224 This is a quotation from *An Account of the Societies*, 1699. The authorship has various been attributed to Yates, Defoe or Woodward. While I do not wish to enter a discussion of this question of authorship here, I will state my own view that Yates (after Portus 1912) was the author and cite this work as such.

225 See The Agreement of the Tower Hamlet Society, Rawlinson Manuscripts 129: 16–27. Folio 16 clearly outlines the goals of the Tower Hamlets society to be 'to consult ... upon the best methods for putting the laws into execution against houses of lewdness and debauchery, and also against drunkenness, swearing and cursing'.

226 The degree of linkage between the SRM and the RSs is contested. The view presented here is that the SRM was a modified form of the RS. This is certainly the view which Burnet (1818) takes, and it is implied, if not stated, by Woodward (1701). In addition to these two sources, the development of the RSs seems to facilitate the creation of the SRM, as noted in this chapter. However, some authors, notably Bahlman (1957), present an alternative view, that the similarities between the RSs and the SRM are coincidental and that they were in fact entirely distinct. Readers interested in Bahlman's argument should refer to Bahlman (1957: 68–70).

227 In ascribing the formation of the first SRM to Stephens, I am taking at face value his claim from Stephens (1700: 4) that 'It was I ... who began our society'. In the face of no evidence to the contrary, and given that his claims were well known enough to have invited refutation, it is reasonable to ascribe the establishment of the first SRM to Stephens. However, readers curious to read an alternative view are directed to Curtis and Speck (1976: 46).

228 Stephens (1691: 10) states that the SRM was originally Anglican, yet the SRM soon developed connections with non-conformists and some SRMs admitted non-conformists to their ranks, while on occasion separate SRMs for non-conformists were created alongside the Anglican SRMs, as happened at Derby (see the SPCK, Abstract Letter No. 288, 28 April 1701). The sermons given by the SRM were often given to separate non-conformist or Anglican audiences, though there were sermons given to both groups at once, such as the annual sermon to the SRM given by Earle in 1704.

229 See Curtis and Speck (1976: 48–49) for more details of the assumptions underlying the SRM.

230 Dunton (1694: 22–25) deals with this issue at length.

231 See Williams (1698), Nicolson (1706) and Penn (1708). Defoe (1704) gives a full account of the storm of 1703.

232 For example, Wright (1715: 12) argues that a growth in immorality is often a prelude to the triumph of Catholicism 'the nearer any age has been approaching toward popery, the more has all manner of iniquity abounded'.

233 See Grant (1700).

234 See Penn (1708: 37–39) for further discussion.

235 For the purpose of this discussion I will focus on the work of the SRM to eradicate bad language. However, the legal situation that applied to bad language also applied to a number of other areas in which the SRM was to become active, such as the prosecution of people not observing the Sabbath, prostitutes and practising homosexuals. For an excellent account of the persecution of homosexuals by the SRM, see Norton (1992).

236 Yates (1699) cites five laws against swearing and cursing and one against

blasphemy that were on the statute books in 1699. See Portus (1912: 240–242) for details.

237 Bahlman (1957: 71).

238 Indeed some societies were formally constituted as single entities, which were in effect both SRM and SPCK societies. See, for example, the Lincolnshire society (Wanley Manuscripts, pages 145–153).

239 This quotation is from the monument to Evelyn at Westbury church.

240 See Lowther Clarke (1959: 15).

241 The SPCK, Abstract Letters No. 1301 (5 September 1709) and No. 2131 (6 July 1710).

242 Indeed, when one considers the work of Skeat and Morrison as presented later in this chapter, it becomes clearer why the public could not differentiate the two societies.

243 See Lowther Clarke (1959: 87).

244 The exception here is the case of churchwardens. The SPCK did seek to root out churchwardens who were lax in their duty of reporting to the justices those who did not attend Sunday services. See Bahlman (1957: 74).

245 The SPCK also sought to spread Anglicanism actively. See the letter of Mr John Sutton of Derbyshire, 1701 (SPCK correspondence archive, letter number 288). The intent in establishing a charity school in this case is clearly to suppress Catholicism and non-conformism.

246 Russell (1697: 9).

247 This table is derived from Portus (1912: 125–127).

248 The Scottish SPCK added the goal of the suppression of the Gaelic language to its teaching activities, identifying the language as being allied to ignorance and Catholicism (Withers, 1982), though the 'English only' policy of the Scottish SPCK was reversed in 1766. While a fuller discussion of this point is beyond the remit of this book, it is interesting to note that the role of the SPCK as language police was not confined to changing attitudes to swearing – they also sought to suppress autochthonous minority languages by schooling and through the use of informers who would report on those who used Gaelic, by encouraging school masters to 'appoint private or clandestine censors to debate such as transgress' the rule that only English was to be used at school (Scottish Records Office document GD 95/10/79). There is evidence that it was not only Scots Gaelic that was targeted by members of the SRM – an anonymous letter from 1704 (Anon. 1704: 2) reports that 'the Bishop of the Isle of Mann, with the joint concurrence of clergy and gentry, is raising a fund for schools with a peculiar intention to improve the inhabitants knowledge of the English tongue' (see Tracts #680, rare books collection, British Library, London).

249 For more information on the Welsh and Scottish SRMs, see Portus (1912: 127, 145–155). For more information on the SRM in the North American Colonies, Gildrie (1994: 202–207) is strongly recommended. It should be noted that the SRM also sent copies of key SRM texts to European countries such as Belgium, Holland and Switzerland – see Woodward (1701: 4–7). While Jamaica did not have an SRM, there is evidence that the SPCK in Jamaica engaged in activities more typical of the SRM. See the Wanley Manuscripts, pages 154–157.

250 Curtis and Speck (1976: 54).

251 This was clearly the understanding of at least some SRM members. For example, Mr Bradshaw of Nantwich, Cheshire, says in 1699 that in his area 'the inundation of vice is owing to toleration' (SPCK correspondence archive, letter number 29). This toleration was caused both by the failure to set up schools to educate the poor appropriately and the 'want of good justices' who would impose the morality laws (the SPCK correspondence archive, letter number 52).

252 The religious nature of the schooling here is essential as Christian thinkers had long assumed that 'belief in God or Jesus Christ implies membership of a uniform and hierarchically constituted social body' (Woodhead 2004: 33). The use of religion by the SRM and the SPCK to enforce class/power distinctions was not at all unusual in Christian society in the early modern period.

253 Wanley Manuscripts, pages 172–173.

254 Watts (1728: 4).

255 See Lowther Clarke (1959: 24).

256 See Lowther Clarke (1959: 26). The play in question was Shakespeare's *Timon of Athens*.

257 Report of White Kennet to the SPCK, quoted in Lowther Clarke (1959: 31).

258 See Lowther Clarke (1959: 43).

259 See Allestree (1731: 99–100).

260 See Allestree (1731: 102).

261 See Allestree (1731: 104).

262 See Allestree (1731: 299).

263 See Allestree (1731: 105).

264 See Allestree (1731: 300).

265 See Allestree (1731: 270–271).

266 See Allestree (1731: 110).

267 See Allestree (1731: 281).

268 Indeed, there are modern books inspired by Allestree's work. For example, see Perry (1980).

269 See Lowther Clarke (1959: 25). Contemporary reports state that 'about two thousand children are actually put to school' in London and Westminster alone (Anon. 1704: 1). The writer is also clear about the effect of the schooling on the language of the children: 'the design of the schools has been successful, so the effect of it, on the morals of the poor hath been still more happy' (Anon. 1704: 2) and 'there is an outward appearance at least of a more sober and regular conversation' amongst the poor.

270 It is worth noting that the Black Rolls contained the names of those accused and subsequently found innocent as well as those accused and convicted. For example, Dunton (1694: 34–35) publishes an early Black Roll in which of the 115 people named and shamed for keeping bawdy houses, only 40 had been subsequently convicted. These Black Rolls were also distributed to be publicly displayed (see Wanley Manuscript, page 162: 'A barber to whom we gave a Black list promised to fix the same in his shop').

271 No extant copies of the report for 1731 or 1736 are known. The publication of distribution figures ceased in 1738.

272 Derived from Portus (1912: 254–255).

273 For example, Bishop Lloyd of Worcester had 2,000 copies of the pamphlet, *A Short Account of the several kinds of Societies* printed. He distributed these freely (see Robertson 1903: 15). The pamphlet is anonymous, though Portus (1912: 223–228) ascribes it to J. Hooke. Woodward (1701) also wrote that the SRM had 'given away, at their own Expense, not less than Fifteen Thousand ... Discourses, besides divers Thousands of ... larger books'. In an anonymous letter from 1704 (Anon. 1704: 3) a member of the SRM reports that 'from one county we are informed that some thousands of books have been disposed of'.

274 *A Short Disswasive from the Sin of Uncleanness*, London, 1701 (Anon.)

275 Archdeacon Nicholson of Carlisle, quoted in *The Life of John Sharp*, Volume 1, page 183.

276 Krutch's (1961: 162) description of the approach of the SRM to the prosecution of sinners.

277 Defoe (1697: 249).

278 See Woodward (1712: 15).
279 Woodward (1701: 12).
280 London Records Office, Repertory 97, folio 160. Further examples of justices both in London and Buckinghamshire being encouraged to execute the anti-immorality laws are given by Bahlman (1957: 51).
281 Woodward (1701: 12).
282 Rawlinson Manuscript number 129, folio 32.
283 See the *Athenian Mercury*, Volume 3, 4 August 1691, page 2, column 1.
284 For example, Bahlman (1957: 54) claims that prosecutions for swearing and cursing surged in Buckinghamshire after the SRM established itself there. The level it reached was higher than in other counties where the SRM had no presence.
285 However, the enforcement of the laws may at times have had unexpected results. Mr Bradshaw of Nantwich writes, in 1700 (the SPCK correspondence archive, letter number 204), that the imposition of the morality laws in Cheshire, where magistrates had not been willing to accept secret depositions against offenders, had led to an upsurge in non-conformism, with some groups having grown 'very insolent, especially the baptists'. While the SRM was relatively non-denominational, not all non-conformist sects viewed their actions as such.
286 Woodward (1701: 10).
287 Woodward (1701: 11).
288 Rawlinson Manuscripts 129, folio 30.
289 Woodward (1701: 12) encouraged members of the SRM to seek out wrong-doers 'by Endeavouring by your self and Friends to encline them to exert their Power in going about into the Streets, Markets and other publick Places, on Week-Days, for the taking up of Drunkards. Swearers &c'.
290 Yates (1699: 9).
291 Portus (1912: 49).
292 Woodward (1701: 29–30).
293 Rawlinson Manuscripts 129, folios 3–8.
294 Both examples from the *Calendar of the Sessions Records, County of Buckingham* 2, 67, 109.
295 Indeed, Dunton (1705: 334–335) claims that one Robert Stephens did indeed earn his living as an informer for the SRM.
296 See Queen Anne's *Proclamation for the Encouragement of Piety and Virtue* 18 August 1708, for example.
297 See Tenison (1699: 5–6) for example.
298 Such as John Cooper, whose death is reported in Woodward (1702).
299 Bissett (1704: 37).
300 See Middlesex Records Office, Sessions Book 491, folios 60–61.
301 See Bahlman (1957: 22).
302 Stephens (1691: 14) complains that, in Middlesex, informers were 'put off, checked, and discouraged for their pains'.
303 Schooling beyond the charity school movement was provided in a number of guises, through private tutors, dame schools, grammar schools and public schools. The collection of teachers could hardly be called a profession nor the whole a system of education. Except where picked up through the intervention of an interested curate or somesuch, education cost the parents. In many families the cost was two-fold – as Porter (1991: 165) notes: 'Lower down the social scale, parents were . . . less eager to send their children to school: they could ill afford the fees, or to forego their labour.'
304 Yates (1699) discusses how existing laws are to be used to prosecute 'Prophaneness and Debauchery'.

305 Derived from Portus (1912: 253–255).
306 The reports from 1725–1729 do not break down the prosecutions brought by the society by category. A mere 22 convictions for cursing and swearing were brought in 1730; 1731 is not available. The last record of prosecutions for cursing and swearing comes in the report of 1732, which records 14 prosecutions being brought by the society.
307 Convictions for Sabbath-breaking represent the bulk of successful prosecutions brought by the society. A possible reason for this is that it was easier to convict a person for Sabbath-breaking as there was usually tangible proof of it, and the 1677 Sunday Observance Act was a particularly effective piece of legislation. This contrasts strongly with convictions for swearing which were difficult to bring, in part because the evidence usually amounted merely to hearsay. See Bahlman (1957: 62) for a fuller discussion of this point.
308 It was under the umbrella of 'lewd and disorderly practices' that the SRM listed its prosecutions of homosexuals. Readers interested in finding out more about the persecution of homosexuals by the SRM are encouraged to read Norton (1992).
309 Woodward (1701: 77).
310 Extract from 'A letter from a minister to his parishioners shewing the indispensable duty incumbent upon all persons to give information to the magistrate as well as against prophane swearing and cursing, as against other crimes and misdemeanours'. This letter is in the British Library bound in Tracts volume 680. The letter lacks an author or date of publication, but is assumed to be from the late 1690s.
311 From the Wanley Manuscripts of the SPCK. However, the extracts printed here are available in reproduction in Gibson (1998: 59–60).
312 Interestingly, *A Help to a National Reformation* warned against entrapment of this sort. However, even though the book had appeared a year before Skeat and Morrison visited Kent, entrapment was still clearly in use by some agents of the SRM.
313 See Pritchard (1864: 156–163).
314 See Pritchard (1864: 156–163).
315 Wanley Manuscripts, pages 161–162.
316 See Curtis and Speck (1976: 56, 58–59) for a discussion of how the prosecutions of the SRM impacted both on the lower class and those members of the middle class which did not share the values of the SRM.
317 This is indeed the pattern of prosecutions undertaken by the SRM – see Speck and Curtis (1976: 58–59).
318 Mandeville (1705: 34).
319 A quote from *Isiah 49:4*, a text used in the penultimate sermon to the Societies for the Reformation of Manners 1737.
320 The SPCK, Abstract Letter Number 299, 19 May 1701.
321 Wesley (1698).
322 Ryther (1699: 62–63).
323 Bedford (1734: 17–18).
324 Tong (1704: 3–4).
325 As indeed did other practices. There are reports that public houses refused to admit constables on the Sabbath, keeping their doors locked so that they could not enter and observe laws being breached. See the SPCK correspondence archive, Cambridge University, letter 77.
326 Bissett (1704: 28).
327 See Bahlman (1957: 60–61).
328 See Porter (1991: 169, 279).
329 Text from *I Timothy 5:22*, used by the Reverend Henry Sacheverell when condemning the SRM in a sermon in 1709.

330 See the SPCK correspondence archive letters 54, 85, 87 and 118 for good examples of the resistance of the clergy to the societies. Letter 118 is particularly interesting as it outlines two objections to the societies from the clergy: (1) that the members of the societies are fanatics; and (2) if the clergy support the campaign they imply, thereby, that they have been negligent in the execution of their duties to date. The clergy also seem to object to the societies on the grounds that they represent a form of repressive Calvinism, saying that the societies were supported by clergy who were 'Scotchmen and loved the Kirk'.

331 Sharp (1704: 17). Note that Sharp writes under the *nom-de-plum* Philalethes.

332 See Bahlman (1957: 85).

333 Sacheverell (1702: 14).

334 See Bahlman (1957: 84–86).

335 A letter from James Vernon in James (1841: 133–134).

336 A letter from James Vernon in James (1841: 133–134).

337 See Bahlman (1957: 91) for evidence of this amendment.

338 For example, see issue 2 of *The Night Walker* (Dunton 1696: 2, 17).

339 See the Parliamentary Report, *The Evidence given at the Bar of the House of Commons upon the complaint of Sir J. Pakington . . .* (1702).

340 See Sacheverell (1710). Of particular note are pages 114, 206, 209 and 236–237.

341 Curtis and Speck (1976: 61).

342 Dowdell (1932: 24–32).

343 Jeckill (1698: iii–iv). To be fair, however, the London Aldermen were generally supportive of the SRM, for example appointing one Francis Higginson as a constable in 1736 at the SRM's behest (see London Records Office, repertory 140, folio 168).

344 The SPCK, Abstract Letters No. 288 (28 April 1701) and No. 301 (10 May 1701).

345 The SPCK, Abstract Letter No. 369 (20 December 1701).

346 See Curtis and Speck (1976: 57).

347 Most notably the beginning of the role of the Lord Chancellor in censoring plays under the provisions of the 1737 Licensing Act, a role that was to endure in Britain until the 1960s. See Porter (1991: 254) and Krutch (1961: 190). However, earlier in the period under discussion, the Master of the Revels and licensing were still in operation. In 1698, Queen Anne specifically instructed the Master of the Revels, Charles Killegrew, not to license or relicense plays which contained 'profane and indecent expressions'. See Krutch (1961: 183–185).

348 Krutch (1961: 165).

349 A point made well by Porter (1991: 231): 'The new audience, paying the piper and calling the tune, was broadly middle class and middle brow. To please them, drama shed the Frenchified gentlemanly-rakish taste of the Restoration, with its sly sexual innuendo, blasphemies and cynicism.'

350 Unless otherwise stated, all quotes and examples in this paragraph are drawn from Porter (1991: 303–307).

351 See also the quotation regarding clothing terms in the conclusion of this chapter.

352 Allestree (1673).

353 In doing so it is argued that Allestree fundamentally changed the view taken of women in English society, adding an emphasis on modesty and passivity that earlier writers had not expressed. See Keeble (2002: 189).

354 See Friedman (1993: 179–200) for an excellent account of the view taken of women in mid-seventeenth-century society. Also, see Capp (2003: 13).

355 Friedman (1993: 179).
356 Allestree (1673: 12).
357 An interesting line of enquiry to pursue to explore why this angelicisation took place is to consider the possibility that bad language afforded the disempowered, in this case women, a chance to assert themselves. There is evidence that women used bad language in just this way – the use of bad language, in public, to upbraid a wayward husband was viewed as a way in which a wronged wife could gain some measure of local support and revenge (see Capp 2003: 89). In a powerfully patriarchal society (Capp 2003: 18–19), using bad language was a way for women to empower themselves. With the possibility of using bad language removed from them, one can only conclude that women were disempowered further.
358 Allestree (1673: 13).
359 Allestree (1673: 29–30).
360 See Keeble (2002: 186–190) for a longer discussion of the changing views of women in the late seventeenth century.
361 Both the quotation and the reference to the *Evangelical* magazine are taken from Porter (1991: 309).
362 These quotations are taken from Murray (1999: 257–259).
363 See Murray (1999: 261) for the original quotations supporting the examples of indelicate speech in the Regency given here.
364 Leigh Hunt, quoted in Murray (1999: 261).

5 Late-twentieth-century bad language: the moral majority and four-letter assaults on authority

365 Marsh (1998: 232–235).
366 Odgers and Eames (1905: 297).
367 Other printed and performed examples of *bloody* preceded Shaw's, but Shaw's use of *bloody* caused the widest scandal and debate by far. See Montagu (1967: 256–257) and Hughes (1998: 186–187).
368 In 1939, it appears that the nominal quota was two per play. See Montagu (1967: 263).
369 Headline from an article discussing the newly launched *Worker's Challenge* in the British newspaper, *Sunday Dispatch*, 25 August 1940.
370 Sergeant McDonald was replaced by William Colledge (aka William Winter) in October 1940. Colledge was a member of the North Somerset Yeomanary.
371 Public Record Office WO 71/1131.
372 I am thankful to Dr M. Doherty, of the University of Westminster, for providing me with this data, which represents a selection of broadcasts from 1940–1944.
373 This example is taken from the edition of *Worker's Challenge* broadcast on 11 September 1940.
374 See Weale (1994: 48).
375 British Broadcasting Corporation, Report WAC R9/9/5, LR/210, *Listening to Enemy Broadcasts*, 20 January 1941.
376 Public Records Office, Report PREM 4/100/1, *Postal Censorship*, 4 April 1942.
377 See Doherty (2000: 91).
378 Morgan (2001: 62).
379 Morgan (2001: 82).
380 Notably Wilfred Pickles. See Morgan (2001: 83).
381 Although, if Tome Sloane, a head of BBC light entertainment in the 1960s, is to be believed, the word *bloody* was first used on a comedy show in *Steptoe and Son* rather than *Till Death Us Do Part*. See Munro (1979: 164).

382 Faithfull and Dalton (1995: 193).
383 Faithfull and Dalton (1995: 339).
384 Faithfull and Dalton (1995: 358).
385 See Thompson (1998: 123–124).
386 See Tracey and Morrison (1979: 26–27) for details.
387 See Marcuse (1964).
388 Wallis (1976).
389 See Tracey and Morrison (1979: 34–35).
390 Milne (1988: 30).
391 BBC producer Sydney Newman quoted in the *Daily Express*, January 1963.
392 This quotation is from *The Variety Programmes Policy Guide for Writers and Producers*, an internal document published by the BBC. The booklet was officially abandoned in 1963.
393 Letter from the BBC in response to a complaint about the Dennis Potter play, *Angels are so Few*, quoted in Tracey and Morrison (1979: 99).
394 Letter from Lord Hill of Luton, Chairman of the BBC (1967–1972) to Mary Whitehouse, quoted in Tracey and Morrison (1979: 112).
395 Letter from Lord Hill to Mary Whitehouse, 20 July 1972, quoted in Tracey and Morrison (1979: 90).
396 See Milne (1988: 79–80) for a fascinating insider view of the deliberations of the Annan Committee.
397 It must be noted, however, that it may well be the case that bad language was a major cause of complaint for those who complained, but those who complained may not have been representative of the population as a whole. The only notable occasion on which this hypothesis was explored was in response to the VALA's criticism of a documentary on Andy Warhol, which was criticised for its use of bad language, nudity and sex. An independent survey of viewers showed that, while non-VALA viewers *were* offended by the bad language of the documentary, the percentage offended by it was very small. See Tracey and Morrison (1979: 117–120).
398 This term is taken from the title of Whitehouse's paper to the Royal Society of Health, Brighton, 22 April 1974.
399 Tracey and Morrison (1979: 91).
400 A phrase used by Richard Neville, an editor of the revolutionary magazine *Oz*.
401 For example, in her speech *Promoting Violence*, given to the Royal College of Nursing, April 1970.
402 Atmore (1811: 157).
403 Whitehouse, M. (1970) *Promoting Violence* (speech).
404 Whitehouse, M. (1970) *Promoting Violence* (speech).
405 VALA (1974: 8).
406 Milne (1988: 87).
407 This section heading echoes the title of Paletz and Harris (1975).
408 Caulfield (1975: 9).
409 Caulfield (1975: 40).
410 Adapted from Paletz and Harris (1975: 963).
411 Paletz and Harris (1975: 976).
412 Caulfield (1975: 117).
413 Quoted in Tracey and Morrison (1979: 77).
414 Quoted in Tracey and Morrison (1979: 77).
415 If this claim appears a little extreme, consider the call in the VALA's *Recommendations as to How Viewers and Listeners Can Best be Represented* for a new type of research. The new type of research was an approach which excluded researchers – data should be gathered from the public, but no attempt should be made by

'sociologists to "interpret" such evidence' (1974: 22). Whether research without researchers is still research is most kindly described as a moot point.

416 The series began formally in 1966, but as the 'pilot' Comedy Playhouse episode of the show aired in 1965 (22 July) I date the show from 1965.
417 Reproduced from Speight (1973b: 133–135).
418 Speight (1973a: 232).
419 Milton Shulman, *Evening Standard*, 21 February 1968.
420 Malcolm Muggeridge, *New Statesman*, 15 December 1967.
421 *The Stage and Television Today*, 22 February 1968.
422 *The Stage and Television Today*, 22 February 1968.
423 Whitehouse (1971: 67–68).
424 Whitehouse (1971: 68).
425 Whitehouse (1971: 71).
426 Whitehouse (1971: 67).
427 Whitehouse (1971: 69).
428 Speight, quoted in Tracey and Morrison (1979: 108).
429 Malcolm Muggeridge, *New Statesman*, 15 December 1967.
430 *Daily Mirror*, 8 August 1968.
431 Whitehouse (1971: 69).
432 This episode has also been referred to as *The Pigeon Fancier*.
433 Letter from Mary Whitehouse to Sir John Eden, Minister of Posts and Telecommunications, quoted in Tracey and Morrison (1979: 111).
434 Letter to Mary Whitehouse from Lord Hill, 2 October 1972, quoted in Tracey and Morrison (1979: 112).
435 For a good overview of the changing nature of blasphemy in English law, and a brief but comprehensive overview of the relevant cases, readers are recommended to read the House of Lords appeal for the *Gay News* case, Law Reports, House of Lords (1979: 617–632).
436 Though it is possible that the exclusion of broadcasters from the Act may not have been entirely successful. Prosecution under provision 1(3a) of the *Obscene Publications Act* may still have been possible. See Munro (1979: 94–97).
437 To give an idea of how the treatment of the shows differed, in the corpus of the VALA writings used in this book, *Steptoe and Son* is not mentioned in the MWC. *Till Death*, on the other hand is mentioned often enough to generate a set of keywords – see pages 223–225.
438 Caulfield (1975: 132).
439 Caulfield (1975: 132).
440 For example, he also appears in the episode *Porn Yesterday*, which is a similar comedy of manners to *Men of Letters*.
441 BBC producer Sydney Newman, quoted in the *Daily Express*, January 1963.
442 Of the 19 bad language phrases/words used in the programme, the father uses 15 of them first, while Harold only initiates three of them. The word *berks* is a word previously used by Harold reported by the vicar. Of the 31 bad language words/phrases uttered in the show, 23 of them are uttered by the father.
443 *Oz* was a revolutionary magazine, the so-called 'school kids' edition of which saw both editors of the magazine successfully prosecuted for obscenity.
444 Mary Whitehouse, quoted in Tracey and Morrison (1979: 11).
445 Unfortunately, the poem cannot be reprinted here, as it has been found blasphemous under English law. To reprint it would still constitute blasphemy.
446 Published originally in *Hymns for Little Children*, 1848. The words of the hymn were written by Cecil F. Alexander.
447 A.J. French, letter in *Gay News* 97, page 8.
448 P.N. Howarth, letter in *Gay News* 97, page 8.
449 C. Harvey, letter in *Gay News* 98, page 8.

450 G.R. Wilson, letter in *Gay News* 99, page 8.
451 M. Whitehouse, quoted in Tracey and Morrison (1979: 7).
452 Barbara Smoker, quoted in *Gay News* 127, page 7.
453 Indeed, the Court of Appeal noted the difficulty on applying a 'law not previously raised in criminal proceedings for half a century and not fully debated for some 60 years or more' (*All England Law Reports* 1978: 179).
454 M. Whitehouse, quoted in Tracey and Morrison (1979: 4).
455 A quote from Lord Diplock, one of the law lords who heard the final *Gay News* appeal in the UK, quoted in *Gay News* 162, page 9.
456 The solicitor of Mary Whitehouse.
457 M. Whitehouse, quoted in Tracey and Morrison (1979: 13).
458 This and the preceding quotation were originally printed in *Buzz* magazine, produced by the Musical Gospel Outreach Trust.
459 Law Reports, House of Lords (1979: 623).
460 Law Reports, House of Lords (1979: 634).
461 Law Reports, House of Lords (1979: 662). The reference to *Regina* v. *Hetherington* is to a key blasphemy case held in 1841.
462 All England Law Reports (1978: 187). The Court of Appeal case is also reported in Law Reports, Queen's Bench Division (1979: 10–31).
463 Law Reports, Queen's Bench Division (1979: 24).
464 Law Reports, House of Lords (1979: 666).
465 There was an earlier Danish edition of the book, published in 1965.
466 The *Little Red Schoolbook*, as quoted in Tracey and Morrison (1979: 136). I quote from Tracey and Morrison as this book, plus the writings of Whitehouse, are the only source of evidence I can reasonably access regarding the contents of the first edition.
467 The *Little Red Schoolbook*, as quoted in Whitehouse (1977: 180).
468 Whitehouse (1977: 181).
469 Whitehouse (1977: 180). Stage One was the name of the publisher of the *Little Red Schoolbook*.
470 Letter from Whitehouse to the DPP, 29 March 1971, quoted in Tracey and Morrison (1979: 135). Note that the use of the phrase 'corrupt and deprave' in the letter is important, as the tendency of something to deprave and corrupt was the crucial test for obscenity under the provisions of the Obscene Publications Act which was in force at the time that Whitehouse wrote.
471 Whitehouse (1977: 180).
472 Whitehouse (1977: 180).
473 The quotation from the original edition is given in Whitehouse (1977: 180). The revised section quoted here is taken from Hansen and Jensen (1971: 97).
474 See Whitehouse (1977: 181) for a quotation from the original, and Hansen and Jensen (1971: 98–102) for the rewritten version.
475 See Whitehouse (1977: 181) for a quotation from the original, and Hansen and Jensen (1971: 103–105) for the rewritten version.
476 It may be the case that changes made to the later edition of the book were not the result of censorship at all, but may, rather, reflect some change of style the editors of the book wished to take the opportunity to make. Hansen and Jensen (1971: 11) do note that they made some changes as a result of suggestions for improvement received from readers of the first edition. However, they do not differentiate these changes from the ones which they were forced to make in order to avoid prosecution. So, where the changes do appear innocuous, it is probably reasonable to guess that these are stylistic changes. If this is the case, it may well be that the few changes which have been made to the first quotation given by Whitehouse are the result of feedback from readers who approved of the book, and nothing to do with obscenity at all. While this

speculation cannot be easily proved, it would make more sense of the changes made to the third paragraph in the quotation given than the desire to avoid a charge of obscenity.

477 Hansen and Jensen (1971: 97–98).

478 See Tracey and Morrison (1979: 135).

479 See Hansen and Jensen (1971: 10).

480 The ruling on the obscenity of the book applied in England and Wales only. A similar trial in Scotland led to acquittal.

481 Andersson and Trudgill (1992: 64) argue that 'Swearing is tied to social restrictions which mirror values of the society. These restrictions are important parts of the structure of society, not merely historical accidents, and can be very deep seated.' I agree with this statement, but would note that (a) values can change and (b) deep-seated values can be uprooted and replaced. What I am claiming in this book is that the purity of the discourse of power has become a deep-seated value of British society, though at one point it was not, at least with reference to BLW use. It became a deep-seated value by a process of legal persecution and the indoctrination of the young with views which supported the idea that power and purity were linked. The only disagreement I would have with Andersson and Trudgill is that the apparent 'values of society' in this case were the values of those with power in society. With this in mind, I would alter their statement to read, 'Swearing is tied to social restrictions which mirror the values of those with overt prestige and power in society.'

482 Andersson and Trudgill (1992: 64–66) discuss the relationship of swearing to the purity principle, whereby (ibid.: 65–66): 'At the individual level, people who are cornerstones in the social structure are expected to keep their appearance and language pure and clean. Individuals on the edge of society – young people, the unemployed, alcoholics and criminals ... can be expected to show less control over their social behaviour and language.' This statement is certainly a perfect encapsulation of the position of the Society for the Reformation of Manners and those who argue for the purity of the discourse of power. My argument, however, is that this purity was enforced on British society by those whose discourse was 'pure' anyway as a means of asserting moral and social power.

483 Again there are parallels between the claims I am making and those made by Milroy and Milroy (1985), though their work does not consider bad language. Milroy and Milroy's work is particularly interesting, however, as they also clearly see the roots of the purity of the discourse of power, albeit as manifested by standardisation, as being in the same period as that identified by me in this book, the late seventeenth/early eighteenth centuries (see in particular Milroy and Milroy 1985: 27–30). Given that they also reference authors who were undoubtedly contributing to the SRM/SPCK discourse of the time (e.g. Swift 1712) I would again suggest that the best way to view the arguments presented in this book are as a further extension of ideas established by Milroy and Milroy.

6 Sea change: the Society for the Reformation of Manners and moral panics about bad language

484 For details of the keyword extraction process, including the p-value used in extracting the keywords, see Chapter 1, pages 18–20.

485 Note that in both this and the following chapter all keywords and key-keywords are shown in lower case only.

486 See Chapter 4, pages 90 and 110–112.

487 The cut-off point of ten is used here solely for the purpose of producing manageable tables.

488 The details of the collocation extraction process are given in Chapter 1, pages 20–21.

489 Note that in providing collocates I have not worked on the basis of lemmatised data. The SRM and MWC were lemmatised, but the lemmatisation process hindered rather than aided the process of interpretation. As will be seen in the collocates listed on page 164, different forms of the same word collocate at times with different keywords. This has been noted by other researchers (e.g. Tognini-Bonelli 2001: 91–98). In turn, different forms of the same keyword associate with distinct sets of collocates. The process of lemmatising this data simply merged together distinct collocational networks and keywords. For an interesting case in point look at the collocations of *swear* and *swearing* on page 164. The two words forms have quite distinct collocational networks associated with them, with the word *curse* being the only one shared as a collocate between the two keywords (though note that the word form *curse* collocating with the word *swear* matches it morphosyntactically as a collocate – a point returned to later in the discussion of coordination and spirals of signification). As such, the process of lemmatisation simply averaged the distinct keywords and collocates and led to a loss of descriptive power. On these grounds, I abandoned lemmatisation.

490 Note that this commodification is further indicated by at least three of the collocates of *guilt* – *double*, *heap* and *treasuring*.

491 In all such figures I will number the examples consecutively and underline the keyword in question. With lengthy sentences, and there are many in the SRMC, I may truncate them as needs demand. Where this occurs, the truncation is marked with a sequence of three periods. All examples given in this chapter are from the SRMC, unless otherwise stated.

492 It is not difficult to find disease metaphors/similes in the SRM texts. Consider the following from Woodward (1701: 15) who comments that vices 'do tend naturally to destroy a city or nation, as the most malignant diseases to (sic) waste and destroy our own bodies'.

493 See page 91 for a fuller discussion of this claim.

494 Or, to use the words of Woodward (1701: 21), people should 'become publick patriots by being publick reformers that you may hereby screen your city and this nation from misery and calamity'.

495 See pages 110–112.

496 Note also that the discourse of disease associated with immorality (as noted with reference to *guilt* previously) is clearly present here, as immorality is identified as a *contagion*.

497 In such cases, where women are the active cause of lewdness and lust they are marked out by a modifier with negative content. Of the 31 examples of *woman/women* in the SRMC, 12 occurrences are modified with the following, negatively loaded, words: *evil* (1), *lewd* (3), *strange* (3), *vice* (1), *vile* (1), *wanton* (1), *wicked* (1) and *whorish* (1). One occurrence has the woman committing *wickedness* (1), while another has a woman *dishonour* (1) her body. In each of these 14 cases, it is female sexual activity that is the cause of the negative depiction of women. Where they simply excite such a feeling in others through their beauty, they are not marked out in such a negative fashion, rather it is the *lust* (4) generated by females in males that is remarked upon. It is clear, from these examples, that it is the perceived link between sex and women that is the cause of negative representations of females in the SRMC.

498 Foremost amongst the offenders are *principal offenders*, yielding the collocate *principal* for *offenders* in the SRMC.

499 Interestingly, *exemplary* is closely associated with *punishment*, with exemplary being the top collocate of *punishment*.

500 Given the outline of the techniques used by the SRM in Chapter 4, the presence of *warrants* and *informations* is particularly interesting here. There are six examples of *warrants* and 36 of *informations*. All of the examples of *warrants* refer to the process of using warrants to prosecute those whose actions were disapproved of by the SRM. All uses of *informations* relate to the process of providing information to bring actions against offenders.

501 *Bringing* is also linked to *legal* and *punishment*. Given that the meaning of *bringing* is related to the meaning of bringing legal proceedings in the SRMC, I include the word in this list of collocates linking back to the corrective action keywords.

502 Indeed, it stretches beyond linguistics to information retrieval and natural language processing tasks in general.

503 I am not the first corpus linguist to have noted that sometimes function words can produce meaningful keywords – Tribble (1999), for example, after shunning the use of stop-lists, found that the word *the* was a meaningful keyword in his study.

504 Of the 64 examples of *etc.* in the SRMC, 33 relate to objects of offence and scapegoats. Of the remaining 31 examples, most (19) refer to legal procedures and agents of the law, as is apparent from the collocates of *etc.* The use of *etc.* in this context is understandable – with the wide array of possible venues for legal action (e.g. magistrates courts, quarter-sessions), agents of the law (judges, magistrates, constables, church-wardens) and fines to be imposed (cash fines, seizure of goods, imprisonment) the writers resort to the use of *etc.* to reduce the size of the list. However, the use of *etc.* in this context is different from that relating to offences and offenders. While in an example such as 'Every constable <u>etc.</u> who does not punish such as are brought before him', the set of people that the *etc.* covers is knowable – it is the set of people authorised by law to punish people – the *etc.* in the case of 'Drunkenness, Whoredom, Excess <u>etc.</u>' is clearly not necessarily knowable and hence more vague, as it depends on the subjective opinion of the members of the SRM regarding which offences could be grouped with drunkenness, whoredom and excess.

505 See pages 108–112 for background information related to this claim.

506 Biber *et al.* (1999: 489).

507 See Biber *et al.* (1999: 497–501).

508 The difference between the number of passive voice uses of *will* between Lampeter A and B is statistically significant at the $p < 0.01$ level, with an LL score of 351.06 indicating an over-representation of passivised uses of *will* in Lampeter B.

509 The difference between the SRMC and Lampeter B is significant at the $p < 0.01$ level, with an LL score of 46.34 indicating a higher level of usage of *will* in the passive voice in Lampeter B.

510 The difference between the SRMC and Lampeter A is significant at the $p < 0.01$ level, with an LL score of 110.87, indicating a higher level of usage of *will* in the passive voice in the SRMC.

511 Biber *et al.* (1999: 500).

512 Hall and Jefferson (1976: 77).

513 Hall *et al.* (1978: 223).

514 See Jenkins (1992: 12) for a further discussion of the inter-relatedness and independence of moral panics.

515 In looking at coordination, I have considered cases where whole phrases are coordinated, e.g. 'the Heavens and the Earth' or heads are coordinated within a phrase, e.g. 'the Swearing and Cursing'. I did not consider the coordination of modifiers in this case study, as I was interested in the coordination of keywords which tend to be heads rather than their modifiers. However, the coordinated

modifiers themselves are typically negative, e.g. 'thy vain and rash Swearing'. There are two further points to make here. First, I consider lists as cases of multiple coordination, e.g. in 'Impiety, Profaneness and Immorality to full abound in our Kingdom', I take *Impiety, Profaneness* and *Immorality* to be coordinated. Finally, there is a further distinction between positive and negative coordination which I do not mention in the main text, as I have yet to discern a clear explanation for it. All of the object of offence keywords shun full phrasal coordination, preferring instead head coordination. One might argue that this promotes convergence further, but I feel that a much larger study, possibly with some form of psycholinguistic experiment as part of it, would be needed to substantiate this view.

516 I accept that the categories I have created here are not inherently negative – one could imagine words with a positive connotation being placed in each category. However, the words under consideration here, for the SRM, had negative connotations, and hence the categories are populated here solely with words which have a negative loading.

517 The word in the SRMC means to retire to a room for the purpose of having sex.

518 Used in the SRMC with the meaning of fractious argument.

519 These figures are derived from the list of collocates given in the appropriate section for each keyword investigated. See Chapter 1, pages 21–24 for a further discussion.

520 While *drunkenness* appears in a greater number of coordinated phrases, whenever *swearing* appears in coordinated phrases it typically coordinates with a larger number of words. Hence while *swearing* appears in 16 coordinated phrases and *drunkenness* occurs in 20, this results in *swearing* being coordinated with 55 other heads while *drunkenness* is coordinated with only 53.

521 For readers with access to the Lampeter corpus, the file is Relb1730. For those without access to Lampeter, the text is Henley (1730).

522 Note in this case that while *common* links to *swearing*, it is in turn linked to by a number of collocates of its own. To this extent, this diagram could be viewed as focused on the node *swearing* and its relationship with *common* and the collocates of *common*.

523 I place this word in verbal acts here, as the word is typically used to refer to the expression of an opinion in the SRMC, e.g.

> In truth, I think 'tis much to be feared, but being very unwilling to fall under the too common Error of not duly considering Human Frailties and Prejudices, or to advance positively any <u>Opinion</u> that may justly bear a dispute with any but those that bring the Reason of Mankind and Religion its self into dispute, (as I hope will appear throughout these Sheets) I submit it to the Judgement of the Causists

or the holding of an opinion leads to the expression of that opinion, e.g. 'The not observing the Lord's Day with Strictness by our own Religious Examples, and the not Promoting it in our People by our Wise and Pious Admonitions, must lodge an ill <u>Opinion</u> in the Mind and open their Mouths against us.'

524 I will remain neutral on the point of whether the collocations select the meaning, or the meaning attracts the collocates. For readers interested in pursuing this debate, Stubbs (1996, 2001) is recommended. What I would say is that, in the cases here, I am arguing that the collocates are being forced into company with words in order to generate new associations, and hence by extension, meanings for those words. With reference to this specific example, I lean towards Stubbs' view.

525 I have included the word *cause* in this list as the original example discusses men making common cause against sin:

> But, in the next place, this Practice is however a high Service to the Community; for Religion being every Man's great Interest, every one's Work or Duty, the Community, according to the Sense of the Civil Law, is injured by the Contempt that is flung upon it, by the open Affronts and Violations of it, which every Man, as in a <u>common</u> Cause, is therefore concerned to prevent.

526 Note that the view that the sin of the out-group will 'infect' the in-group was discussed on pages 157–159. In this example, the SRM argues that those who are otherwise blameless of wrong-doing will become part of the out-group by failing to act against the out-group, as they will thus facilitate the sins of the out-group and condemn them to continue to sin:

> And if any of their Body, after this matter is plainly laid before them, and they are convinced 'tis their Duty to be diligent in the furthering it, wilfully neglect to excite all sorts of People, especially those belonging to their Charge, of what Rank or Quality soever, to do their Duty likewise in promoting, in their respective Stations, the Execution of the Laws against Profaneness and Debauchery, they can give a good Account of their Conduct to those of their particular Charge, who have no concern to discharge their Duty herein, only for want of their being admonished of it, and are not Partakers, in some degree, in the <u>Common</u> Guilt of the Nation, which, as our Neglect of our Duty in this particular Instance, of not Promoting a Reformation, will increase, so it may be a means notwithstanding our present respite from Destruction, to draw down God's judgements upon the Kingdom, if we continue to make no better use of the Peace we have with our Neighbours, than to fight with our crying Enormities against our God; which as I think few Nations, if any, have had in these last Ages greater Reason to dread, so, I suppose, all will grant, that none seem to have greater reason to use all proper means to prevent, than those who expect to give Account, not only for their own Sins, but for the Sins of so many others besides, if they wilfully suffer them to perish in them by their refusing to use the necessary means of preventing their living and dying in them.

527 The practices are bad ones, e.g. 'lewd discourse'.

528 Indeed in both the discourse of the SRM and that of Mary Whitehouse, as reviewed in the next chapter, the qualities of the out-group are often implied by the contrast created with the in-group (and vice versa). This mechanism should come as no surprise as it is a well-acknowledged device used to emphasise and define otherness, in this case the otherness of the out-group. See Hall (1997: 234–236).

7 Mutations: the National Viewers' and Listeners' Association moral panic

529 See Chapter 1, for a description of key-keywords.

530 Note that some semantic fields contain only one word. This is because the fields were initially developed for the full keyword list. When this is used, the fields with only one member gain further members. For example, the people field in the scapegoat category gains words such as *fox* and *hoggart*.

531 The keywords which are names that fall into this category are *hugh*, *greene*, *normanbrook*, *trevelyan*, *hoggart* and *fox*. These keywords link to the names Sir Hugh

Greene, Lord Normanbrook, John Trevelyan, Professor Richard Hoggart and Mrs Avril Fox. All were viewed, in one way or another, as key opponents by Whitehouse.

532 See Chapter 6, pages 159–161.

533 For some excellent, if harrowing, first-hand accounts of discipline in such schools see www.archivist.f2s.com/cpa/writtenaccounts.htm.

534 See later in this chapter for a discussion relating to Whitehouse's assumptions regarding the Christian nature of Britain (pages 214–215).

535 See Pilkington (1962) and Newsom (1963).

536 See Whitehouse (1977: 28–29).

537 For a brief outline of Hoggart's attack on the VALA, see Munro (1979: 132).

538 A claim made of a US report produced by the American Presidential Commission on Obscenity and Pornography, 1970.

539 A claim made of the Arts Council Report on Censorship of the Arts, 1969.

540 A claim made of Enid Wistrich's report for the Greater London Council's Film Viewing Committee on the abolition of censorship in films intended for over-18-year-old viewers, 1975.

541 For example, by 1974 the American Psychiatric Association had removed homosexuality from its list of recognised diseases.

542 See the discussion of pronouns later in this chapter for a further discussion of Whitehouse's claim to speak for a majority of people in Britain (pages 214–216).

543 Billy Graham is a conservative American Southern Baptist evangelical preacher given to travelling the world trying to attract mass conversions. Cardinal Heenan was the doctrinally conservative Catholic primate of all England in the period 1963–1975.

544 Dr John A.T. Robinson was an English bishop who embraced liberal causes – he appeared for the defence in the *Lady Chatterley* trial, for example. He was also doctrinally liberal, and his book *Honest to God* (1963) espoused a number of radical ideas (e.g. the non-existence of a personal God). Werner Pelz was a sociologist and author of *The Scope of Understanding in Sociology* (1974).

545 See Biber *et al.* (1999: 1048, 1060–1062) for a discussion of the use of enclitics in speech.

546 The phrase *blue film* is used to refer to pornographic films. At the time when Whitehouse was writing, *x* was a certificate awarded to films limited to an adult audience. Such films were limited because they contained bad language, sex or violence, either singly or in combination.

547 See Biber *et al.* (1999: 329–330) for a discussion of the vagueness of this category of pronouns.

548 I include the keyword *us* in this analysis. While it is not a key-keyword, the inclusion of *us* in this discussion seems appropriate in the context of discussing the way in which Whitehouse manipulates first person plurals.

549 The words *who* and *what* are key-keywords. I will also discuss *which* here as the word groups logically with the two other *wh*-forms under discussion.

550 The third example in this figure is from Whitehouse's book *Cleaning Up TV* (1967) and is from the foreword written by the Bishop of Hereford.

551 See, for example, Biber *et al.* (1999: 1033–1034).

552 The phrase 'men and women' occurs 30 times in LOB, accounting for the great majority of coordinations of the words *men* and *women*. The phrase 'boys and girls' occurs 15 times, once again accounting for the majority of all co-ordinations of the nouns *boys* and *girls* in LOB. Note also that a stroke notation is used here to present a coordinated pair where the direction of the coordination is unimportant, i.e. boys/girls refers to both 'boys and girls' and 'girls and boys'.

553 The phrase 'men and women' occurs 45 times in the MWC, accounting for the majority of coordinations of the nouns *men* and *women*.

554 The covering of genitalia on works of art by prudish Popes is an example that springs to mind. The chiselling off of the genitals on the Epstein statue above the grave of Oscar Wilde on the grounds of decency is another.

555 See Garside and Rayson (1997).

556 Readers interested in the semantic tagging system and tagset should look at www.comp.lancs.ac.uk/ucrel/usas/.

557 Note that all of the LL scores listed in this table are well in excess of the threshold for the $p < 0.1$ threshold.

558 See Chapter 5.

559 Bourdieu (1984: 461).

Postscript

560 See www.asa.org.uk/news/documents/upl_5.pdf.

561 A portion of each fine is kept by the arresting officer. The word of the arresting officer is sufficient evidence to secure a conviction.

562 See www.ananova.com/news/story/sm_1146030.html?menu=news.scienceand discovery.

563 Mediawatch is the new name for the VALA.

Bibliography

Abbott, W.C. (1937–1947) *The Writings and Speeches of Oliver Cromwell (5 volumes)*, Cambridge, MA: Harvard University Press.

All England Law Reports (1978), Volume 3, London: Butterworths.

Allestree, R. (1673) *The Ladies Calling*, London.

—— (1731) *The Whole Duty of Man*, London.

Andersson, L. and Trudgill, P. (1992) *Bad Language*, London: Penguin.

Anon. (1698) 'A letter to A. H. Esq'.

Anon. (1701) *A Short Disswasive from the Sin of Uncleanness*, London.

Anon. (1704) *A letter from the society for the propagation of Christian knowledge in London to a correspondent in the country*, London.

Anon. (1740) *A Memorial and Proposal Concerning Reformation of Manners, and for Exciting to Meetings for Religious Exercise Among Christians*, Edinburgh.

Arber, E. (1875–1894) *A Transcript of the Registers of the Company of Stationers of London*, 5 volumes, London.

Asten, G. and Burnard, L. (1998) *The BNC Handbook: Exploring the British National Corpus with SARCA*, EUP.

Atmore, C. (1811) *The Whole Duty of Man*, Liverpool.

Bahlman, D.W. (1957) *The Moral Revolution of 1688*, New Haven: Yale University Press.

Bailey, L.A. and Timm, L.A. (1976) 'More on women's – and men's – expletives', *Anthropological Linguistics*, 18(9): 438–449.

Baker, J.P. (2004) 'Querying keywords: questions of difference, frequency and sense in keywords analysis', *Journal of English Linguistics*, 32(4): 346–359.

Bald, R.C. (1938) 'Arthur Wilson's *The Inconstant Lady*', *The Library*, 19: 296–299.

Bawcutt, N.W. (1996) *The Control and Censorship of Caroline Drama: the Records of Sir Henry Herbert, Master of the Revels 1623–73*, Oxford: Oxford University Press.

Bedford, A. (1706) *The Evil and Danger of Stage Plays: shewing their natural tendency to destroy religion, and introduce a general corruption of manners, etc.* Bristol.

—— (1734) *A Sermon Preached to the Societies for the Reformation of Manners*, London.

Bellarmine, R. (1610) *Apologia Roberto Bellarmino pro Responsione sua ad Librum Jacobi Magnae Brittaniae*, Rome.

Biber, D., Johansson, S., Leech, G., Conrad, S. and Reppen, R. (1999) *The Longman Grammar of Spoken and Written English*, London: Longman.

Bissett, W. (1704) *Plain English*, London.

Bourdieu, P. (1984) *Distinction: a Social Critique of the Judgement of Taste*, London: Routledge.

Bray, A. (1996) *Homosexuality in Renaissance England*, New York: Columbia University Press.

Bray, T. (1709) *For God or for Satan*, London.

Bray, W. (1827) *Memoirs of John Evelyn*, Vol. IV, London: Simpkin Marshall.

Burnet, B. (1818) *A History of My Own Time*, Oxford.

Cameron, D. (1995) *Verbal Hygiene*, London: Routledge.

Capp, B. (2003) *When Gossips Meet: Women, Family and Neighbourhood in Early Modern England*, Oxford: Oxford University Press.

Caulfield, M. (1975) *Mary Whitehouse*, Oxford: Mowbrays.

Cheshire, J. (1982) *Variation in an English Dialect*, Cambridge: Cambridge University Press.

Claridge, C. (1997) 'A century in the life of multi-word verbs', in M. Ljung (ed.) *Corpus-based Studies in English. Papers from the 17th International Conference on English Language Research on Computerized Corpora*, Amsterdam: Rodopi, Amsterdam, pp. 69–85.

Clark, Peter (1976) 'The ownership of books in England, 1560–1640: the example of some Kentish townsfolk', in L. Stone (ed.) *Schooling and Society: Studies in the History of Education*, Baltimore: Johns Hopkins University Press, pp. 95–111.

Clarkson, L. (1659) *The Right Devil Discovered*, London.

Clegg, C.S. (1997) *Press Censorship in Elizabethan England*, Cambridge: Cambridge University Press.

—— (2001) *Press Censorship in Jacobean England*, Cambridge: Cambridge University Press.

Coates, J. (2003) *Men Talk: Stories in the Making of Masculinities*, Oxford: Blackwell.

—— (2004) *Women, Men and Language*, London: Longman.

Cohen, S. (1972) *Folk Devils and Moral Panics* (first edition), London: McGibbon and Kee.

—— (2002) *Folk Devils and Moral Panics* (third edition), London: Routledge.

Collier, J. (1688) *A Short View of the Immorality and Profaneness of the English Stage*, London.

Coppe, A. (1650) *The Flying Fiery Roll (and Roulle)*, Parts One and Two, London.

—— (1651a) *A Remonstrance*, London.

—— (1651b) *Coppe's Return to the Ways of Truth*, London.

Cosin, R. (1591) *An Apologie: of and for sundrie proceedings by jurisdiction ecclesiasticall*, London.

Coward, B. (1994) *The Stuart Age*, London: Longman.

Cressy, D. (1977a) 'Levels of illiteracy in England 1530–1730', *Historical Journal*, (XX): 1–23.

—— (1977b) 'Literacy in seventeenth-century England: more evidence', *Journal of Interdisciplinary History*, (VIII): 141–150.

—— (1980) *Literacy and Social Order: Reading and Writing in Early-Modern England*, Cambridge: Cambridge University Press.

Crystal, D. (2001) *The Cambridge Encyclopedia of the English Language*, Cambridge: Cambridge University Press.

Curtis, T.C. and Speck, W.A. (1976) 'The Societies for the Reformation of Manners: a case study in the theory and practice of moral reform', *Literature and History*, (3): 45–64.

D'Urfey, T. (1694) *The Comical History of Don Quixote*, London.
—— (1698) *The Campaigners*, London.
Daille, B. (1995) *A Combined Approach for Terminology Extraction: Lexical Statistics and Linguistic Filtering*, Lancaster University: UCREL.
Defoe, D. (1697) *An Essay Upon Projects*, London.
—— (1702) *Reformation of Manners, A Satyr*, London.
—— (1704) *The Storm*, London.
Dennis, J. (1726) *The Stage Defended*, London.
Doherty, M.A. (2000) *Nazi Wireless Propaganda*, Edinburgh: Edinburgh University Press.
Dowdell, E.G. (1932) *A Hundred Years of Quarter Sessions*, Cambridge: Cambridge University Press.
Dunning, T. (1993) 'Accurate methods for statistics of surprise and coincidence', *Computational Linguistics*, 19(1): 61–74.
Dunton, J. (1694) *Proposals for a National Reformation of Manners*, London.
—— (1696) *The Night-Walker, Or, Evening Rambles In Search After Lewd Women*, London.
—— (1705) *The Life and Errors of John Dunton*, London.
Dutton, R. (2000) *Licensing, Censorship and Authorship in Early Modern England*, Basingstoke: Palgrave.
Eiskovits, E. (1998) 'Girl talk/boy talk in adolescent speech', in J. Coates (ed.) *Language and Gender: a Reader*, Oxford: Blackwell, pp. 42–54.
The Evidence given at the Bar of the House of Commons upon the complaint of Sir J. Pakington against William, Lord Bishop of Worcester, and Mr Lloyd, his son. Together with the Proceedings of the House of Commons thereupon, (1702) London.
Faithfull, M. and Dalton, D. (1995) *Faithfull*, London: Penguin.
Firth, J.R. (1957) *Papers in Linguistics, 1934–1951*, Oxford: Oxford University Press.
Fraser, A. (2002) *King Charles II*, London: Phoenix.
Friedman, J. (1987) *Blasphemy, Immorality and Anarchy: the Ranters and the English Revolution*, London: Ohio University Press.
—— (1993) *The Battle of the Frogs and Fairford's Flies*, New York: St Martin's Press.
Garside, R. and Rayson, P. (1997) 'Higher-level annotation tools', in R. Garside, G. Leech and A. McEnery (eds) *Corpus Annotation: Linguistic Information from Computer Text Corpora*, London: Longman, pp. 179–193.
Gibson, W. (1998) *Religion and Society in England and Wales 1689–1800*, Leicester: Leicester University Press.
Gildrie, R.P. (1994) *The Profane, the Cival and the Godly: the Reformation of Manners in Orthodox New England, 1679–1749*, Pennsylvania: The Pennsylvania State University Press.
Goode, E. and Ben-Yahuda, N. (1994) *Moral Panics: the Social Construction of Deviance*, Oxford: Blackwell.
Grant, F. (1700) *A Discourse Concerning the Execution of the Laws Made Against Profaneness*, Edinburgh.
Greg, W.W. (1967) *Companion to Arber*, Oxford: Oxford University Press.
Hall, S. (1997) 'The spectacle of the other', in S. Hall (ed.) *Representation, Cultural Representations and Signifying Practices*, London: Sage.
Hall, S. and Jefferson, T. (eds) (1976) *Resistance Through Rituals: Youth Sub-Cultures in Post-War Britain*, London: Hutchinson.

Hall, S., Critcher, C., Jefferson, T., Clarke, J. and Roberts, B. (1978) *Policing the Crisis: Mugging, the State and Law and Order*, London: Macmillan.

Hansen, S. and Jensen, J. (1971) *The Little Red Schoolbook* (revised edition), London: Stage One.

Head, B. (1977) 'Sex as a factor in the use of obscenity', Honolulu: Paper presented at the Linguistics Society of America Summer Meeting.

Heinemann, M. (1980) *Puritanism and Theatre: Thomas Middleton and Opposition Drama under the Early Stuarts*, Cambridge: Cambridge University Press.

Henley, J. (1730) *Light in a Candlestick, to All that are in the House*, London.

Hill, C. (2001) *The Intellectual Origins of the English Revolution*, Oxford: Oxford University Press.

Hoey, M. (1991) *Patterns of Lexis in Text*, Oxford: Oxford University Press.

Horne, T.A. (1978) *The Social Thought of Bernard Mandeville*, London: Macmillan.

Horneck, A. (1690) *Sirenes* (second edition), London.

Hughes, G. (1998) *Swearing: a Social History of Foul Language, Oaths and Profanity in English*, Oxford: Blackwell.

Hundt, M., Sand, A. and Siemund, R. (1998) *Manual of Information to Accompany the Freiburg-LOB Corpus of British English ('FLOB')*, Online, available at: www.hit.uib.no/icame/flob/index.htm.

Isaacs, T. (1982) 'Anglicans and the Reformation of Manners', *Journal of Ecclesiastical History*, 33(3): 191–411.

James, G.P.R. (1841) *Letters Ilustrative of the Reign of William III, Volume 2*, London.

Jay, T. (1992) *Swearing in America*, Amsterdam: John Benjamins.

—— (1999) *Why We Curse*, Amsterdam: John Benjamins.

Jeckill, T. (1698) *A Sermon Preach'd before the Societies for Reformation of Manners*, London.

Jenkins, P. (1992) *Intimate Enemies: Moral Panics in Contemporary Great Britain*, New York: De Gruyter.

'J.F.' (1693) *A New Proclamation*, London.

Johansson, S., Leech, G. and Goodluck, H. (1978) *Manual of Information to Accompany the Lancaster-Oslo/Bergen Corpus of British English, for Use with Digital Computers*, University of Oslo.

Keeble, N.H. (2002) *The Restoration*, Oxford: Blackwell.

Kennedy, G. (1998) *An Introduction to Corpus Linguistics*, Longman: London.

Kidder, R. (1698) *Life of Anthony Horneck*, London.

Kishlansky, M. (1997) *A Monarchy Transformed: Britain 1603–1714*, London: Penguin.

Krutch, J.W. (1961) *Comedy and Conscience after the Restoration*, New York: Columbia University Press.

Kučera, H. and Francis, W.N. (1967) *Computational Analysis of Present-Day American English*, Providence: Brown University Press.

Labov, W. (1966a) *The Social Stratification of English in New York City*, Washington: Center for Applied Linguistics.

—— (1966b) 'Hypercorrection by the lower middle class as a factor in linguistic change', in W. Bright (ed.) *Sociolinguistics*, The Hague: Mouton.

Lakoff, R. (1975) *Language and a Woman's Place*, New York: Harper and Row.

Lambert, S. (1987) 'The printers and the government, 1604–1637', in R. Myers (ed.) *Aspects of Printing from 1600*, Oxford: Oxford Polytechnic Press, pp. 1–28.

Law Reports, House of Lords (1979) The Incorporated Council of Law Reporting for England and Wales, London.

Law Reports, Queen's Bench Division (1979) The Incorporated Council of Law Reporting for England and Wales, London.

Louw, B. (2000) 'Contextual prosodic theory: bringing semantic prosodies to life', in C. Heffer, H. Sauntson and G. Fox (eds) *Words in Context: a Tribute to John Sinclair on his Retirement*, Birmingham: University of Birmingham.

Lowther Clarke, W.K. (1959) *A History of the SPCK*, London: SPCK.

McEnery, A.M. and Wilson, A. (2001) *Corpus Linguistics* (second edition), Edinburgh: Edingburgh University Press.

McEnery, A.M., Baker, J.P. and Hardie, A. (2000) 'Swearing and abuse in modern British English', in B. Lewandowska-Tomaszczyk and P.J. Melia (eds) *Practical Applications of Language Corpora*, Hamburg: Peter Lang, pp. 37–48.

Mair, C., Hundt, M., Leech, G. and Smith, N. (2002) 'Short term diachronic shifts in part-of-speech frequencies', *International Journal of Corpus Linguistics*, 7(2): 245–264.

Mandeville, B. (1705) *The Grumbling Hive: or, knaves turn'd honest*, London.

Marcuse, H. (1964) *One Dimensional Man*, London: Routledge.

Marsh, J. (1998) *Word Crimes*, Chicago: University of Chicago Press.

Millwood-Hargrave, A. (2000) *Delete Expletives?* London: Advertising Standards Authority.

Milne, A. (1988) *The Memoirs of a British Broadcaster*, London: Coronet Books.

Milroy, J. and Milroy, L. (1985) *Authority and Language*, London: Routledge.

Montagu, A. (1967) *The Anatomy of Swearing*, London: Macmillan.

—— (1973) *The Anatomy of Swearing* (second edition), London: Macmillan.

Morgan, K.O. (2001) *Britain Since 1945: the People's Peace*, Oxford: Oxford University Press.

Munro, C.R. (1979) *Television, Censorship and the Law*, Farnborough: Saxon House.

Murray, V. (1999) *High Society in the Regency Period, 1788–1830*, London: Penguin.

Neale, J.E. (1957) *Elizabeth I and her Parliaments, 1584–1601*, London: Jonathan Cape.

Newsom, J. (1963) *Half Our Future*, London: Her Majesty's Stationery Office.

Nicolson, W. (1706) *A Sermon Preached at Bow Church, London on Monday, December 30th 1706, before the Societies for the Reformation of Manners*, London.

Norton, R. (1992) *Mother Clap's Molly House: the Gay Subculture in England 1700–1830*, London: The Gay Men's Press.

Odgers, W.B. and Eames, J.B. (1905) *A Digest of the Law of Libel and Slander*, London: Stevens.

Oftedal, M. (1973) 'Notes on language and sex', *Norwegian Journal of Linguistics*, 27: 67–75.

Paletz, D. and Harris, W. (1975) 'Four-letter threats to authority', *Journal of Politics*, 37(4): 955–979.

Patterson, A. (1984) *Censorship and Interpretation: the Conditions of Writing and Reading in Early Modern England*, Madison: University of Wisconsin Press.

Pelz, W. (1974) *The Scope of Understanding in Sociology: Towards a More Radical Reorientation in the Social and Humanistic Sciences*, London: Routledge.

Penn, T. (1708) *A Sermon Preached before the Society for the Reformation of Manners in the Parish Church of Wendover in the County of Bucks.*, London.

Penn, W. (1745) *A Call to Repentence, Recommended to the Inhabitants of Great Britain in General: with a brief address to the magistrates intrusted with the execution of the laws against prophaneness and immorality*, London.

Perry, M. (1980) *The Whole Duty of Man, in Today's English*, London: Ark Publishing.

Phillips, M. (1985) *Aspects of Text Structure: an Investigation of the Lexical Organization of Text*, New York: Elsevier.

Pierce, T. (1671) *A Collection of Sermons*, Oxford.

Pilkington, H. (1962) *The Future of Sound Radio and Television*, London: Her Majesty's Stationery Office.

Plum, H.G. (1972) *Restoration Puritanism*, London: Kennikat Press.

Porter, R. (1991) *English Society in the Eighteenth Century*, London: Penguin.

Portus, G.V. (1912) *Caritas Anglicana*, London: Mowbrays.

Pritchard, S. (1864) *A History of Deal*, Deal.

Rayson, P. (2003) *Matrix: a Statistical Method and Software Tool for Linguistic Analysis Through Corpus Comparison*, unpublished thesis, Lancaster University.

Robertson, D. (1903) *Diary of Francis Evans, Secretary to Bishop Lloyd, 1699–1706*, Oxford.

Robinson, A.T. (1963) *Honest to God*, London: SCM Press.

Russell, J. (1697) *A Sermon Preach'd at St. Mary le Bow, June 28*, London.

Ryther, J. (1699) *A Sermon Preach'd to the Society for the Reformation of Manners*, London.

Sacheverell, H. (1702) *The Character of a Low-Churchman*, London.

—— (1710) *The Tryal of Dr. Henry Sacheverell, before the House of Peers for High Crimes and Misdemeanors, upon an Impeachment by the Knights, Citizens, and Burgesses in Parliament Assembled … 27 day of February 1709/10, and from thence Continued by Several Adjournmetns {sic} until the 23rd day of March Following*, House of Commons, London.

Schmied, J. (1994) 'The Lampeter corpus of Early Modern English tracts', in M. Kytö, M. Rissanen and S. Wright (eds) *Corpora Across the Centuries*, Amsterdam: Rodopi, pp. 81–89.

Scobell, H. (1658) *A Collection of Acts and Ordinances*, London.

Scott, M. (1999) *WordSmith Tools*, Oxford: Oxford University Press.

—— (2000) 'Focusing on the text and its key words', in L. Burnard and T. McEnery (eds) *Rethinking Language Pedagogy from a Corpus Perspective*, Frankfurt: Peter Lang, pp. 103–122.

—— (2003) *WordSmith Tools Manual*, online, available at: www.lexically.net/wordsmith/version4/.

Scott, T. (1620) *Vox Populi*, London.

Sharp, J. (1704) *Plain Dealing in Answer to Plain English*, London.

Sinclair, J.McH. (1966) 'Beginning the study of lexis', in C.E. Bazell., J.C. Catford, M.A.K. Halliday and R.H. Robins (eds) *In Memory of J.R. Firth*, London: Longman, pp. 410–431.

Sinclair, J.McH., Jones, S. and Daley, R. (1970) *English Lexical Studies: Report to OSTI on Project C/LP/08*, Department of English, Birmingham University.

Sindall, R. (1990) *Street Violence in the Nineteenth Century: Media Panic or Real Danger?*, Leicester: Leicester University Press.

Smith, M.E. (1995) 'John Fletcher's response to the gender debate: the woman's prize and the taming of the shrew'. *Papers on Language and Literature*, 31: 38–60.

Speck, W.A. (1977) *Stability and Strife, England 1714–1760*, Cambridge, MA: Harvard University Press.

Speight, J. (1973a) *Alf Garnett Till Death Us Do Part Scripts*, London: The Woburn Press.

—— (1973b) *It Stands to Reason*, London: M&J Hobbs.

Stephens, E. (1691) *The Beginning and Progress of a Needful and Hopeful Reformation of England with the first Encounter of the Enemy Against it, his Wiles Detected and his Design ('t May be Hop'd) Defeated*, London.

—— (1700) *A Seasonable and Necessary Admonition to the Gentlemen of the first Society for the Reformation of Manners, Concerning Reformation of Themselves, of the Bishops, and of the House of Commons*.

Streitberger, W.R. (1978) 'On Edmond Tyllney's biography', *Review of English Studies*, 29.

Stubbs, M. (1996) *Text and Corpus Analysis: Computer Assisted Studies of Language and Institutions*, Oxford: Blackwell.

—— (2001) *Words and Phrases*, Oxford: Blackwell.

—— (2002) 'Two quantitative methods of studying phraseology in English', *International Journal of Corpus Linguistics*, 7(2): 215–244.

Swift, J. (1709) *Project for the Advancement of Religion, and the Reformation of Manners*, London.

—— (1712) *Proposal for Correcting, Improving and Ascertaining the English Tongue*, London.

Tenison, T. (1699) *His Grace the Lord Archbishop of Canterbury's Letter to the Right Reverend the Lords Bishops of his Province*, London.

Thompson, K. (1998) *Moral Panics*, London: Routledge.

Tickell, J. (1651) *The Bottomless Pit Smoaking in Familisme*, London.

Tognini-Bonelli, E. (2001) *Corpus Linguistics at Work*, Amsterdam: John Benjamins.

Tong, W. (1704) *A Sermon Preached . . . Before the Societies for Reformation*, London.

Tracey, M. and Morrison, D. (1979) *Whitehouse*, London: Macmillan.

Tribble, C. (1999) *Writing Difficult Texts*, unpublished thesis, Lancaster University.

Trudgill, P. (1972) 'Sex, covert prestige and linguistic change in the urban British English of Norwich', *Language in Society*, 1: 179–195.

—— (2000) *Sociolinguistics: an Introduction to Language and Society*, London: Penguin.

Usher, R.G. (1913) *The Rise and Fall of the High Commission*, Oxford: Clarendon.

VALA (1974) *Recommendations to the Annan Inquiry into the Future of Broadcasting*, VALA.

Walker, S. (1711) *Reformation of Manners Promoted by Argument, in Several Essays, etc.*, London.

Wallis, R. (1976) 'Moral indignation and the media analysis of VALA', *Sociology*, 10: 271–295.

Ward, A.W., Waller, A.R., Trent, W.P., Erskine, J., Sherman, S.P. and Van Doren, C. (1907–1921) *The Cambridge History of English and American Literature: an Encyclopedia in Eighteen Volumes*, Cambridge: Cambridge University Press.

Watts, I. (1728) *An Essay towards the Encouragement of Charity Schools . . . to which is prefix'd an address to the supporters of these schools*, London.

Weale, A. (1994) *Renegades: Hitler's Englishmen*, London: Weidenfeld & Nicolson.

Webb, S. and Webb, B. (1903) *The History of Liquor Licensing, Principally from 1700 to 1830*, London: Longman.

Wesley, S. (1698) *A Sermon Concerning Reformation of Manners*, London.

Whitehouse, M. (1967) *Cleaning Up TV*, London: Blandford.

—— (1971) *Who Does She Think She Is?*, London: New English Library.

—— (1977) *Whatever Happened to Sex?*, Hove: Wayland.

Williams, D. (1698) *A Sermon Preached at Salters Hall to the Societies for the Reformation of Manners, May 16th 1698*, London.

Wither, G. (1624) *Schollers Purgatory*, London.

Withers, C.W.J. (1982) 'Education and anglicisation: the policy of the SSPCK toward the education of the Highlander', *Scottish Studies*, 26: 37–56.

Woodhead, L. (2004) *An Introduction to Christianity*, Cambridge: Cambridge University Press.

Woodward, J. (1697) *Sermon Preach'd Before the Lord Mayor at Guildhall Chapel, August 1, 1697*, London.

—— (1701) *Account of the Rise and Progress of the Religious Societies*, London.

—— (1701) *The Divine Joy of Religion*, London.

—— (1702) *A Sermon Preach'd . . . at the Funeral of Mr. John Cooper*, London.

—— (1712) *The Divine Right of Civil Government*, London.

Wright, S. (1715) *A Sermon Preached Before the Societies for the Reformation of Manners*, London.

Yachnin, P. (1991) 'The powerless theatre', *English Literary Renaissance*, 21: 49–74.

Yates, (first name unknown) (1699) *An Account of the Societies*, London.

Index

LaVergne, TN USA
20 November 2009
164821LV00001B/4/P